Exploring the World of JAPANESE CRAFT SAKÉ

Nancy Matsumoto
Michael Tremblay
Foreword by John Gauntner

TUTTLE Publishing

Tokyo | Rutland, Vermont | Singapore

The Wide World of Sake

by John Gauntner

When I arrived in Japan in 1988, there was one book about sake in English: *Sake: A Drinker's Guide*, by Hiroshi Kondo. Today, there are many more—each with its own angle, niche and allure. Yet a good dollop of overlap is inevitable. In fact, lately, there is quite a bit of sake information out there. Beyond books there are blogs, newsletters, articles, podcasts and videos. Live *kura* tours, interviews and online seminars are part of this mix too. When it comes to sake, it seems like everybody's got a gig these days. This is not surprising, as sake is such an interesting field of study, and it's also a welcome development, since on the familiarity front, sake has some catching up to do.

But the printed word still rules. Sure, modern electronic media are here to stay. And with the plethora of information out there, a printed book on sake needs to have something special to offer. The something special found in this book is conveyed in three words: depth, breadth and vibrancy.

The authors go *deep* into each topic, deeper than most might surmise is possible with sake. They cover a range of subjects, from the four basic ingredients of rice, water, yeast and *koji* mold to the societies of craftsmen and craftswomen that are the backbone of the industry. They infuse each technical, historical and cultural theme with color and energy that flows from the people we meet through their stories. As they travel across Japan together, visiting breweries, research facilities and rice fields, their perspectives intertwine to create stories of sake, richly illustrated with accounts of discussions with people—real people that have all played seminal roles in the subject being presented. Like a great sake, this book is well balanced, with all the necessary elements clearly discernible. Nancy and Michael are very clearly enamored with sake, and clearly driven to uncover every detail they can.

In the rapidly growing but still-niche sake market, newcomers are still trying to figure it all out. What are the grades, the rules, the brewing methods, what makes it unique and what should I be drinking? Most conversations about sake are related to simple technical issues, while discussions about the people that have made it what it is are all too rare.

Ironically, the latter topics are the truly interesting ones. The quirks of brewery owners, governmental policies and circumstances unique to every era have shaped sake into what it has become. And the people that guided sake through the labyrinths of history, and sometimes even bent things to their own will, are often the very factors that make us fond of one sake over another. Yet the human angle alone is just not enough; we still need the technical descriptions too, the history of those developments, and the relationship of all those to just how sake tastes, smells and can be best enjoyed.

Nancy and Michael have our backs; they have it all covered, and in finely wrought balance. And, to wrap it all up, at the end of every chapter, they tell us just what to go out and drink to best illustrate and thereby best remember the gist of each topic. It all makes for a comprehensive education indeed!

If the authors leave us with anything in this book, it is a thirst for more—more information, more stories and certainly for more sake. Let them take you on this journey through the annals of the world of sake. You'll not likely want to return.

John Gauntner
Author of *The Sake Handbook* and *Sake Confidential*, publisher of *Sake Industry News*, Co-founder of *Sake World* at sake-world.com

Why We Wrote This Book

by Nancy Matsumoto and Michael Tremblay

Nancy

The idea for this book was hatched, naturally, over many glasses of sake. We were at Toronto's Omai restaurant, a casual Korean-Japanese place with high culinary standards. It's the kind of place where neo-soul and French house music play on the sound system and you can order salmon-maple-daikon handrolls wrapped in Ariake Bay nori and eight-spice fried chicken with ramp aioli to go with your yuzu beer, Tengumai *yamahai junmai* or locally brewed Izumi unpasteurized sake.

The scene was a good example of the increasing diversity of food and drink available in Toronto and North America, and the growing popularity of sake worldwide. The day I moved my primary residence from New York City to Toronto to join my husband in October 2016, sake educator John Gauntner's first Toronto Sake Professional Course was wrapping up. That night, as a graduate of the course, I attended a packed farewell party for the group on the patio at ki modern Japanese + bar, the home base of my coauthor, Michael. He heads the beverage department at ki and curates the largest sake program in Canada.

The international sake community was small, but growing rapidly. Over the past decade, exports of Japanese sake set record levels, doubling in growth and nearly tripling in value. Among those countries that have welcomed sake imports, the US is the leading export market and China is the fastest growing. So it didn't seem at all surprising that my sake sensei was in town to spread the word.

Sake embodies some of the things I love most about Japan: the contrast between old, traditional ways and endlessly imaginative reinvention, and an intense dedication to craft. Sake's identity is inseparable from the country's history, culture and language. To open a bottle of sake is to catch a glimpse into that sometimes turbulent history, and chart the evolution of taste it represents. But to understand it fully, it helps to have some guidance.

So I took John Gauntner's Sake Professional Course in Las Vegas in 2015, and his Advanced Sake Professional Course in Tokyo in 2018 and Michael's course on sake regionality in 2019. I continued to write about and deepen my understanding of sake. John, meanwhile, has gone on to educate thousands; his course is now one of a number of programs that offer sake education and certification.

Michael

My own Sake Scholar course is among that growing number of classes available to sake fans and drink professionals today. The program was three years in the making, during which time I mapped out every region of Japan and its unique geography, sake-rice varieties, water, yeast and culture so that I could connect the sake dots and put together a course that delves into sake regionality. This book does that too, but without going down the sake rabbit holes I get into in the course.

When I started working at ki in 2005 I didn't know much about sake but had a great passion for wine. No one in Toronto knew much about sake, and the number of imports available for purchase was limited. In many respects I was in the right place at the right time, at the beginning of Toronto's burgeoning love for sake. I took both of John Gauntner's sake professional courses, and it was like little sake fireworks going off in my head—I was hooked. My favorite thing to do with customers at ki is to take them on a trip to a region of Japan through a bottle of sake, to make them feel like they're tucked in an izakaya restaurant in the mountains of Nagano, following the Nakasendo road through the Japanese Alps. I hope that this book, too, transports you deep into Japan's rural

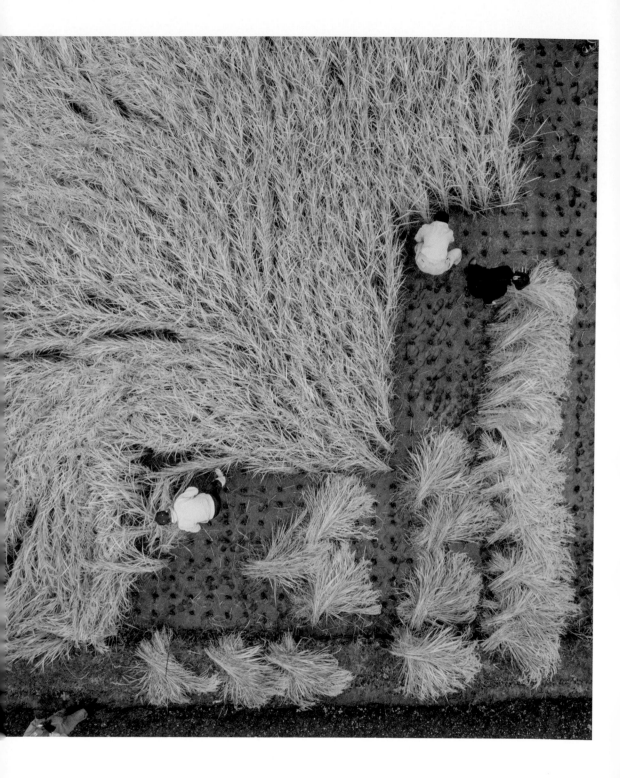

Left Golden ears of Yamada Nishiki rice at harvest time. **Below** Lineup of sakes made with flower yeasts, from Amabuki Brewery.

sake country. As every master brewer will tell you, there's no end to the learning when it comes to sake brewing. Then they'll quote brewer Tatsue Shimohara, who retired from Daishinshu Brewery in Nagano Prefecture at the age of ninety-one. When he was sixty-six, he said, "I've been brewing sake for fifty years, but every year, I feel like I'm in first grade again." The same is true, we believe, for the sake fan: just when you think you've figured the drink out, a humbling new wrinkle appears, and the hunt is on again, for a deeper level of sake understanding and enjoyment.

What You'll Find inside This Book

This book is based on two years of research and writing, one sake-brewing year in Japan, visits to thirty-five breweries across Japan and North America and conversations with many more. It's designed to take you through the sake-making process, from paddy to glass. We'll meet the farmers, brewers and brewing families who practice this ancient craft. We'll also meet others key to the process of sake making with whom you may be less familiar: the pioneers of new brewing techniques and yeast and rice varieties, and the merchants who trade in sake's indispensable *koji* mold—the unique fermentation that lies at the heart of sake. Along the way, we'll meet the former systems engineer who runs some of the most forward-looking sake bars in Japan, the professor of brewing and fermentation whose life mission is to discover exciting new yeasts, and the maker whose inspiration comes in part from the natural wines of the former Soviet republic of Georgia.

After reading our first chapter on the king of rice varieties, Yamada Nishiki, you may think sake sounds terribly elitist. But sake made with Yamada Nishiki rice can be found just as easily in "one-cup" products sold at 7-Eleven, or the boisterous *gaado shita* (literally "under the girders") pubs found squeezed beneath the Tokyo railway tracks as it can be in Michelin-starred restaurants. To us, "sake culture" spans two poles that stretch from small-town back-alley izakayas to next-level *nihonshu* dens and fine-dining temples.

The first half of this book tells the story of our favorite beverage from its elemental beginnings: rice, water and earth. We'll take you back to the birth of *ginjo* in the early 1980s, when advances in rice-polishing techniques and yeasts ushered in a golden age of premium sake. We'll look at the different types of water used in sake brewing, a perennial favorite topic of master brewers. And we'll introduce you to brewers who are taking their cues from France and ushering in a focus on regionality.

The second half is devoted to the alchemy of magical molds and yeasts, the people who research or trade in them and the master brewers—both men and women—who transform them, along with a few simple ingredients, into something magical.

If you're brand new to sake, you might want to spend time with our Sake Primer (pages 9–37) to absorb the basics of sake's history, how it is brewed

and its different components. Alternatively, feel free to dive right into our stories. At the end of each chapter, we have included a suggested sake-tasting flight to go with the theme of the chapter, so that as you're reading or after you've finished, you can travel to the prefectures and breweries we describe through the suggested bottles. Skip to chapter 20 if you want to experience some of our favorite sake-bar moments, or to chapter 21 to try some sake-friendly recipes from the brewing families we visited, complete with their recommended pairings. We survey the rapidly growing international sake scene in chapter 22, and bring it all back home for a final *kanpai* toast in chapter 23. Whatever your particular sake interest, we hope you will find something about it to satisfy your needs in this book.

We hope you enjoy the ride with us.

A Note on the Text

While we have chosen to write all personal names in the Western style (first, or given name followed by the surname), the one exception to this rule is well-known Japanese historical figures who are better known by their Japanese name order, or often just by their first name (e.g., Oda Nobunaga, Toyotomi Hideyoshi, Katsushika Hokusai). In such cases, we have adopted the Japanese custom of last name first, then given name.

In the case of historical figures who are famous in sake history but not known to the general public (e.g., Senzaburo Miura), we have elected to stick to the Western name order.

Yamagata Prefecture's Mitobe Brewery shows off the qualities of two rice varieties, Dewasansan (left) and Omachi (right).

A Sake Primer

The Origins of Sake

Sake is so intertwined with the history of Japan that it appears in its foundational myths, first as an offering to divine spirits, who were presumed to delight in the drink. Mentions of sake can be found in the earliest histories of Japan, *The Kojiki* (Record of Ancient Things) and *The Nihongi* (Chronicles of Japan), which date back, respectively, to the seventh and eight centuries. In one such story, the god of Omiwa Shrine in Nara is revealed to the legendary first-century-BC Emperor Sujin in a dream. He advises his mortal subject that an offering of sake will quell the plague then sweeping across Japan. The sake has the desired effect, and Omiwa—Japan's oldest standing shrine—has ever since been thought to enshrine the god of sake and of master brewers. Today the close associations between sake and Shintoism live on, and sake plays a role in purification rites, rituals, festivals and other auspicious occasions. In the Heian period (794–1185), sake brewing was carried out by Buddhist monks, who over time gave up these duties to commercial sake makers. Enjoying sake became a pastime not just for the aristocracy but for the ordinary citizen as well.

The tradition of *naorai*, a ritual in which participants commune with the gods through the shared drink of sake, is perhaps the Shintoist feature that most closely resembles the Christian ritual of Eucharist, or Holy Communion. But unlike wine, sake's purity and divinity extends to the ingredients with which it is made. In every sake brewery, you will find a miniature shrine (*kamidana*) affixed to a wall, bearing offerings of sake. This is where sake makers pray for safety and success in brewing. And in every brewer you will find a reverence for sake's ingredients—rice, water and *koji* mold—that is imbued with Shinto and Buddhist overtones.

What Is Sake?

Sake, also known as *nihonshu*, is an alcoholic beverage made with fermented rice.

Ingredients that are used in sake include rice, water, koji mold (*koji-kin*) and yeast. Brewer's alcohol is an optional ingredient.

sakamai

table rice

Sakamai, or sake-specific rice, is different than table rice. It has a well-defined starchy heart and fewer fats and proteins.

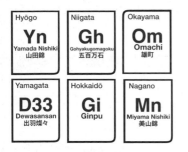

Rice There are more than a hundred different strains of sake rice used throughout Japan, depending on the climate and altitude of the region.

Yeast There are many different strains of sake yeast used throughout Japan, either native to or developed in different regions of the country. They include commercially available, proprietary and wild (or ambient) yeasts.

Water Mountains cover more than 75 percent of Japan's land mass. Rain and snow percolate through them to purify the brewing water used by most sake brewers.

October 1 is known as Sake Day, or *Nihonshu no Hi*, the first day of sake brewing.

Sake can be made by using a single rice variety or by blending different rice strains. The same goes for yeast strains.

Japan is considered sake's home country. Sake has been made here, in some way, shape or form, for 2,600 years.

There are more than 100 sake-specific rice strains, also known as *shuzo kotekimai*, used to craft sake. The advantage of these strains compared to table rice is they have a well-defined starchy heart at the center of the grain, giving brewers greater control over how much of the outer husk's proteins and fats to remove. Brewers care most about preserving the starch, which will be converted to fermentable sugars. But leaving some of the outer husk can also aid in fermentation and add savory layers to the sake. The growing number of sake-specific rice strains is due to regional efforts to develop better local strains or revive older ones. Each rice variety has unique attributes it can bring to sake. On this and the next page you can find information about the most popular rices given in the form of a periodic table.

Top Five Sake Rice Strains

Hyogo	Niigata	Nagano	Okayama	Yamagata
Yn	**Gh**	**Mn**	**Om**	**D33**
Yamada Nishiki	Gohyakugomagoku	Miyama Nishiki	Ōmachi	Dewasansan
山田錦	五百万石	美山錦	雄町	出羽燦々
Yamadaho x Tankan Wataribune 1923 / 1936	Kikusui x Shin No.200 1938 / 1957	Takane Nishiki x y 1978 /--	1859 / 1866	Miyama Nishiki x Hana Fubuki 1985 / 1997

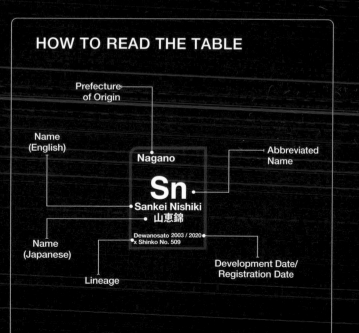

HOW TO READ THE TABLE

Prefecture of Origin

Name (English)

Nagano

Abbreviated Name

Sn

Sankei Nishiki
山恵錦

Dewanosato 2003 / 2020
x Shinko No. 509

Name (Japanese)

Lineage

Development Date/ Registration Date

Akita

Ask

Akita Sake Komachi
秋田酒こまち

Akikeishu 251
x Akikeishu 306 — 1992 / 2003

Hokkaido

Gi

Ginpu
吟風

Kirara No.397 — 1989 / 2000
x Hattan Nishiki No.2

Fukushima

Yk

Yume no Kaori
夢の香

Dewasansan
x Hattan Nishiki — 1991 / 2003

Hiroshima

Hn^1

Hattan Nishiki No.1
八反錦 1号

Hattan No.35
x Akitsu-Ho — 1973 / 1983

Iwate

Gg

Ginginga
吟ぎんが

Dewasansan
x Akita Sake No.49 — 1991 / 2002

Nagano

Ht

Hitogokochi
ひとごこち

Shirotae Nishiki
x Shinko No.444 — 1987 / 1997

Hyogo

Ai

Aiyama
愛山

Aifune No.117
x Yamao No.67 — 1941 / --

Hyogo

Hn

Hakutsuru Nishiki
白鶴錦

Yamada Nishiki
x Yamadabo — 1995 / 2007

Yamagata

Ds

Dewanosato
出羽の里

Ginfubuki x
Dewasansan — 1994 / 2004

Aomori

Hf

Hanafubuki
華吹雪

Okuhomare — 1974 / 1988

Miyagi

Kn

Kura no Hana
蔵の華

Yamada Nishiki
x Tohoku No.140 — 1987 / 1997

Niigata

Kt

Koshi Tanrei
越淡麗

Yamada Nishiki — 1989 / 2004
x Gohyakumangoku

Water

The average bottle of sake consists of 80 percent water. Brewing water is very important to sake making, and brewers pride themselves on the purity of their source. The hardness of their water affects the sake profile. Harder water contains more minerals like calcium and magnesium, which are nutrients for the yeast. Historically, hard water was important for ensuring strong and thorough fermentation, but with the advent of temperature control and improved brewing techniques, brewers have learned to make great sake with both hard and soft water.

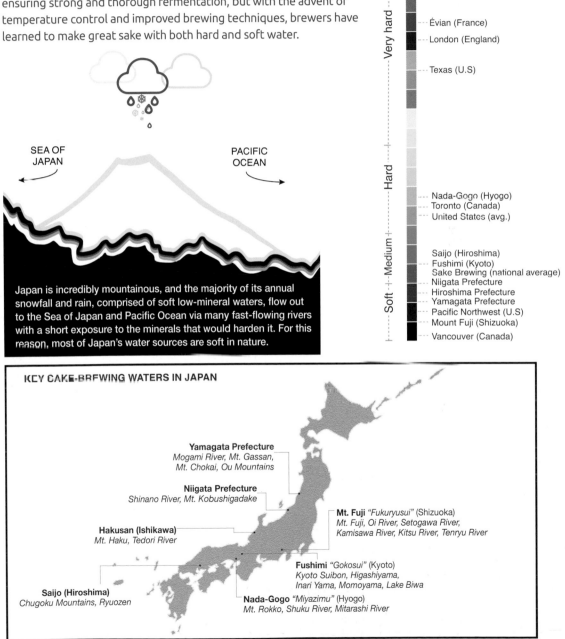

SEA OF JAPAN

PACIFIC OCEAN

Japan is incredibly mountainous, and the majority of its annual snowfall and rain, comprised of soft low-mineral waters, flow out to the Sea of Japan and Pacific Ocean via many fast-flowing rivers with a short exposure to the minerals that would harden it. For this reason, most of Japan's water sources are soft in nature.

Badoit (France)

Very hard
- Évian (France)
- London (England)

Texas (U.S)

Hard

- Nada-Gogo (Hyogo)
- Toronto (Canada)
- United States (avg.)

Medium

- Saijo (Hiroshima)
- Fushimi (Kyoto)
- Sake Brewing (national average)
- Niigata Prefecture
- Hiroshima Prefecture
- Yamagata Prefecture
- Pacific Northwest (U.S)
- Mount Fuji (Shizuoka)
- Vancouver (Canada)

Soft

KEY SAKE-BREWING WATERS IN JAPAN

Yamagata Prefecture
Mogami River, Mt. Gassan, Mt. Chokai, Ou Mountains

Niigata Prefecture
Shinano River, Mt. Kobushigadake

Mt. Fuji *"Fukuryusui"* (Shizuoka)
Mt. Fuji, Oi River, Setogawa River, Kamisawa River, Kitsu River, Tenryu River

Hakusan (Ishikawa)
Mt. Haku, Tedori River

Fushimi *"Gokosui"* (Kyoto)
Kyoto Suibon, Higashiyama, Inari Yama, Momoyama, Lake Biwa

Saijo (Hiroshima)
Chugoku Mountains, Ryuozen

Nada-Gogo *"Miyazimu"* (Hyogo)
Mt. Rokko, Shuku River, Mitarashi River

How Sake Is Made

PROCESSING THE RICE, AND KOJI MAKING

Rice Polishing
Almost all breweries purchase unpolished brown rice either milled by a third party or in-house by the brewery, to the desired polish ratio.

Rice Washing
After polishing, rice is quickly washed to remove any residual bran.

Rice Soaking
Rice is cold soaked to adjust its moisture level, usually to 30% of its total weight. This helps prevent cracking during the steaming process.

Rice Steaming
Steaming gelatinizes rice grains, making it easy for koji mold to access their starchy hearts.

Koji Making
Koji mold is applied to about a fifth of the rice used to make a batch of sake. Koji mold produces enzymes that transform the rice's starch into sugar.

FERMENTATION

Moto / Shubo
Also known as the "yeast starter." This is where steamed rice, koji, water and yeast are blended in a small tank to develop a healthy yeast population.

2 - 4 WEEKS

18 - 35 DAYS

Main Fermentation
More steamed rice, koji and water are added in three stages, called *sandan shikomi*. The koji continues to churn out sugar, which the yeast feeds on, producing alcohol, CO_2 and heat.

POST FERMENTATION

60°C - 65°C
140°F - 150°C

Adding Brewer's Alcohol
In premium sake, an optional step taken to extract more aromatics from the *moromi* (fermenting mash) before filtration.

Pressing
Rice lees are separated from the liquid sake. The *assakuki* (filtration press) is the most common method. Other methods include using a *fune* (boat press) and *shizuku* (drip pressing).

Adding Water
An optional step taken to reduce the alcohol level to the desired percentage, which can help balance the sake. Undiluted bottles are called *genshu*.

Filtration
In addition to pressing, sake can also be clarified further using a number of different methods, including activated charcoal paper, membrane, diatomaceous earth (DE) or cellulose filters.

Pasteurization
An optional step where sake is quickly heated to kill off microbes that can cause the sake to spoil without proper cold storage. A stabilizing process that allows for easier export.

MATURATION, BOTTLING AND SHIPPING

-5°C - +5°C
23°F - 41°F

Blending
Brewers blend in order to maintain a consistency of style between multiple tanks. Brewers may also blend two sakes made with different rice strains, polishing ratios, or yeast strains.

Maturation & Storage
Depending on the style the producer is aiming for, and to allow the sake to stabilize and come into balance, the sake may be matured in bottle or tank for a number of months (or even years), and stored in a refrigerated warehouse.

Bottling and Labeling
The sake is bottled and labeled under sterile conditions. Bottles are treated to minimize light damage. Some are shipped in decorative boxes designed to prolong shelf life as long as possible.

Shipping
Most sake is transported via shipping container. An increasing number of importers ship using refrigerated containers. Seasonal specialty styles are sometimes shipped via air transport.

The Kimoto Method of Brewing

As brewers have sought to recapture the handcrafted tastes of traditional sake, the *kimoto* method of brewing—which produces umami-rich flavors and a layered complexity—has seen a resurgence in popularity. This yeast-starter method dates back to Hyogo Prefecture in the early Edo period (1603–1868), when brewers began intuitively harnessing invisible microbes to kick-start fermentation. The word *kimoto* reflects this spontaneous birth: the character for ki (生) means "life," and moto (酛) means "origin." Like a sourdough starter or the crushed-grape *pied de cuve* starter used in traditional winemaking, the goal is to create a healthy population of yeast. First, brewers place koji-inoculated rice and water in shallow tubs called *hangiri* where, several times a day, they pulverize the mixture with long wooden *kai*, or paddles. This helps distribute the enzymes produced by the koji which in turn help break down the steamed rice. Ambient nitrate-reducing bacteria and lactic-acid bacteria, present on the wooden paddles and tubs, creates nitrous acid and lactic acid that clear out unwanted microbes and allow the wild yeast to thrive and begin fermentation. Once the starter (*shubo* or *moto*), is established it is transferred to a larger tank, where more rice, water and koji are added to create the *moromi*, or main mash. The yeast population continues to multiply, and the fermentation process is well on its way.

Today there are many different variations on this method. One notable labor-saving advance was developed in the 1950s by Dr. Kenkichi Kodama, a microbiologist and member of the Kodama Brewery family, who invented a large drill bit to replace the taxing process of using wooden poles to break down the rice. While most kimoto sakes tend to be full-bodied with lactic, creamy notes, the Akita kimoto method developed by Dr. Kodama tends to yield a lighter profile. In the early twentieth century, brewing scientists discovered it was possible to make a similar starter without laborious paddle mixing, resulting in what came to be known as the *yamahai* method. While many kimoto and yamahai sakes share a similar set of profiles, complexity and lots of umami and creamy notes, yamahai can sometimes edge out its kimoto cousin with added gamey and earthy flavors, since some brewers like to age them a little to bring out these funkier elements.

THE BIRTH OF MOTO TIMELINE

12th–15th Centuries
Brewing expertise is centered in religious temples.

NARA
Late 14th Century
The early precursors to the kimoto starter are invented: *bodaimoto*, *nimoto* and *mizumoto*.

Late 16th Century
Civil unrest leads to the destruction of temples and the decline of the monk brewing styles. Rise of Itami as sake capital.

17th Century
Kanzukuri ("winter brewing") method is developed.

NADA
Late 17th Century
Emergence of kimoto making.

c.1900
Sokujo ("quick starter") developed by Eda Kenjiro, involving the addition of lactic acid to speed up starter development and creating a cleaner sake profile.

HIROSHIMA (NRIB)
1909
Yamahai is developed.

Mid-20th Century
A high-temperature variant of sokujo, called *koontoka moto*, is developed.

AKITA
1950s
Dr. Kenkichi Kodama develops the Akita kimoto method.

Grades

Sake grades are based on the polishing ratio of the rice. The more of the outside fat- and protein-containing husk that is polished off, the lower the ratio and the higher the grade. The number you see on the label is always what is left. If you like the savory, more cereal-driven sakes, go with a higher number. If you like the delicate, wine-like aromas that sake can have, go with a lower number.

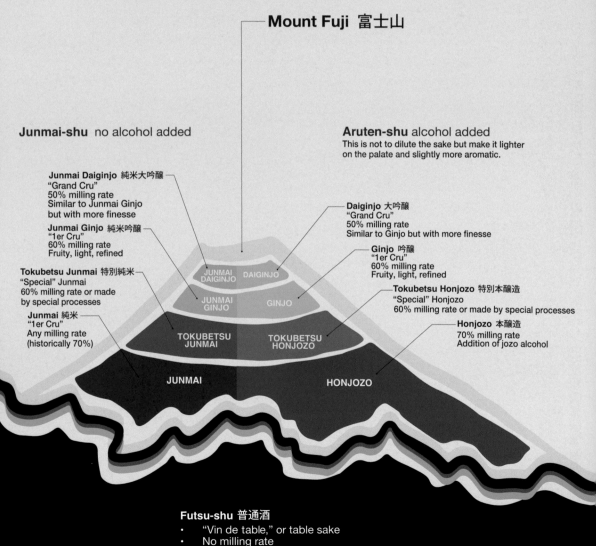

Mount Fuji 富士山

Junmai-shu no alcohol added

Aruten-shu alcohol added
This is not to dilute the sake but make it lighter on the palate and slightly more aromatic.

Junmai Daiginjo 純米大吟醸
"Grand Cru"
50% milling rate
Similar to Junmai Ginjo but with more finesse

Junmai Ginjo 純米吟醸
"1er Cru"
60% milling rate
Fruity, light, refined

Tokubetsu Junmai 特別純米
"Special" Junmai
60% milling rate or made by special processes

Junmai 純米
"1er Cru"
Any milling rate
(historically 70%)

Daiginjo 大吟醸
"Grand Cru"
50% milling rate
Similar to Ginjo but with more finesse

Ginjo 吟醸
"1er Cru"
60% milling rate
Fruity, light, refined

Tokubetsu Honjozo 特別本醸造
"Special" Honjozo
60% milling rate or made by special processes

Honjozo 本醸造
70% milling rate
Addition of jozo alcohol

JUNMAI DAIGINJO · DAIGINJO
JUNMAI GINJO · GINJO
TOKUBETSU JUNMAI · TOKUBETSU HONJOZO
JUNMAI · HONJOZO

Futsu-shu 普通酒
- "Vin de table," or table sake
- No milling rate
- Addition of brewer's alcohol
- Approximately 60% of production

Sake Styles and Other Key Terms

Arabashiri あらばしり
The first one third of sake to come out of the press. Typically free-run sake from a *fune* box press.

Happo-shu or Awazake 発砲酒 or あわ酒
Sparkling sake. *Awazake* is also a term used to refer to bottle-fermented sparkling sake.

Genshu 原酒
Not diluted with water before bottling.

Hiyaoroshi ひやおろし
Autumn-released *nama-zume* sake.

Kijoshu 貴醸酒
A sweet sake made by replacing a percentage of the brewing water with already-brewed sake.

Kimoto 生酛
A very old labor-intensive fermentation starter using ambient lactic acid bacteria and wooden poles to mash the rice into a paste.

Koshu 古酒
Aged sake, usually at least a year old. The aging can be done intentionally by the brewer or refer to old sake that has not been consumed.

Muroka 無濾過
Not charcoal filtered. The sake is clear but you can expect a greater flavor intensity.

Nama-chozo 生貯蔵
Sake that is stored as *nama*, matured and then pasteurized only once before shipping.

Namazake 生酒
Unpasteurized sake.

Namazume 生詰
Single pasteurized sake that is then stored and matured. The usual second pasteurization is omitted and the sake is bottled. Hiyaoroshi is an example of this.

Niqori にごり
Cloudy sake. A sake that has been roughly filtered. Note: "unfiltered" is incorrect!

Shiboritate 搾りたて
Fresh, just-pressed sake.

Taruzake 樽酒
Sake that has been matured in cedar barrels (*taru*), which give a woody and spicy fragrance to the sake.

Yamahai 山廃
A type of fermentation starter where ambient lactic acid bacteria is encouraged to propagate. The sakes are often layered, savory or gamey.

Comparing Sake, Wine and Beer

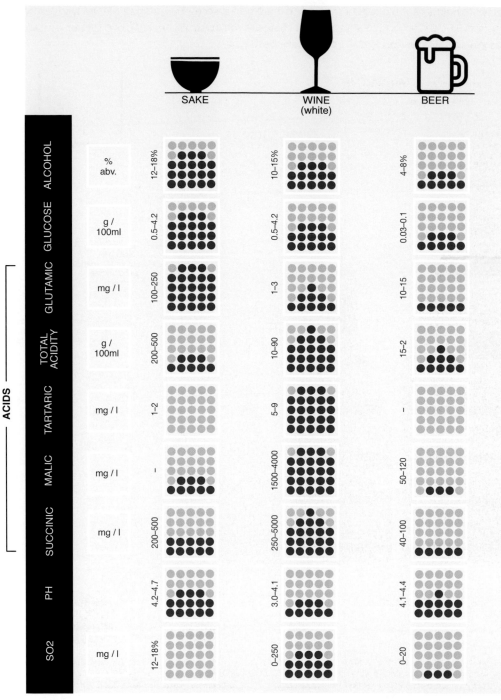

	units	SAKE	WINE (white)	BEER
ALCOHOL	% abv.	12–18%	10–15%	4–8%
GLUCOSE	g / 100ml	0.5–4.2	0.5–4.2	0.03–0.1
GLUTAMIC	mg / l	100–250	1–3	10–15
TOTAL ACIDITY	g / 100ml	200–500	10–90	15–2
TARTARIC	mg / l	1–2	5–9	–
MALIC	mg / l	–	1500–4000	50–120
SUCCINIC	mg / l	200–500	250–5000	40–100
PH		4.2–4.7	3.0–4.1	4.1–4.4
SO2	mg / l	12–18%	0–250	0–20

ACIDS (bracket covering GLUTAMIC, TOTAL ACIDITY, TARTARIC, MALIC, SUCCINIC)

Data based on: A Comprehensive Guide to Japanese Sake, Japan Sake and Shochu Makers Association, 2011.

Bottle Sizes and Measurements

The measurements below date from the Edo era and are based on the *masu*, a small 180 ml wooden box used to measure grains and soy sauce among other things. If you are a history buff, this system is really interesting, as you can still see its legacy today in sake bottle sizes.

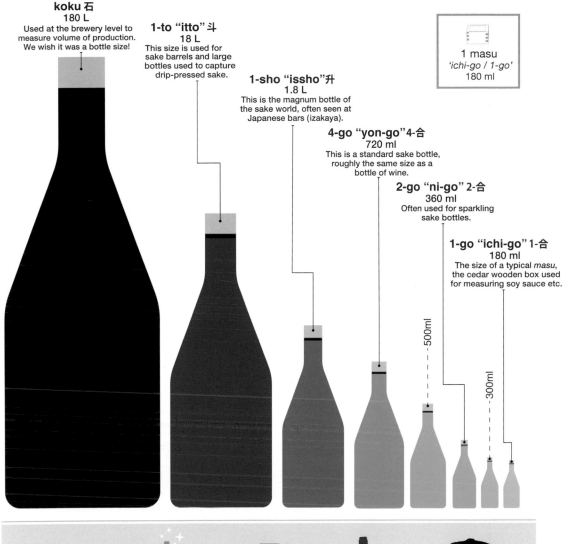

koku 石
180 L
Used at the brewery level to measure volume of production. We wish it was a bottle size!

1-to "itto" 斗
18 L
This size is used for sake barrels and large bottles used to capture drip-pressed sake.

1-sho "issho" 升
1.8 L
This is the magnum bottle of the sake world, often seen at Japanese bars (izakaya).

4-go "yon-go" 4-合
720 ml
This is a standard sake bottle, roughly the same size as a bottle of wine.

2-go "ni-go" 2-合
360 ml
Often used for sparkling sake bottles.

1-go "ichi-go" 1-合
180 ml
The size of a typical *masu*, the cedar wooden box used for measuring soy sauce etc.

1 masu
'ichi-go / 1-go'
180 ml

500ml

300ml

Cup 180 ml
Hugely popular since they are easy to carry on trains and double as a drinking vessel.

Sparkling Bottles 720 ml
Reinforced glass to withstand the pressure created by awa (sparkling) sake made like champagne.

Carton 1.8 L
Often used for bulk, regular sake.

Tobin 18 L
Used to collect drip-pressed sake.

Sake Taru (barrel) 18 L
Historically used to transport sake, but today they are often seen at shrines and used at cask-opening ceremonies.

Reading the Label

The many terms found on sake labels will help you determine its classification, its flavor profile and how it was made.

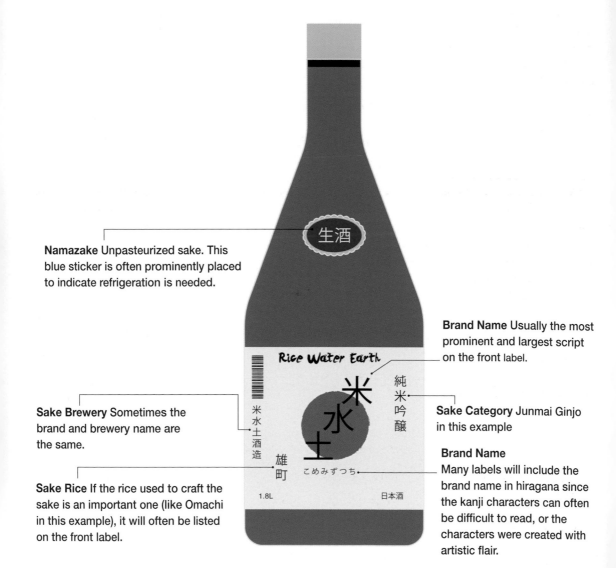

Namazake Unpasteurized sake. This blue sticker is often prominently placed to indicate refrigeration is needed.

Sake Brewery Sometimes the brand and brewery name are the same.

Sake Rice If the rice used to craft the sake is an important one (like Omachi in this example), it will often be listed on the front label.

Brand Name Usually the most prominent and largest script on the front label.

Sake Category Junmai Ginjo in this example

Brand Name Many labels will include the brand name in hiragana since the kanji characters can often be difficult to read, or the characters were created with artistic flair.

生酒

Rice Water Earth

純米吟醸

米水土

こめみずつち

米水土酒造

雄町

1.8L

日本酒

BACK LABEL There are many terms that can be found on the back label that can help tell what to expect when you try the sake. Here are several of the most frequently used terms.

Brewing Year (BY) May be indicated in the Gregorian calendar (e.g., 2020) or, in this case, the Japanese calendar year, Reiwa 2.

Ingredients Typically indicating the type of rice used.

Nihonshu-do / Sake Meter Value (SMV) Indicates the sweetness or dryness. Generally, the higher the number (e.g., +10) the drier.

Acidity Like the Nihonshu-do, the higher the number, the drier the sake will taste. The range is usually between 1.0 and 2.0.

Yeast Certain yeasts can have a profound effect on the sake's profile. Sometimes indicated on the label.

Production Date / Bottling Date

Rice Water Earth
R2BY　米水土
純米吟醸　生酒

原料米 / 赤磐 雄町

精米歩合 / 65%

アルコール分 / 17度以上18度未満

日本酒度 / +5

酸度 / 1.6

アミノ酸度 / 1.0

酵母｜協会9号

瓶詰年月
21.09

Type of Sake (ginjo, daiginjo, junmai, etc.)

Production Method (nama, nigori, yamahai, genshu, kimoto, etc.)

Seimai Buai / Polishing Rate This percentage tells you what is left of the rice after polishing.

Alcohol Percentage In this case, indicated as a range between 17% and 18%.

Amino Acidity This indicates the level of amino acids. The higher the number, the more savory umami-driven flavors you can expect.

Japanese Sake Seishu ("clear sake" 清酒) is also an official term used.

OTHER TERMS TO LOOK OUT FOR

Naka-dori 中取り The middle fraction of pressed sake, considered the best part.

Kasu Buai 粕歩合 Refers to the percentage of rice solids remaining of the original amount of rice used to make a tank, after pressing the sake.

Hi-ire 火入 Pasteurized sake.

Ki-ippon 生一本 Sake that was brewed in a single brewery. In earlier decades, many breweries made sake for the big brands, which would blend these small batches with others to produce blends marketed nationally. This term is a nostalgic reference to those days.

Hiyaoroshi 冷やおろし An autumn-released sake, typically not pasteurized a second time.

Karakuchi 辛口 Dry taste.

Kojimai 麹米 Rice used for koji making.

Kakemai 掛米 Rice added as regular steamed rice.

Sake Vessels

With so many sake grades, styles and profiles available, there is also a wide selection of serving vessels, some with histories dating from the Edo period or earlier. Below is a list of the main sake vessels and their materials. Whether earthenware, glass or metal, they all bring out different nuances in a sake!

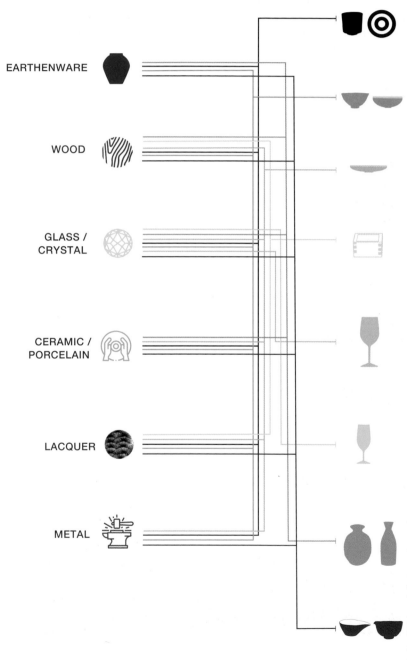

EARTHENWARE

WOOD

GLASS / CRYSTAL

CERAMIC / PORCELAIN

LACQUER

METAL

CHOKO 猪口
Comes in all shapes, sizes and designs, often accompanied by a *tokkuri* flask. A large white porcelain version with two concentric blue circles at the bottom of the cup is a *kikichoko* professional taster's cup.

GUINOMI ぐい呑み
These sake cups tend to be larger than a *choko*, although there isn't a regulation as to when a choko becomes a guinomi.

SAKAZUKI 盃
A flat, saucer-like cup dating back to the 10th century, used at weddings and New Year parties.

MASU 升
Typically made of Japanese cedar or cypress, this cup was originally used to measure grains and sauces. It usually measures one *go*, or 180 ml.

WINE GLASS
Great for aromatic types of sake. The bowl of the glass and narrowed rim captures and enhances aromas.

SAKE GLASS
An offshoot of the wine glass, specifically made for sake. Reidel, a wine glass maker, has a range of sake glasses. Specialty glass companies like Shotoku and Sugahara also make sake-specific glasses. Kaburaki, a venerable porcelain maker from Ishikawa, also makes a line of sake glasses (Kutani-ware).

TOKKURI 徳利
Used for vinegar storage before the advent of smaller versions in the Edo era. Depending on its material, it is great for heating and serving *kanzake* (warm sake). It can be used for *reishu* (chilled sake).

KATAKUCHI 片口
This vessel is bowl shaped with a spout for pouring. It can be used for chilled and room-temperature sake.

Serving Temperatures

One of the many fine attributes of sake is the wide range of temperatures at which it can be served. Playing with sake temperature is something the Japanese have done since the Edo period, when names such as *hanahie* ("flower chilled"), with subtle references to seasonal shifts, were given to different serving temperatures. Heating a sake can bring out different aspects of its personality. What temperature to serve a sake at really comes down to personal preference. While we've recommended some ideal service temperatures for each grade and style, we encourage you to try experimenting with different temperatures to help figure out what your own preferences are.

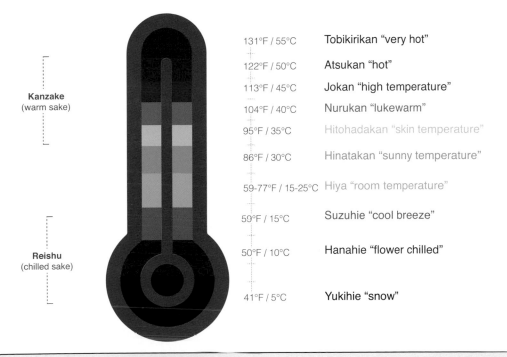

Kanzake (warm sake)

Reishu (chilled sake)

131°F / 55°C	Tobikirikan "very hot"
122°F / 50°C	Atsukan "hot"
113°F / 45°C	Jokan "high temperature"
104°F / 40°C	Nurukan "lukewarm"
95°F / 35°C	Hitohadakan "skin temperature"
86°F / 30°C	Hinatakan "sunny temperature"
59-77°F / 15-25°C	Hiya "room temperature"
59°F / 15°C	Suzuhie "cool breeze"
50°F / 10°C	Hanahie "flower chilled"
41°F / 5°C	Yukihie "snow"

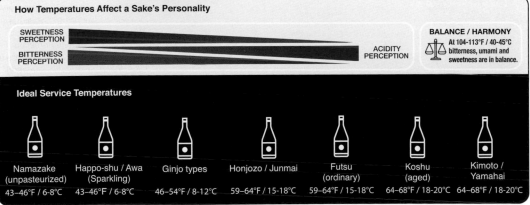

How Temperatures Affect a Sake's Personality

SWEETNESS PERCEPTION

BITTERNESS PERCEPTION

ACIDITY PERCEPTION

BALANCE / HARMONY At 104-113°F / 40-45°C bitterness, umami and sweetness are in balance.

Ideal Service Temperatures

Namazake (unpasteurized)	Happo-shu / Awa (Sparkling)	Ginjo types	Honjozo / Junmai	Futsu (ordinary)	Koshu (aged)	Kimoto / Yamahai
43–46°F / 6-8°C	43–46°F / 6-8°C	46–54°F / 8-12°C	59–64°F / 15-18°C	59–64°F / 15-18°C	64–68°F / 18-20°C	64–68°F / 18-20°C

Basic Sake Characteristics

Wine and sake professionals often use the criteria of appearance, aromas, flavors and one's overall opinion to assess a product. This is an effective way to train your palate and ability to recall a wide range of tastes and aromas.

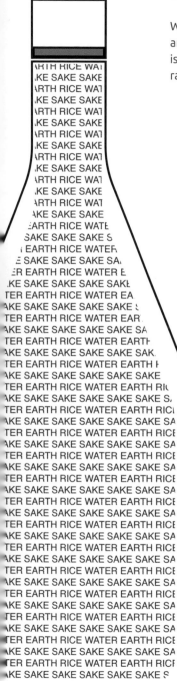

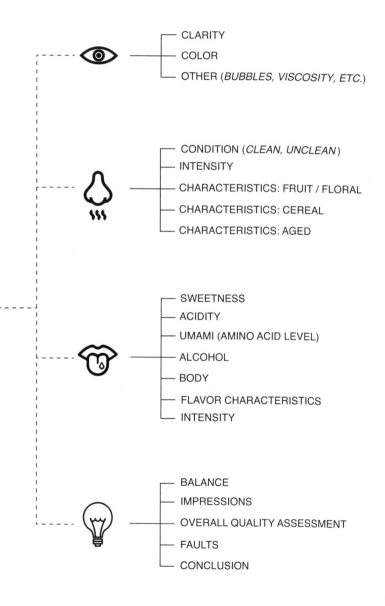

- CLARITY
- COLOR
- OTHER (*BUBBLES, VISCOSITY, ETC.*)

- CONDITION (*CLEAN, UNCLEAN*)
- INTENSITY
- CHARACTERISTICS: FRUIT / FLORAL
- CHARACTERISTICS: CEREAL
- CHARACTERISTICS: AGED

- SWEETNESS
- ACIDITY
- UMAMI (AMINO ACID LEVEL)
- ALCOHOL
- BODY
- FLAVOR CHARACTERISTICS
- INTENSITY

- BALANCE
- IMPRESSIONS
- OVERALL QUALITY ASSESSMENT
- FAULTS
- CONCLUSION

Tasting Sake

There are six characteristics of sake that help define it: sweetness, acidity, umami, alcohol, body and texture. A sake's personality comes from the interplay of these components with one another.

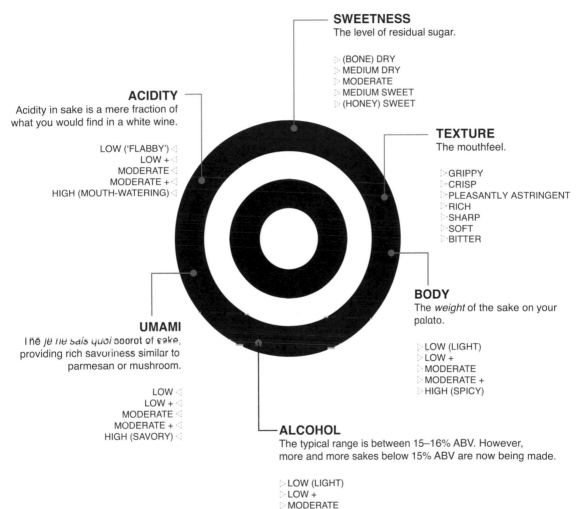

SWEETNESS
The level of residual sugar.

▷ (BONE) DRY
▷ MEDIUM DRY
▷ MODERATE
▷ MEDIUM SWEET
▷ (HONEY) SWEET

ACIDITY
Acidity in sake is a mere fraction of what you would find in a white wine.

LOW ('FLABBY') ◁
LOW + ◁
MODERATE ◁
MODERATE + ◁
HIGH (MOUTH-WATERING) ◁

TEXTURE
The mouthfeel.

▷ GRIPPY
▷ CRISP
▷ PLEASANTLY ASTRINGENT
▷ RICH
▷ SHARP
▷ SOFT
▷ BITTER

UMAMI
The *je ne sais quoi* factor of sake, providing rich savoriness similar to parmesan or mushroom.

LOW ◁
LOW + ◁
MODERATE ◁
MODERATE + ◁
HIGH (SAVORY) ◁

BODY
The *weight* of the sake on your palate.

▷ LOW (LIGHT)
▷ LOW +
▷ MODERATE
▷ MODERATE +
▷ HIGH (SPICY)

ALCOHOL
The typical range is between 15–16% ABV. However, more and more sakes below 15% ABV are now being made.

▷ LOW (LIGHT)
▷ LOW +
▷ MODERATE
▷ MODERATE +
▷ HIGH (SPICY)

Tasting Sake: Appearance

Assessing sake is often done using two vessels. The *kikichoko* is a traditional professional sake taster's cup that's been used for more than a century to assess sake at national sake competitions. It is a white porcelain cup with two concentric blue rings on the bottom of it. These allow you to better detect any color or turbidity in the sake. While the kikichoko is great for checking out a sake's appearance, a wine glass can help tasters more readily perceive and assess aromas and flavors. If you are using a wine glass, tilt the glass to a forty-five-degree angle over a white background to assess its appearance.

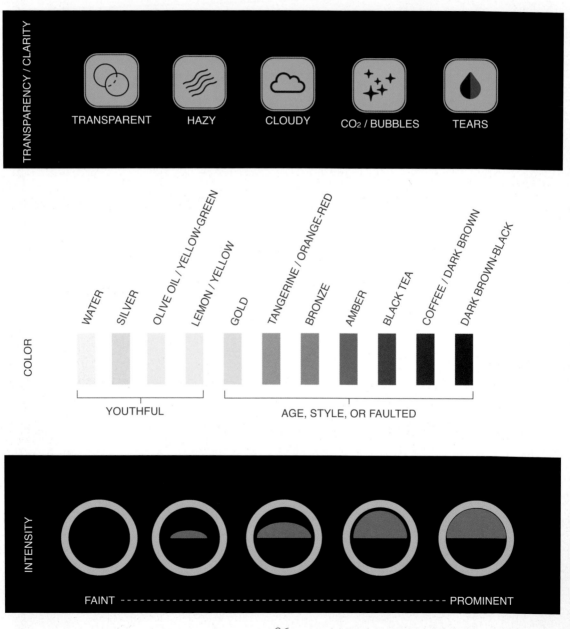

TRANSPARENCY / CLARITY

TRANSPARENT   HAZY   CLOUDY   CO₂ / BUBBLES   TEARS

COLOR

WATER   SILVER   OLIVE OIL / YELLOW-GREEN   LEMON / YELLOW   GOLD   TANGERINE / ORANGE-RED   BRONZE   AMBER   BLACK TEA   COFFEE / DARK BROWN   DARK BROWN-BLACK

YOUTHFUL   AGE, STYLE, OR FAULTED

INTENSITY

FAINT - PROMINENT

Tasting Sake: Aromas

Sake aromas range widely, from fruity to floral, or reminiscent of mushrooms, yogurt or baking spices.

INTENSITY

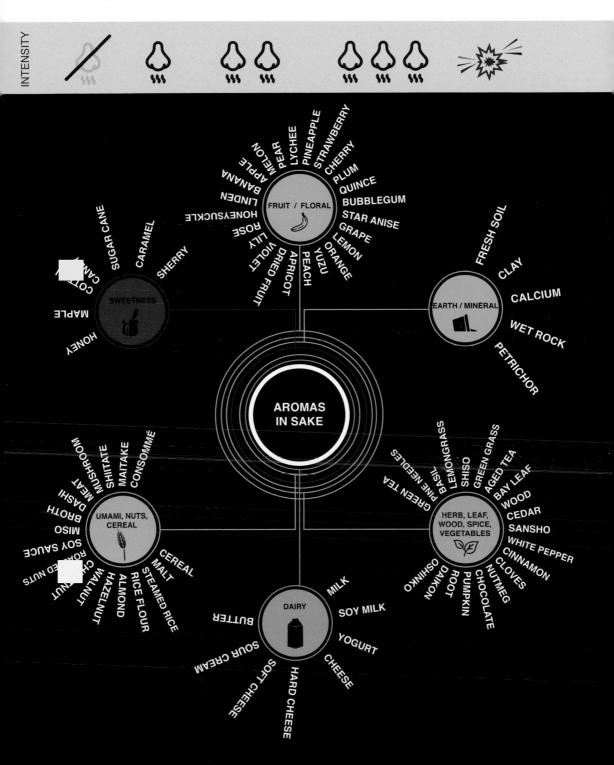

Tasting Sake: Palate

By assessing the palate we mean recognizing the various components in a sake and how they relate to one another. Are they in harmony? Is one particularly prominent? Exploring these traits will help you build a mental profile of the sake.

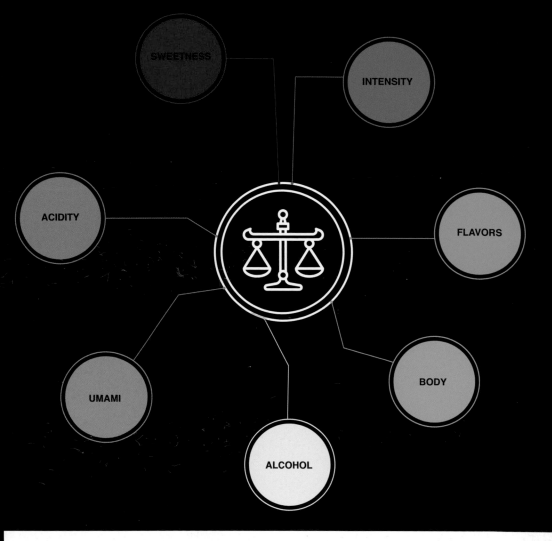

Tasting Sake: Conclusion

Now that you have noted the appearance, aromatic profile and palate of the sake, you can form an opinion of the sake. This tasting method allows you to deduce the quality of the sake based on the balance or imbalance of its components. Tasting this way can also help determine the sake styles that you prefer. Jotting down the aspects you enjoy will develop your skills at communicating your likes and dislikes.

"so-so"   "wow!"

Tasting Lexicon

Writing a useful tasting note takes practice but can be a lot of fun. This is an example of how to structure a tasting note. Be sure to inject your own personality and opinions in it.

TODAY'S DATE / BOTTLE DATE / BREWING YEAR

BRAND _____

BREWERY _____

PREFECTURE/REGION _____

GRADE / STYLE _____

RICE _____

POLISH RATE _____

NOTES _____

CLARITY

☐	☐	☐
Crystal / Water	Usunigori	Nigori

COLOR

☐	☐	☐	☐	☐	☐
Water	Olive Oil	Lemon	Gold	Amber	Coffee

OTHER _____

CONDITION

☐	☐	☐
Fresh / Clean	Pungent	Unfresh / Not Clean

INTENSITY

☐	☐	☐
Obsolete	Moderate	Room Filling

CHARACTERISTICS

FRUIT / FLORAL _____

tropical / red fruits _____

stone fruit / citrus _____

flowers _____

HERB / LEAF / WOOD _____

SPICE / VEGETABLE _____

EARTH / MINERAL _____

UMAMI / NUTS / CEREAL _____

SWEETNESS / DAIRY _____

OTHER _____

	Bone Dry	Mid Dry	Moderate	Sweet	Honey
SWEETNESS	☐	☐	☐	☐	☐

	Low	Low +	Moderate	Moderate +	High
ACIDITY	☐	☐	☐	☐	☐
UMAMI	☐	☐	☐	☐	☐
ALCOHOL	☐	☐	☐	☐	☐

	Light	Light +	Moderate	Moderate +	Full
BODY	☐	☐	☐	☐	☐

CHARACTERISTICS

OTHER _____

Identifying Sake Faults

UV LIGHT
Sake is quite sensitive to UV light. Over time, the unpleasant aroma of burnt hair can develop from the reaction of light with proteins and amino acids in the sake. Beware of sake that has been sitting on liquor-store shelves for long periods.

MICROBIAL
Sake is made with several microorganisms. Many things can go wrong during sake making that can cause unpleasant aromas of compost, mold, chemical adhesives, or rancid dairy products, among others.

BUBBLES
Caused by refermentation. This one is tricky, since several producers create their sake with a hint of spritz on the palate on purpose. Unintended bubbles could be accompanied by haziness or cloudiness.

OXIDATION
Oxidized sake usually smells and tastes flat and stale. It can also contribute to *hineka* (see below).

4VG
4-vinyl guaiacol is a part of a group of phenols that includes vanillin. It develops through bacterial spoilage during koji making. Its hallmarks are aromas of burnt rubber or smoke.

VINEGAR
Acetic acid is created in small doses during fermentation and can sometimes become more prominent in a sake's profile.

HINEKA
Hineka refers to sulfurous, rotten cabbage–like and pickled-vegetable aromas, indicating a bottle that has been improperly stored and undergone oxidation.

HIOCHI
A type of lactic acid bacteria that can develop post fermentation. The sake will be cloudy and possess an imbalanced acidity and perceptible, undesirable aromas.

NAMA HINEKA
The meaty aroma known as *nama hineka* is caused by improper storage of unpasteurized sake.

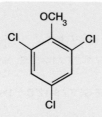

TCA
TCA is a chemical that manifests as a musty, wet-cardboard smell often associated with "corked" wine. It likes wood, found in many sake breweries.

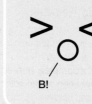

DIACETYL
A cheesy aroma (think cottage cheese) caused by sake-making contamination.

ZATSUMI
Rough, unpolished and unbalanced sake that includes elements of bitterness and astringency.

Sake Storage

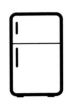

KEEP COOL
Generally, below 54°F / 12°C. For namazake, below 46°F / 8°C.

STORE UPRIGHT
Most sake is bottled with a screw-top cap. Minimizing the length of contact with the synthetic materials of the cap is best.

PROTECT FROM LIGHT
If it doesn't already come in a box, wrap your sake in newspaper to minimize contact with light.

SHELF LIFE
As a rule, sake should be consumed relatively soon after purchasing. Lighter styles like ginjo will lose their fresh aromas and flavors faster than a yamahai junmai. Of course, a lot depends on personal preference. Some people like to experiment with aging different bottles to see what outcomes are possible.

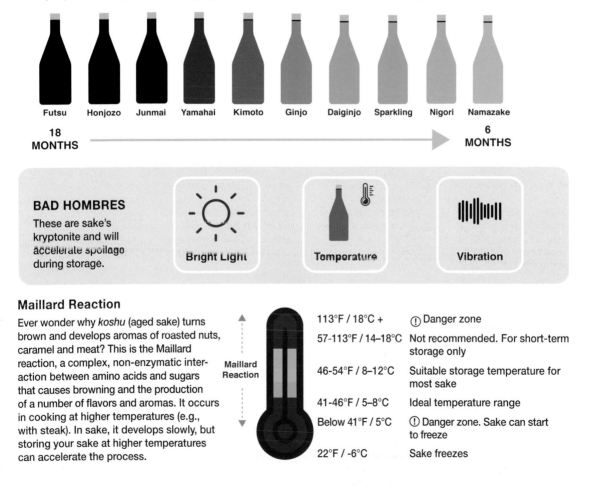

| Futsu | Honjozo | Junmai | Yamahai | Kimoto | Ginjo | Daiginjo | Sparkling | Nigori | Namazake |

18 MONTHS ———————————————————————→ **6 MONTHS**

BAD HOMBRES
These are sake's kryptonite and will accelerate spoilage during storage.

Bright Light

Temperature

Vibration

Maillard Reaction

Ever wonder why *koshu* (aged sake) turns brown and develops aromas of roasted nuts, caramel and meat? This is the Maillard reaction, a complex, non-enzymatic inter-action between amino acids and sugars that causes browning and the production of a number of flavors and aromas. It occurs in cooking at higher temperatures (e.g., with steak). In sake, it develops slowly, but storing your sake at higher temperatures can accelerate the process.

Maillard Reaction

113°F / 18°C +	ⓘ Danger zone
57-113°F / 14–18°C	Not recommended. For short-term storage only
46-54°F / 8–12°C	Suitable storage temperature for most sake
41-46°F / 5–8°C	Ideal temperature range
Below 41°F / 5°C	ⓘ Danger zone. Sake can start to freeze
22°F / -6°C	Sake freezes

Food and Sake

Versatility Power
Sake has a chameleon-like ability to provide the perfect match for a wide range of cuisines. It has an innate ability to enhance and complement food while often staying in the shadows. It's not only great with or in food, but also in cocktails and at a broad range of service temperatures.

Three things to take away about sake and food pairing:

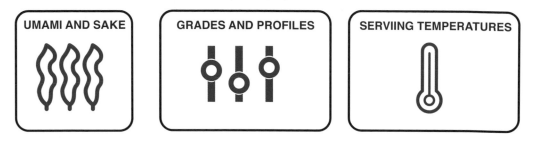

UMAMI AND SAKE

GRADES AND PROFILES

SERVIING TEMPERATURES

We can sense many (thousands of!) aromas, but we can only perceive five basic tastes:

SWEET   SOUR   SALT   BITTER   UMAMI

Considerations
Ideally a dish, whether made by a professional chef or a home cook, balances these five basic tastes. When sake is thrown into the equation, how will it change this balance? How will the dish affect how the sake tastes? Remember that every person's tastes are different and subjective.

It's all in the balance...the balance of sweetness, bitterness, acidity, umami and salt, in addition to other components like fat and spiciness, in finding a sake that doesn't tip the scale but rather works with it.

Flavor Learning
According to scientist Dr. Kristin Connor, we develop our first taste preferences in the womb! And our flavor learning is trained by early and repeated exposures, from the womb, to breast milk, to the introduction of solid foods. It is one of the reasons we all taste differently!

Umami: Sake's Secret Ingredient

Umami was discovered in 1908 by a Japanese chemist named Kikunae Ikeda. It became the fifth taste after Ikeda isolated the taste from sea kelp (kombu). It's a difficult taste to describe, often simply expressed as "delicious" or "savory." And, unlike the other tastes (salt, sweet, bitter, sour), it is hard to isolate as it's often accompanied by other components like salt. Foods with high umami have one important thing in common: they have a very high level of amino acids, especially glutamic acid.

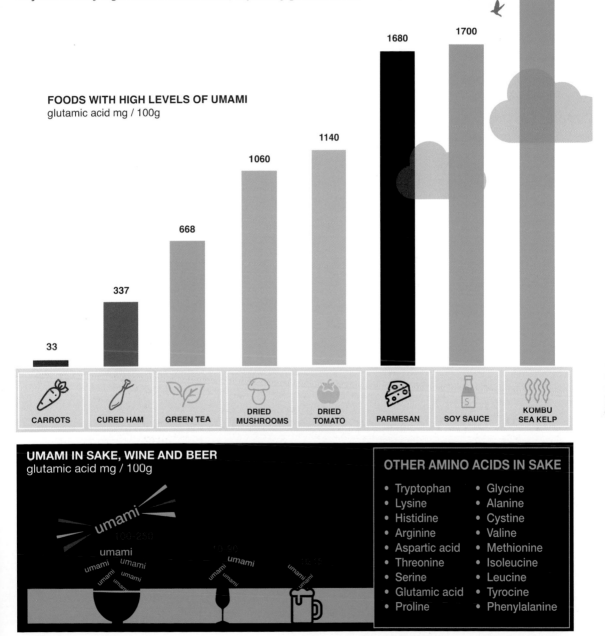

FOODS WITH HIGH LEVELS OF UMAMI
glutamic acid mg / 100g

Food	glutamic acid mg / 100g
CARROTS	33
CURED HAM	337
GREEN TEA	668
DRIED MUSHROOMS	1060
DRIED TOMATO	1140
PARMESAN	1680
SOY SAUCE	1700
KOMBU SEA KELP	>2000

UMAMI IN SAKE, WINE AND BEER
glutamic acid mg / 100g

umami umami umami umami umami umami umami umami umami umami umami umami

OTHER AMINO ACIDS IN SAKE

- Tryptophan
- Lysine
- Histidine
- Arginine
- Aspartic acid
- Threonine
- Serine
- Glutamic acid
- Proline
- Glycine
- Alanine
- Cystine
- Valine
- Methionine
- Isoleucine
- Leucine
- Tyrocine
- Phenylalanine

Umami by Sake Grade

In general, sakes with a higher polishing ratio have less umami than those with a lower polishing ratio. Umami-rich glutamic acid and other amino acids generate umami from the proteins present in the outer husks of rice. So, less polished rice = more umami!

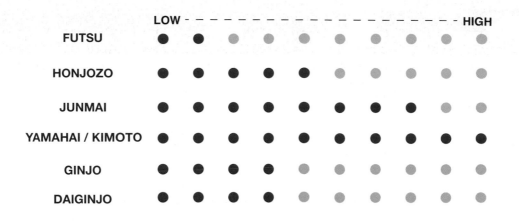

LOW – – – – – – – – – – – – – – – – – – HIGH

FUTSU
HONJOZO
JUNMAI
YAMAHAI / KIMOTO
GINJO
DAIGINJO

SYNERGISTIC EFFECT OF UMAMI
One of the reasons that sake is so food friendly is the bond it forms with dishes that have umami.

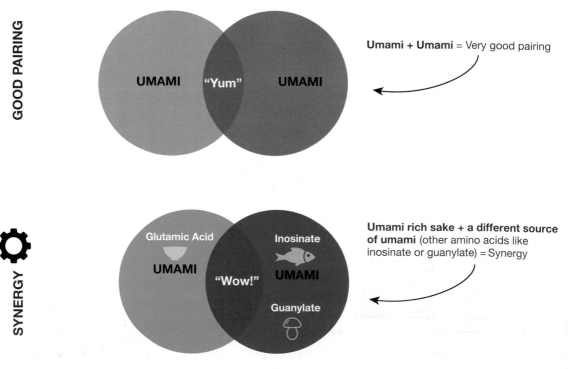

GOOD PAIRING

UMAMI "Yum" UMAMI

Umami + Umami = Very good pairing

SYNERGY

Glutamic Acid

UMAMI "Wow!" UMAMI

Inosinate

Guanylate

Umami rich sake + a different source of umami (other amino acids like inosinate or guanylate) = Synergy

Sake and Fish

Most seafood has moderate-to-high levels of umami, which creates that synergistic effect when paired with sake. Sake's low iron and zero sulfite content allows sake to complement fish dishes and play down any negative fishiness (*namagusai*).

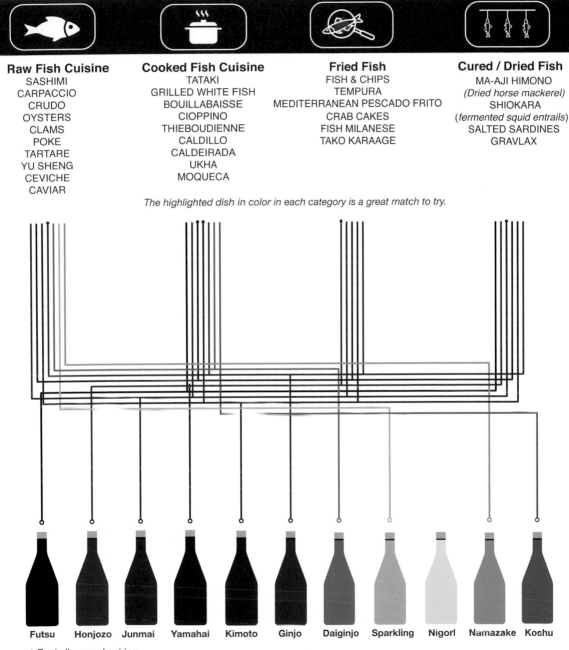

Raw Fish Cuisine
SASHIMI
CARPACCIO
CRUDO
OYSTERS
CLAMS
POKE
TARTARE
YU SHENG
CEVICHE
CAVIAR

Cooked Fish Cuisine
TATAKI
GRILLED WHITE FISH
BOUILLABAISSE
CIOPPINO
THIEBOUDIENNE
CALDILLO
CALDEIRADA
UKHA
MOQUECA

Fried Fish
FISH & CHIPS
TEMPURA
MEDITERRANEAN PESCADO FRITO
CRAB CAKES
FISH MILANESE
TAKO KARAAGE

Cured / Dried Fish
MA-AJI HIMONO
(Dried horse mackerel)
SHIOKARA
(fermented squid entrails)
SALTED SARDINES
GRAVLAX

The highlighted dish in color in each category is a great match to try.

Futsu Honjozo Junmai Yamahai Kimoto Ginjo Daiginjo Sparkling Nigorl Namazake Koshu

● *Best all-around pairing*

Sake and Cheese

Yes, cheese and sake are a match made in heaven! From the creamy fresh to the pungent and umami-laden aged cheeses, the various sake profiles can offer exemplary pairings.

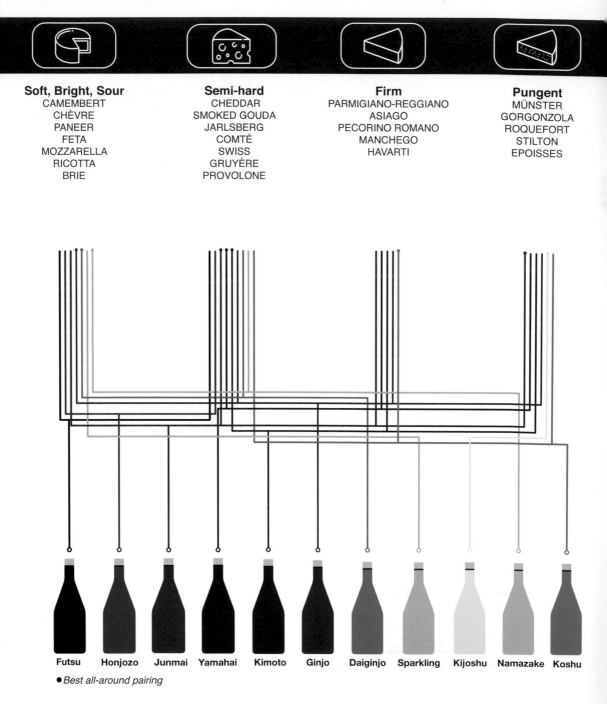

Soft, Bright, Sour
CAMEMBERT
CHÈVRE
PANEER
FETA
MOZZARELLA
RICOTTA
BRIE

Semi-hard
CHEDDAR
SMOKED GOUDA
JARLSBERG
COMTÉ
SWISS
GRUYÈRE
PROVOLONE

Firm
PARMIGIANO-REGGIANO
ASIAGO
PECORINO ROMANO
MANCHEGO
HAVARTI

Pungent
MÜNSTER
GORGONZOLA
ROQUEFORT
STILTON
EPOISSES

Futsu   Honjozo   Junmai   Yamahai   Kimoto   Ginjo   Daiginjo   Sparkling   Kijoshu   Namazake   Koshu

● *Best all-around pairing*

Sake with Meats & Vegetables

It doesn't matter if it's white meat, dark meat, poultry or vegetables, sake is a friend to all!

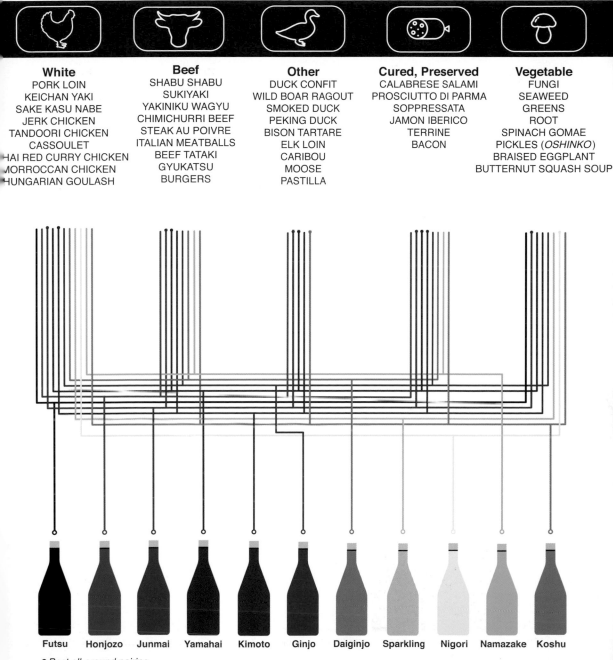

White
PORK LOIN
KEICHAN YAKI
SAKE KASU NABE
JERK CHICKEN
TANDOORI CHICKEN
CASSOULET
THAI RED CURRY CHICKEN
MORROCCAN CHICKEN
HUNGARIAN GOULASH

Beef
SHABU SHABU
SUKIYAKI
YAKINIKU WAGYU
CHIMICHURRI BEEF
STEAK AU POIVRE
ITALIAN MEATBALLS
BEEF TATAKI
GYUKATSU
BURGERS

Other
DUCK CONFIT
WILD BOAR RAGOUT
SMOKED DUCK
PEKING DUCK
BISON TARTARE
ELK LOIN
CARIBOU
MOOSE
PASTILLA

Cured, Preserved
CALABRESE SALAMI
PROSCIUTTO DI PARMA
SOPPRESSATA
JAMON IBERICO
TERRINE
BACON

Vegetable
FUNGI
SEAWEED
GREENS
ROOT
SPINACH GOMAE
PICKLES (*OSHINKO*)
BRAISED EGGPLANT
BUTTERNUT SQUASH SOUP

Futsu   Honjozo   Junmai   Yamahai   Kimoto   Ginjo   Daiginjo   Sparkling   Nigori   Namazake   Koshu

● *Best all-around pairing*

Part I
Rice, Water, Earth

The deeper we get into our travels through the mountains and plains of Japan, the better we are able to visualize the inner architecture of sake. In its texture and rich aroma, we see its solid foundation in the fertile rice fields. In its transparent beauty, we see the clear spring water and snowmelt that nourishes those fields, and brews the rice they produce. In its freshness, we see the mountains that purify this water as it travels through ancient geological strata. This first part of our book is dedicated to these three elemental ingredients of sake: rice, water and earth.

The introduction of rice-paddy cultivation from mainland Asia 3,000 years ago was the start of Japan's transformation into an agrarian society. Rice, and its planting and harvesting rituals, came to be closely associated with the imperial family. And since the emperor was considered a direct descendant of the gods, rice and its brewed and fermented incarnation, sake (酒), took on sacred status. Over time, it became the iconic staple grain of Japan. The bento box, delicately vinegared sushi or the one-bowl *donburi* meal are all beloved culinary symbols of Japanese identity.

Water is important because while the key sake elements of rice, yeast, *koji* mold and even the skill of the sake maker are transportable, massive quantities of water are not. And the water needs of sake breweries are massive: about fifty times the weight of the rice used to make sake. In addition to imparting its mineral backbone to sake, earth, like water, is central to the ancient idea of *jizake*, or local sake. Today, both earth and water are invoked to describe the still-contentious idea of "terroir" in sake.

Chapter One

Yamada Nishiki: The Grand Cru Sake Rice

Standing shin deep in rice paddy mud, we're trying not to think about the leeches lurking below as we plant our precious seedlings. We've come on a pilgrimage to this six-mile-square (15 km²) hamlet in Yokawa, Hyogo Prefecture, for a first-hand glimpse at the agricultural source of premium sake. Hyogo is the birthplace of the king of sake-rice varieties, Yamada Nishiki (山田錦), and the land where it grows best, yielding some of the most elegant, aromatic and refined sake being made today.

More Yamada Nishiki is grown in Japan than any other sake rice, and 60 percent of what's grown is from this prefecture. Hyogo and Yamada Nishiki are to sake what Kentucky and Kentucky bluegrass are to thoroughbred horse breeding, where the fertility of land, nature and human experience come together to create something exceptional.

But even within Hyogo, Yamada Nishiki has been painstakingly classified into increasingly rarefied levels—twenty-four if you merge paddy rankings and rice-quality grades. This paddy, where our toes are sunk in mud, is categorized as a *Toku-A* (special class) rather than the lesser but still high-quality *Toku-B* or *Toku-C* fields that form the *Toku-jo* (top special class) category.

Yokawa is one of only five Toku-A towns, and so is nearby Tojo. What makes rice grow so well in these fields is a combination of soil and microclimate. They're protected by gentle hills and the Rokko Mountains to the southeast. The hills, mountains and proximity to the sea create crucial fluctuations between day- and nighttime temperatures, ideally a ten-degree swing during the roughly thirty days between "heading" (the appearance of ears of grain) and harvest. Both the plant's grains and their starchy inner hearts are large and not easily broken, which helps produce a sake profile that can range from delicately alluring to hedonistically deep and full-bodied. As a microclimate it's close to those that help high-quality pinot noir vines thrive in California's Russian River and Anderson valleys.

This visit to Yokawa is the start of a journey through Japan to trace the evolution of sake from paddy to glass. We'll meet the brewery owners, the master brewers, the farmers and the yeast and *koji-kin* (mold or fungus) merchants who keep the business of making Japan's national drink afloat. We'll also trace sake's 2,000-year journey from a drink for Shinto gods and the aristocracy to its evolution as the comforting tipple of the middle class; the business's contraction during and after the economic miracle that opened Japanese ports to foreign wines and spirits, and the better-than-ever premium sake that brewers are now producing today.

Above A barrel containing Hyogo Prefecture *junmai daiginjo*, brewed from the prefecture's best Yamada Nishiki rice.

Right Women in traditional dress plant Yamada Nishiki seedlings in the nutrient-rich clay soil of Yokawa, Hyogo Prefecture.

These Yamada Nishiki seedlings are started in flats between March and May at a nursery in Yokawa; a tag identifies them as Yamada Nishiki. Less than an inch (2.5 cm) high, the seedlings will be nurtured until they are tall enough to clear the level of the flooded fields.

"We" are Nancy Matsumoto, a third-generation Japanese American journalist and sake writer, and Michael Tremblay, a Canadian sake sommelier and a member of the elite group of global Sake Samurai who spread sake culture throughout the world via education, importation or sales of sake. Nancy came to sake through writing about Japanese food, culture, agroecology and her Japanese American heritage. Michael has a background in wine and teaches a sake regionality class. While Nancy wants to tell the story of sake as an agricultural and artisanal product, and is most interested in the intersection of food and sake, Michael is a sake geek's geek, the sake educator who has mapped the known reaches of the sake universe from the sake yeast galaxy to the periodic table of sake rices. His brain sees the world in brightly colored infographics, charts and classification systems, while Nancy's sees it as a never-ending series of stories to capture in words, alongside food and drinks to sample. Which is how we ended up writing this book together.

On this late-May morning, though, our minds are more focused on staying upright while we slip and slide in the thick mud, barefoot. The leech warnings that have been issued aren't helping either: "If the bloodsucker bites you for long time [sic], a raw wound and itch will remain for days."

Before learning about the bloodsuckers, Michael thought he was dressing for the occasion by wearing khaki shorts and a bright blue T-shirt bearing a dinosaur clenching a *kikichoko*, or professional sake taster's cup, in its jaw. But lined up next to our coworkers, five women dressed in the traditional farmer's garb of indigo-dyed kimono, steeply angled straw hats and bright red obi sashes and forearm protectors, he looks every inch the novice *gaijin* (foreigner). The ladies, whose presence has been arranged for a promotional photo, politely refrain from comment.

The seedlings we're planting are slender, bright green shoots that go white at their roots like leeks or green onions. They're cultivated indoors between March and May in large yellow plastic flats in Yokawa greenhouses and are ready for planting when they are about six inches (15 cm) tall. This is the point at which they can easily clear the level of the flooded rice field and minimize any weeds competing for soil nutrients.

Yamada Nishiki is a hybrid variety that made its debut in 1936 after the Hyogo Prefectural Agricultural Institute, in a bid to expand local sake rice varieties, successfully crossed two rice strains, Yamadabo (commonly known in northern Japan as Yamadaho) and Tankan Wataribune. Both are prized for their sake-brewing qualities and high yields. The characters for Yamada (山田) mean "mountain" and "rice field," an apt description for a rice born in the fields tucked behind the Rokko mountain range. Nishiki (錦) means "brocade," referring either to the treasured nature of this premium grain, or the way its long, golden-sheafed stalks resemble a rich brocade rippling in the wind. Though farmers in many other prefectures have tried their hand at growing the prized grain, Yamada Nishiki is native to Hyogo soil. And since all of it is derived from the original late-1930s planting, it possesses an unparalleled purity of lineage, taste, and aroma.

In addition to an ideal microclimate, the region is blessed with deep clay soil that has evolved from a 35-million-year-old petrified forest. Rich in montmorillonite (a common clay mineral), limestone, magnesium and potassium, it excels at retaining the moisture and nutrients that rice plants need to thrive. The mud that hugs the three-foot (1 m)-long roots does for these Yamada Nishiki fields what the reddish marl and sandstone of the grand cru vineyards of Burgundy do for its chardonnay wines: they provide the ideal medium for nurturing the best product a master brewer or vigneron could hope for.

Planting rice by hand is arduous, but it brings us closer in spirit to the Japanese rice farmers who have for thousands of years engaged in *taue* (田植え), rice planting. Even Japanese who have never set foot in a rice field feel a tug of nostalgia at the sight of farmers stooping low, sun beating off straw hats and bare shins, hands sinking into the mud to gently press each tender seedling into place.

Rice consumption may have diminished as Western cuisine has made inroads, but for the Japanese, this grain is still very much a cultural touchstone.

Keeping a Prized Rice in the Prefecture

Not long after Yamada Nishiki's debut, sake makers understood its potential to become a glittering star in the sake world. To a significant degree, brewing excellence is equated with gold medals won at important national sake competitions. For this reason, breweries will pour extraordinary effort into brewing their "competition sake," which has a very specific profile, one that can be quite different from the kind of sake the brewery is known for, or prefers to brew. The reason is simple: awards grab media attention, boost sales and confer bragging rights—they are one of the sake brewer's best marketing tools.

For years now, the formula for any serious competition sake has been YK35, shorthand for Yamada Nishiki rice brewed with Kumamoto yeast. The rice is polished to 35 percent, which means that 65 percent of the grain's outer husk has been polished off. The "Y" part undoubtedly works: approximately 90 percent of all gold medal–winners at the yearly National New Sake Appraisal competition have been made with Yamada Nishiki. But we're getting ahead of ourselves; you'll read more about this type of sake in the next two chapters.

Even before the development of Yamada Nishiki,

A newly planted paddy in Yokawa. The region's climate and mineral-rich soil both contribute to its high-caliber rice.

the southwestern part of Hyogo, known as the Banshu region, was famous for its high-quality sake rice, and helped fuel the rise to prominence of the neighboring Nada sake brewers (see chapter 9). One unique feature associated with Banshu is the *muramai seido*, or village contract system that sake brewers and rice farmers developed beginning in about 1887. Farmers ensured a steady supply of high-quality Hyogo rice in exchange for the breweries' promise of stable yearly purchases from farmers. In order to stay competitive, both parties knew they had to keep making a better and better product. So they worked together to improve rice quality, and in times of disaster, helped each other out as family members would. It was a well-ordered, highly effective system. By the time Yamada Nishiki and its complicated paddy rankings came to be, the village contract system was firmly entrenched. The top farmers all had exclusive contracts with Nada brewers, effectively barring outsiders from access to Banshu's prime Yamada Nishiki fields.

Today, if you visit the Toku-A villages of Yokawa or Tojo you'll see the flags of famous Nada breweries waving from the small Yamada Nishiki plots, like those of conquering nations proclaiming their ownership of foreign lands.

Yet while Hyogo brewers have locked up most of this prized rice crop, our itinerary includes trips to two breweries far from Hyogo—Sohomare Brewery in Tochigi Prefecture and Kikuhime Brewery in Ishikawa Prefecture. Through no small

The Omi Shonin (近江商人)

One brewery story that we often heard on our travels was that of the sake-brewing and migration of the *Omi shonin*, or Omi merchants. The group's name comes from its place of origin, the feudal domain of Omi, today known as Shiga Prefecture. It's located in the Kansai region, where the main island of Honshu narrows between Kyoto and Nagoya. From around the thirteenth century, the Omi merchants were itinerant peddlers who traveled the length and breadth of Japan hawking wares ranging from tatami to mosquito nets and medicine, and returned home laden with purchases from the various regions they visited.

The Omi merchants supported the local communities they did business with, funding civic and infrastructure projects and building a record of integrity. They have been credited with creating the blueprint for Japan's modern business and industrial structure. One of their business philosophies came to be known as *sanpo yoshi*, or "three-way satisfaction," and anticipated the idea of corporate social responsibility by centuries. The term refers to the practice of always seeking the price or approach that is good for the buyer, good for the seller and good for society. The approach worked: during the mid-nineteenth century, the Omi network included business entities with as many as fifteen branches across the entire country,

according to Doshisha University professor of Japanese economic history, Kunitoshi Suenaga.

Between the seventeenth and nineteenth century, many Omi merchant families moved to the north and east, coinciding with Japan's transition from the feudal to the modern age, and the growing power and consumer demand of the capital, Edo (today's Tokyo).

The half-dozen brewing families we meet who are descended from the Omi shonin include those behind Tonoike, Senkin and Sohomare breweries in Tochigi, Terada Honke in Chiba, Dewazakura in Yamagata and Hachinohe in Aomori.

Left An Omi merchant travels on foot with his wares. **Right** Aomori's Hachinohe Brewery, founded in 1740, traces its roots back to these early entrepreneurs, as do five other breweries that we visited.

effort, both were able to lay claim to a portion of the rice from the prefecture's most coveted Yamada Nishiki rice fields.

The Wandering Samurai Family: Sohomare Brewery

Sohomare was established in 1872 by the Kono family in the Haga district, and uses only Toku-A Yamada Nishiki rice for its junmai, ginjo and daiginjo labels. Fifth-generation owner Jun Kono is partial to the old-fashioned kimoto style of brewing. For this product line, he may blend three different vintages and four varieties of yeast (and over ten batches for his junmai daiginjo kimoto) to produce sake that is creamy, rich and elegant.

On the January afternoon of our visit, Sohomare staff member Masahiro Sekimoto greets us at Utsunomiya Station to drive us to the brewery. Sunlight glints off the Kanto Plain that in the spring will turn green with Gohyakumangoku rice, one of the two types that Sohomare uses for its sake. We cross the Kinu River, the source of Sohomare's well water. In the distance, to the northwest, is Mt. Nantai, which Sekimoto, an old-timer who has worked for Sohomare for over twenty-five years, points out to us. The volcanic peak rises over Nikko, the favored mountain retreat of the Tokugawa shogunate, where its founding member, Tokugawa Ieyasu, is enshrined in gilded splendor.

We're shown into an annex next to the brewery known as the *ishigura*, or stone warehouse, named after its walls made of Tochigi's volcanic Oya stone, which can only be found in a 600-million-

In Chiba, twenty-third-generation owner Keisuke Terada's Omi merchant family's migration to the northeast came during the Edo shogunate's spending spree on infrastructure improvements designed to speed the flow of goods into the capital. The previously wild and unpredictable Tone River, which ran through Chiba and emptied into Tokyo Bay, underwent extensive engineering and construction work. As a result of these changes the Katori region of Chiba—which was blessed with good, hard, well water—became an attractive place from which to sell goods, including sake, to Edo. The Terada family moved their brewery there in 1673.

Jun Kono of Sohomare explains that his family began in the Shiga town of Hino. When the Omi daimyo (lord) that Kono's family was associated with was called to Aizu (present-day Fukushima Prefecture) by the Edo government, the lord's son also moved north. He settled closer to Edo in Utsunomiya (the present-day capital of Tochigi and Japan's gyoza capital). The Kono family, too, chose to follow the lord's son to Utsunomiya. "So many Omi merchants decided to move with him," says Kono, "that today there is now a street called Hino Street in Utsunomiya City. We are one of those families from that time. We've been here since 1872."

Omi families were organized around the products they specialized in. The Hino branch, which Kono traces his roots back to, was closely associated with sake. "To this day, there are many sake breweries in Tochigi, Ibaraki, Saitama and Gunma prefectures that are from Omi families in Shiga," Kono tells us. Of his own business practices, Kono says, "They have been handed down through generations, and they happen to be Omi values."

ton deposit near Utsunomiya. Following damage in the Great East Japan earthquake of 2011, Kono's wife, Junko, commissioned her former architecture professor at the University of Tokyo, Hidetoshi Ohno, to modernize it and build a sleek, modern wood-clad main building next door. We're seated at one end of an extra-long wooden table under exposed beams, where Kono and his son Michihiro serve us sencha tea in Mashiko-ware cups. The famous pottery village is nearby; Kono's father, a painter as well as brewery president, was a close friend of the influential Mashiko potter Shoji Hamada. To eat, we're offered local Tochiotome green-house-grown strawberries, vivid red and bursting with flavor, served in beautiful speckled glass dishes.

Like many sake-brewing families, Kono's carries with it centuries of history tied to Japan's important political and historical events. Originally from Ehime Prefecture, his samurai family was allied with the Mori clan. But in 1600, their side was defeated in the civil war that led to the long, peaceful reign of the Tokugawa shogunate. In order to escape possible death at the hands of the victors, the family fled to a remote mountain district of Gifu Prefecture, as Kono says, "to hide ourselves for several generations." The Konos even changed their name, taking the head of the family's wife's name, Takemura. Another move to Shiga Prefecture followed, where the family was able to reassume the Kono name and take up miso and vinegar making. The Konos are just one of six brewing families we will meet on our journey that are descended from a unique class of businesspeople known as the Omi merchants (see page 44).

Turning to the topic of Yamada Nishiki, Kono says, "Before the 1990s, brewers outside Hyogo Prefecture couldn't buy Toku-A Yamada Nishiki." In the early 1950s, through careful relationship building with the Hyogo branch of the Japan Agricultural Cooperative, known as the JA, Kono's father began buying Yamada Nishiki, though his son is not sure what part of Hyogo it came from. Then, around the 1980s, Sohomare began bringing in Toku-A Yamada Nishiki, gradually increasing the amount in the 1990s. "You drink sake with them

[the agricultural power brokers]," Kono says simply. "It's like any other connection, it's about going there, talking, building human relationships." By the early 1980s the Konos were buying 80 percent of the Hyogo Yamada Nishiki coming into three breweries in Tochigi, negotiated through the JA.

Today 90 percent of the Yamada Nishiki they buy is Toku-A from Yokawa or Tojo villages, although since it is aggregated by the JA, they do not know specifically which farmers grow their rice. And, Kono explains, "Yamada Nishiki rice fields in Hyogo are grouped into three categories: Toku-A-a, Toku-A-b, Toku-A-c. All three of them are called Toku-A. But when I use Toku-A, it means Toku-A-a." Within Toku-A, he feels that Yokawa's is superior to that of other Toku-A growing villages. All of this hair-splitting makes the US agriculture department's prime meats categorization system, with its mere eight grades, seem a dull tool in comparison.

Arts, Crafts and Drinking Sake with the Right People: Kikuhime Brewery

The Toku-A Yamada Nishiki rice that we helped plant back in May will eventually make its way to Kikuhime Brewery in Ishikawa Prefecture, another brewery known for its top-quality Yamada Nishiki sake. Like Sohomare, it has managed to establish a more direct relationship with the farmers that grow its Yokawa rice. But unlike Sohomare, which negotiates with the JA to source its Toku-A rice, Kikuhime has managed to become the only brewery

Left Kimoto making at Tochigi Prefecture's Sohomare Brewery. The wave pattern on the *koji* rice maximizes the surface area, which helps control moisture. **Below** A billowing, cloth-covered *koshiki*, or rice steamer.

to 2019. It also has a dedicated rice-polishing facility that opened in 1987, making Kikuhime one of the first sake breweries to own a computer-operated rice-polishing machine.

After a tour of the facilities with brewer Shigeyuki Matsumoto and rice-polishing expert Toshiyuki Ide, we're ushered into the cool, tatami-matted sitting room of a traditional wood-beamed home. Seventeenth-generation president Tatsushi Yanagi, a lean, tanned man with a thatch of snowy white hair, sits cross-legged at a sunken hearth. He beckons for us to join him as he reaches for an oversized, graceful iron kettle connected to a chain and a massive wooden hook that descends from the ceiling. His grandmother, he explains, had the iron kettle made for his grandfather by the craftsman Morihisa Suzuki, who went on to be designated an Intangible Cultural Asset of Japan in 1974. "I'm seventy-one, and this was made when I was in elementary school, so it's about sixty years old," Yanagi tells us.

The Kaga region in which the brewery is situated

outside of Hyogo Prefecture to join the tight-knit village contract system. Kikuhime's sterling reputation, and the question of how it muscled its way into this clubby circle has brought us to the brewery, which is located in the south of the Kaga region of Ishikawa Prefecture.

Among aficionados, Kikuhime sake holds quasi-mythical status. Sake taste arbiter Beau Timken, owner of a shop called True Sake in San Francisco, says he once told a friend he wanted to be "embalmed in Kikuhime daiginjo when the great one punches my ticket." The friend, another sake expert, replied, "By the time you die I will have drunk it all. That sake is one of the best I have had."

On our late-July visit we

is known for its fertile soil and highly evolved culinary and artistic practices. During the Edo period (1603–1868) this wealthy territory was presided over by the Maeda clan, who actively cultivated this artisan culture. Yanagi is an exemplar of it, a man who at one time fired three hundred sake cups annually in the three electric kilns that he owns to give to

travel by local trains due south from the prefectural capital of Kanazawa City, through vivid green rice fields and sleepy towns, alighting at Tsurugi, where the Tedori River's swift flowing water coming off of Mt. Haku slows and morphs into an alluvial fan. After a short walk through Tsurugi Shinmachi, the brewery materializes in the sweltering heat. It's a large complex with three different brewing plants dating from three different eras, Meiji, Showa and Heisei, and spanning the years from 1868 through

friends as gifts; who braids *shimenawa* (the protective Shinto reed ropes used to ward against evil spirits); and who even built the handsome wooden *kamidana* household shrine that hangs on the wall above us. He is also brash, outspoken and short-tempered. His style of making sake, he says with a raucous laugh, is, "Make the best in Japan; I won't allow second best." Depending on where you stand in the sake industry, his candor is either refreshing or infuriating; acquaintances take his pronouncements with several pinches of salt.

Yanagi tips the iron kettle to pour hot water into a vermillion-colored teapot, making rapid and vigorous circular motions, like a Las Vegas high-roller warming up to shoot craps. As he pours tea into hand-thrown cups, he recounts the history of the brewery. "It began during the Tensho era (1573–1592), about the same time that guns came to Japan." Yanagi measures time not according to minutes, hours or years, but according to the timeline of his family and his country.

"There are two types of sake makers," says Yanagi. "One is the merchant-trader family, and the second is landowners who have access to rice. Our family were the landowners." At a time when Japan's economy was still rice based, the Yanagis transported rice grown by tenant farmers to Osaka's Dojima Rice Exchange, a precursor to Japan's modern banking system. To add value to their rice, they brewed sake with a portion of the harvest.

"This region was run by peasant farmers," Yanagi explains, referring to the former Kaga domain's unruly and rebellious fifteenth-century theocracy that included farmers and Buddhist priests. When they tired of the local military governor, they staged what became known as the 1487 Kaga Rebellion, ousting him and therefore expanding their power. "When they fought with the Oda clan's army, they won in one fell swoop, and sent them packing!" Yanagi says with great delight. Left unspoken is the eventual takeover of Kaga by the powerful lord Nobunaga Oda in the late sixteenth century.

Jumping forward in time to the twentieth century, Yanagi displays a similar disregard for conventional power structures. Kikuhime's rise—from a small family brewery in the 1960s making a strong drink favored by lumberjacks, to a nationally and interna-

Left Kikuhime's Tatsushi Yanagi.
Below Iron kettle made by craftsman Morihisa Suzuki.

tionally recognized brand—was one that had to overcome the hegemony of large sake makers from Hyogo and Kyoto prefectures. "Even elementary-school primers claim the main sake-making regions are Nada and Fushimi," Yanagi says disdainfully, referring to those prefectures' most famous brewing regions. "They were brainwashing people in elementary school, when it was really the *jizake* (local sake of the countryside) that was reviving

sake!" (see chapter 2 for more on the "jizake boom.)

But how did Yanagi, in the late 1970s, become not only one of the first brewers outside Hyogo to procure top-grade Yamada Nishiki, but also a member of the muramai seido system? Kikuhime now has relationships with one hundred small farmers in seven Yokawa villages.

Ide passes us a sheet of paper identifying all the Hyogo villages that grow top grade toku-jo rice. There, among the big sake makers, including Kenbishi, Kikumasamune and Hakutsuru, is the name Kikuhime. Next to each village is an "A."

"Yokawa is Mecca!" Yanagi says with a victorious cackle. "The very top level. It's just like in Burgundy, where you can tell by the soil where the highest quality fields are." The way it came about, he says, was that he wanted the very best Yamada Nishiki. But to go through the farmer's cooperative, he says, "you don't know what rice you're getting. Every year it comes from some place different. We wanted it to be fixed, from the same place every year. We want only the best!" Later, when we asked Sohomare president Jun Kono how Yanagi had managed this trick, he laughed, and said, "He drank more sake!"

Yanagi says that it wasn't just logging more drinking hours that won him favor, it was also making sure he was drinking with the right people. "I used political strength, too," he says, mentioning the name of Hyogo's former deputy governor. Yanagi was able to meet with farmers, "but since they are part of the JA and not in decision-making positions," interrupts Ide, to try to gloss over his boss's indiscretion, "we had to make a strong plea from above." The farmer's cooperative is still the middleman but over time—mainly it seems, by continuing to show up in the fields until the farmers accepted them—the brewery was able to establish direct relationships with them.

If the lengths that brewery owners will go to in order to lay their hands on Toku-A Yamada Nishiki are extreme, their reasoning is sound. Yanagi's recollection of his first sip of Kikuhime sake made with Yokawa Yamada Nishiki is as clear as a bell. "It was in 1979 when the Yokawa rice first came in. The weather was bad, and the rice wasn't good. There's a term, *housaku fuzou*, referring to a bad harvest year, when the rice is too hard to be broken down during fermentation, allowing bad-actor bacteria to enter the tank and rot the batch. It was that kind of year."

"And yet, in a year of bad harvest, the sake we made was the best." This special rice, which he had worked so hard to procure from the mecca of Japan's rice-growing regions, in other words, possessed the supernatural power to transcend the deficiencies that climate and poor luck had inflicted upon it. It truly was the king of sake rice.

Yamada Nishiki Flight

Sake name: Kikuhime "BY"
Sake type: Daiginjo
Brewery: Kikuhime, Ishikawa Prefecture
An outstanding representation of Yamada Nishiki: elegant, silky smooth and finely balanced.

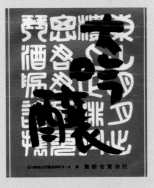

Sake name: Tatsuriki "Akitsu"
Sake type: Junmai daiginjo
Brewery: Honda Shoten, Hyogo Prefecture
Honda Shoten's mission is to express the soils of northern Harima, home to the best Yamada Nishiki fields, including those of Yokawa. Made in the YK35 style used for most competition sake.

Sake name: Kuheiji "Eau du Desir"
Sake type: Junmai daiginjo
Brewery: Banjo, Aichi Prefecture
Though based in Aichi, the brewery has a brewing facility in Hyogo to express the bounty of its prime Yamada Nishiki rice fields. The brewery self-identifies as a domaine, the Burgundian term for a winemaker's small vineyard-winery.

49

Chapter Two

The Birth of Ginjo

The year was 1980 and Japan was ascendant. Its electronics and auto manufacturers had blanketed the world with their reliable, affordable products, and the growth potential of the Japanese economy seemed limitless. In the beverage world, Tokyo liquor wholesalers were looking for new and interesting niche products to satisfy consumers with swelling wallets and appetites. Small-batch sake from different regions of Japan had begun to appear in the capital over the last decade, touching off a *jizake* (地酒) "local sake" boom. Yet all was not well in the world of sake. Increasingly, an influx of alluring foreign wines and spirits commanded the attention of the nouveau riche.

North of the noisy capital, in mountainous, Yamagata Prefecture, a team of brewers at Dewazakura Brewery had been hard at work for five years. Their goal: to revolutionize the sake market the way the newly introduced Sony Walkman was transforming the way people listened to music. After peaking in 1975, sake sales had fallen every year since. "The sake business was in bad shape," recalls president Masumi Nakano, whose father Seijiro was then in charge, with master brewer Hirota Togashi. "We needed something new."

Their elusive goal—arresting, aromatic sake made with highly polished rice, brewed at low temperatures—wasn't a brand new type of sake. Since the introduction of rice-polishing machines in the early 1930s, top brewers had been experimenting with these *ginjo*-style brews, not for the drinking public, but "to advance the technical boundaries of sake," Nakano explains. It was also a bid to win prestigious national sake competitions.

Building an Affordable Ginjo Sake

As early as 1934, for example, Kodama Brewery in Akita—up against more than 5,000 other entries—

took home first place in the annual National New Sake Appraisal competition for a junmai-daiginjo-style sake featuring a 40 percent polishing ratio. The problem was that these competition sakes, with their transparent, florid beauty and rice milled down to what seemed at the time extravagant levels, were expensive and technically challenging to produce. The trick was brewing an affordable sake like this for everyday consumption.

Since its founding in 1892, Dewazakura, neither large nor deep-pocketed, had established a reputation for technical excellence. If anyone could figure out how to mass produce competition-style sake, it was Nakano and his team. "My father challenged himself to make a cup of sake that would cost about what a cup of coffee at the time cost," recalls Nakano. "If an *isshobin* (a 1.8 liter/2 quart bottle), say, cost two-thousand yen, then one glass would run about three hundred to five hundred yen. That was his goal."

Nakano's father set about assembling a team of craftsmen that included carpenters, electricians, machinists and experts in refrigeration technology to help overcome technical hurdles. One of the

50

Left The *futa-koji* method of making *koji* rice, in small batches held in shallow wooden trays. This tray is destined for a *ginjo* sake starter tank at Yamagata's Dewazakura Brewery. **Above** The Yamagata rice fields that supply Dewazakura sake. **Right** The Dewazakura Brewery team.

costliest aspects of ginjo brewing was keeping the brewing tanks at suitably low temperatures.

Nakano borrowed a tank-cooling system from his friends at nearby Takeda Winery, which involved wrapping rubber hoses around 3,000–5,000-liter (800–1,300 gallon) tanks and running cold water through them. He also invested in an armada of refrigerators to keep his delicate sake in pristine condition. They started storage at 50°F (10°C), then 41°F (5°C). Today, the standard storage temperature is 23°F (-5°C). Refrigeration during transport to customers also had to be planned and carefully carried out.

But the largest part of the team's effort—"the most brain power," says Nakano—was lavished on perfecting the *koji*, or mold-inoculated rice for the new brew in a way that would sustain yeast activity over a longer fermentation period and enhance aromas. The late researcher Hideo Abe from the National Research Institute of Brewing (NRIB) played an influential advisory role in the project. Abe, who entered the sake-brewing world in the 1950s, not only helped shaped modern ginjo, but was one of the sake world's most colorful characters. After working in sake wholesaling, brewery management and as a key advisor to breweries in the Tohoku region, he had come to know just about everyone in the industry. He played the stock market and was a regular Las Vegas gambler. A long-time advisor to the International Sake Association, he also served as a bridge to the West.

For the *kurabito* (蔵人), or brewery workers, brewing ginjo was nerve-wracking. So much money and so many expectations were riding on each tank. "Everyone felt nervous using these new techniques," says Nakano, "but that nervousness is good for making high-quality sake!"

The new sake was called Oka, and it was a hit, touching off a new mania known as the "ginjo boom." (Japan loves "booms," or fads, and there's a long history of them, from the hula-hoop boom of the late 1950s, the bowling boom in the early 1970s, and the golf boom of the go-go 1980s. There were booms before the term "boom" was even coined, like the dark mania for lovers' double suicides in the first quarter of the eighteenth century. It was so

powerful that the government issued a law forbidding such behavior.) Polished to a then-unheard-of-for-the-mass-market 55 percent, Oka introduced a new gorgeousness to sake in the form of a light-bodied, crisp brew with fruity and floral aromas. It was a much more refined, delicate and aromatic sake than what Japan was used to.

To say it was a hit, however, glosses over the prefecture-wide support that made success possible. "We didn't make a profit for five years," Nakano explains. "At first it was the local Yamagata distributors and retailers who came out in support of the product. The profits came because it sold well here, where we weren't paying freight charges." Oka's reputation slowly spread nationally, finally making the leap abroad when it became the first sake to be offered by Britain's oldest wine merchant and supplier to the royal family, Berry Bros. & Rudd. Remarkably, *Oka ginjo* also indirectly contributed to Japan's $25 billion-a-year cosmetics industry when, to enhance a luxury facial serum, Max Factor created a ginjo-like aroma that mimicked the scent of the sake.

Today, Nakano says the technical leap his brewery made was possible because his father stood on the shoulders of giants, the family ancestors and master brewers before him who had continually pushed boundaries.

Ginjo's Backstory

To truly understand the world that ginjo was born into, one has to have a sense of both the pre- and postwar cultures of Japan. So stark are the differences between these two different eras that they each have their own shorthand

At the museum of Otokoyama Brewery in Asahikawa, Hokkaido, there are Edo-era ukiyo-e woodblock prints that depict sake's presence in pleasure quarters, at sumo tournaments and among warriors. In this Utagawa Kuniyoshi print, Otokoyama and Kenbishi barrels can be seen.

Toshihiko Koseki and the Role of Prefectural Research Centers

Sake-making know-how has been advanced throughout history through networks of master brewers, academics, and friendship circles, and national research institutions such as the National Tax Agency and the National Research Institute of Brewing have played important roles. It's also important to note the role of prefectural industrial research centers in sake-making advances.

In the 1980s, a young civil servant with the Yamagata Industrial Technology Center called Toshihiko Koseki arrived on the scene and launched a prefecture-wide effort to elevate the sake of Yamagata Prefecture. He would inspire a generation of young Tohoku owner-*toji*, including Tomonobu Mitobe of Mitobe Brewery, Akitsuna Takagi from Juyondai and Yusuke Sato of Aramasa.

Yamagata is a mountainous prefecture that sprawls over 3,600 square miles (9,000 km²). In feudal times it was home to four different *han*, or domains, each with its own version of *Yamagata-ben*, or Yamagata dialect, which are still alive today in some rural areas. Tomonobu Mitobe can speak only his own central Yamagata dialect. One winter, early in his career, Mitobe accompanied Koseki on his yearly talks to all the breweries of Yamagata. "The older toji only spoke in dialect, and tended to be hesitant, even nervous among outsiders," says Mitobe. Koseki would slip effortlessly into each of the local dialects, teaching, gathering information, and cementing bonds between regions. "Suddenly, everything became smooth because the brewers opened their hearts up to him," says Mitobe. "It was a kind of chemistry that was so impressive to me."

The united outlook that Koseki was able to achieve in Yamagata is not one found in all parts of Japan, but is the hallmark of certain areas that—perhaps not coincidentally—have been lauded for innovation and high-quality sake, such as Yamagata and Hiroshima.

reference: *senzen* (戦前, "before the war") and *sengo* (戦後, "after the war"). The setback that World War II represented to the sake industry and sake culture in general cannot be underestimated.

During the Meiji era (1868–1912) an estimated thirty thousand sake breweries operated throughout Japan, a number that dwindled to about four thousand during the prewar Taisho era (1912–1926). Most of them were small, family run businesses. (Today, there are an estimated 1,200 working breweries in Japan). Every town had a brewery, and most of them catered strictly to the local community. There were exceptions to this rule, though—nationally famous brands whose histories stretch as far back as the Edo period (1603–1868). At the venerable Otokoyama Brewery in Hokkaido, for example, you can see woodblock prints by Edo artists Kitagawa Utamaro and Kuniyoshi Utagawa showing wooden casks displaying the logos of Otokoyama and the Hyogo brewery Kenbishi, in the pleasure quarters of the capital.

In the prewar era, rice was, as it had always been, a precious commodity. At one time it was a form of currency with which tenant farmers paid their feudal landlords in tribute. During Japan's rapid industrialization in the late-nineteenth and early twentieth centuries the government made sure there was a steady supply of cheap rice from domestic and colonial sources to feed workers. But for most of Japan's history, rice was a commodity in short supply, so sake could only be brewed when there was excess rice available. And since rice has always been an important source of tax revenue, it has historically been managed and regulated by the national tax bureau. The National Tax Agency (NTA) or its precursor, the Ministry of Finance's tax

RICE POLISHING MANIA

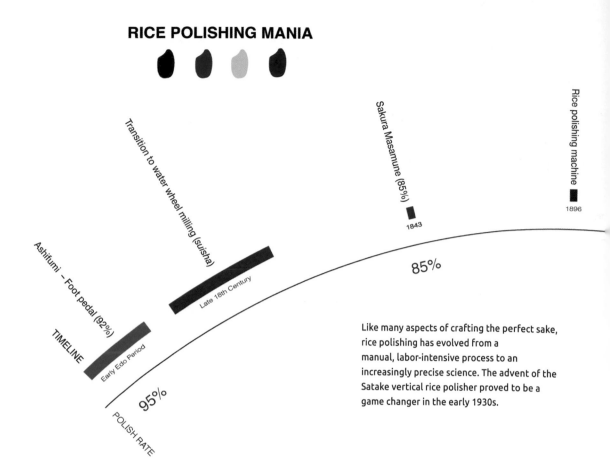

Rice polishing machine

1896

Sakura Masamune (85%)

1843

85%

Transition to water wheel milling (suisha)

Late 18th Century

Ashitumi – Foot pedal (92%)

TIMELINE

Early Edo Period

95%

POLISH RATE

Like many aspects of crafting the perfect sake, rice polishing has evolved from a manual, labor-intensive process to an increasingly precise science. The advent of the Satake vertical rice polisher proved to be a game changer in the early 1930s.

bureau, designed both pre- and postwar sake classification systems. The agency is also in charge of issuing brewing licenses. The National Research Institute of Brewing, meanwhile, which was launched under the Ministry of Finance in 1904, is now an independent institution that produces top technical experts like Hideo Abe, the fermentation scientist who was instrumental in the creation of Oka ginjo. It's hard for Americans to imagine the IRS employing top flight oenologists or brewing and fermentation experts or wielding this much power over an entire beverage industry.

During the Second Sino-Japanese War (1937–1945), the quantities of rice and sake sent to soldiers disrupted Japan's supply system so much that makers adopted a highly diluted product derisively

known as "goldfish sake" because it was thin enough for goldfish to swim in. During World War II, as the country's population headed toward starvation, half of Japan's breweries were shut down and the government directed growers to produce only table rice. Sake making, still considered a wartime necessity, became concentrated in the hands of big industrial makers with the large infrastructure needed to meet national demands.

Rice shortages persisted during the postwar period, and so in 1949 the liquor law was changed, making legal what became known as *sanbai jozo-shu*, or triple-volume sake. Brewers added equal parts distilled alcohol and water to sake, along with glucose syrup, acidulants, glutamic acid and other additives, effectively tripling its volume for a

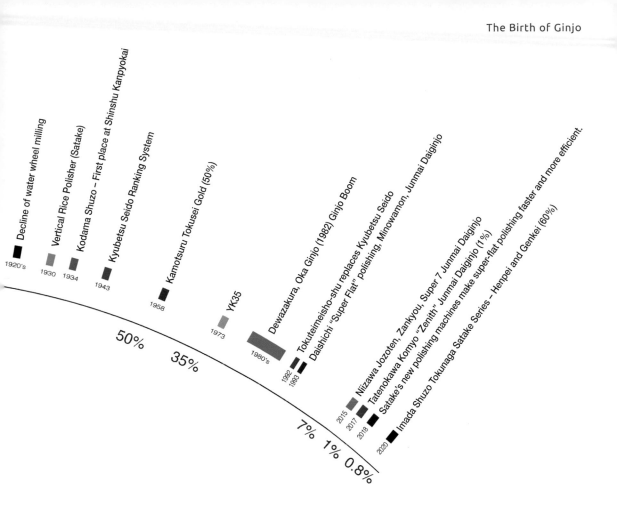

Decline of water wheel milling — 1920's
Vertical Rice Polisher (Satake) — 1930
Kodama Shuzo – First place at Shinshu Kanpyokai — 1934
Kyubetsu Seido Ranking System — 1943
Kamotsuru Tokusei Gold (50%) — 1958
YK35 — 1973
1980's
Dewazakura, Oka Ginjo (1982) Ginjo Boom — 1982
Tokuteimeisho-shu replaces Kyubetsu Seido — 1983
Daishichi "Super Flat" polishing, Minowamon, Junmai Daiginjo
Niizawa Jozoten, Zankyou, Super 7 Junmai Daiginjo — 2015
Tatenokawa Komyo "Zenith" Junmai Daiginjo (1%) — 2017
Satake's new polishing machines make super-flat polishing faster and more efficient. — 2018
Imada Shuzo Tokunaga Satake Series – Henpei and Genkei (60%) — 2020

50%   35%   7%   1%   0.8%

nominal increase in cost. The manufacture of *sanzo-shu* (shorthand for *sanbai jozo-shu*) continued, estimates Kazuhiro Maegaki, president of Kamo-izumi Brewery, until the late 1960s. "The era when sake makers could buy a lot of rice and use it freely only began fairly recently," he says. "Breweries had a predetermined amount of rice they could use in one year. So the only way to earn a profit was to make more sake out of the rice that they had."

Not only that, says Nakano, people wanted and needed triple-volume sake. "Japan had lost the war and it was a very hard time," he says. "Ginjo was too weak for them—they needed stronger medicine."

As much as they wanted to experiment with making more refined, highly milled sake, makers' hands were tied by the availability of rice, and the country's wish to drown its sorrows in a stronger, familiar sake. The taste for old-style *futsu* "regular" sake, in fact, continues to this day, especially in rural Japan. It's also important to note that the addition of a small amount of distilled alcohol today in pre-mium *honjozo* sake can make beautifully expressive sake. It's unfortunate that it is often unfairly dismissed in an era of *junmai* primacy.

By the 1970s, the rapidly expanding economy brought new types of consumer demand. That 1970s jizake boom we referred to earlier, of bringing back local sake? Although prewar brewing technol-ogy was primitive and the sake made then should not be overly glorified, this trend was part of an effort to revive some of the diversity of local sake types that had existed prewar. An emphasis on

current president Naotaka Miyasaka, recalls how his father Masaru and the legendary master brewer Chisato Kubota traveled to Kamotsuru Brewery in Hiroshima in the early 1930s to learn about the soft-water brewing techniques they had heard so much about. When they returned, Kubota taught these methods to all of the brewers in his region.

In the early 1950s, Dewazakura's future president Seijiro Nakano was sent by his family to the Miyasaka Brewery in Nagano to study and work. He lived with the Miyasaka family, learning lessons in how to run a brewery from Masaru Miyasaka, and meeting Masaru's son Kazuhiro, who was then working in Miyasaka's sales department. When Seijiro became president, he sent his *kurabito* to Miyasaka to learn how to make master brewer Kubota's elegant ginjo sakes.

regionality, combined with new brewing techniques led to breweries such as Koshi no Kanbai in Niigata kicking off a frenzy for local sake with its palate-shocking, clean, complex, light and dry style, known as *tanrei karakuchi* (crisp and dry).

It Takes a Lot of Villages

It was during this jizake boom, perhaps even a little earlier, that Dewazakura Brewery's Seijiro Nakano and a tight-knit group of progressively minded Yamagata brewing friends, including Yonetsuru and Eiko Fuji breweries, began sharing notes on their efforts to make a more premium, technically advanced brew. All of them helped push ginjo-style sake forward. "We've always believed that the sharing and exchange of information is important," explains Masumi Nakano. "When you do that, everyone benefits, and you all rise together."

Close bonds, either through friendship circles or the *toji* (brewing master) guilds, founded on the shared desire to elevate their craft, have throughout sake history been key vehicles of progress. Kazuhiro Miyasaka, born in 1928, company advisor to Miyasaka Brewing Co. in Nagano Prefecture (producers of the Masumi line of sake) and father of

The relationship with the Miyasaka family made such an impact on Nagano that he named his only son Masumi after its flagship brand. Masumi Nakano is now friends with current Miyasaka Brewery president Naotaka Miyasaka; Nakano's daughter and her husband, Akari and Shotaro Nakano, are close with the next-generation son of the Miyasakas, Katsuhiko. Many in their friendship circle are fellow brewery heirs and former classmates at the National Research Institute of Brewing (NRIB).

For the generation of brewery owners who were not master brewers themselves, NRIB seminars were a good way to meet other brewers. Kazuhiro Miyasaka's friendship with Shigeo Saura of Urakasumi began this way. In the 1960s, Saura helped Miyasaka's then-small brewery become the largest in Nagano by steering him to breweries that were closing, to buy up brewing rights. The two also cemented their friendship by each holding a copy of the other's complete yeast library, says Naotaka Miyasaka. This paid off after the March 2011 earthquake, tsunami and nuclear disaster. Urakasumi Brewery lost power to its yeast bank freezer for several weeks, losing its entire supply. After power was restored, Miyasaka delivered its entire intact collection back to Urakasumi. Today, the sons of these presidents, Naotaka Miyasaka and Koichi Saura, are presidents of Miyasaka and Urakasumi themselves, continuing the close family friendship.

The Tokyo University of Agriculture (Nodai for short) is Japan's most famous educational institution for brewers. It's also a place where lifelong bonds are formed. When Masumi Nakano was a student there in the early 1980s, his father was launching his trailblazing mass-market Oka ginjo.

But the center of the ginjo brewing universe was far away. "Hiroshima brewers were right at the top," Nakano recalls. They won all the competitions with their new-style, high-polish ginjo sakes, redolent of ripe apples, the aroma an intoxicating by-product of Yeast No. 9, isolated in Kumamoto in the 1950s; highly milled rice; and low-temperature fermentation. At the forefront of the Hiroshima brewers was Kamotsuru, which won a streak of eighteen gold medals beginning in 1973, and gave rise to the aforementioned prizewinning formula, YK35. "We all tried to emulate them," says Nakano.

To follow the story, we turn to Hiroshima, a city with seemingly little to recommend it as a sake-brewing powerhouse until two highly innovative men figured out how to overcome geographical and regional handicaps, and pave the way for the modern ginjo movement.

Ginjo Flight

Sake name (Japan): Dewazakura "Oka"
Sake name (US): "Cherry Bouquet"
Sake type: Ginjo
Brewery: Dewazakura, Yamagata Prefecture
The first mass-market ginjo, Oka sparked the ginjo boom of the eighties and is still popular today.

Sake name: Masumi "Nanago"
Type: Junmai daiginjo nama chozo
Brewery: Miyasaka, Nagano Prefecture
Made with local Miyama Nishiki rice and the brewery's own line of No. 7 yeast.

Sake name: Urakasumi "Hirano"
Type: Yamahai junmai daiginjo
Brewery: Saura Co., Miyagi Prefecture
Named after the late toji Juichi Hirano, who first came to the brewery in 1949, and trained brewers well into the aughts.

Chapter Three

Hiroshima and the Saijo Brewers (The Birth of Ginjo Part II)

On a brilliant, blue-skied Saturday in February we hop on a Sanyo Line train from Hiroshima Station headed east to the village of Saijo. Dewazakura and the northern Japan region of Tohoku may have captured bragging rights for issuing the first mass-marketed *ginjo* sake in the 1980s, but the true cradle of ginjo culture is in Hiroshima. We're here to delve into that history, check out the cluster of seven breweries that dot the main street of this historically important sake town, and visit one of its leading citizens, Kamoizumi Brewery president Kazuhiro Maegaki.

The arrangements for our visit have involved an unusually heavy volume of emails back and forth with Maegaki, who has just assumed the presidency of the family brewery, founded in 1912. What is our schedule? Can we join the family for lunch or dinner? What time will we arrive? Our plans to arrive in Saijo early and stroll around before heading to Kamoizumi change when we learn that Maegaki himself would like to meet us at the station.

Alighting from our train in just under an hour we head for the exit turnstiles. There, we spot Maegaki, an impish grin on his face and a secret up his sleeve. With him is Kamoizumi's French sales representative Gautier Moysset, dressed like his boss in a dark-colored half-zip sweater over a button down shirt. "We have surprise visitors for you!" announces Maegaki. The reason for the flurry of emails becomes clear as we turn the corner. There, we find Michael's fellow Canadian, Sake Samurai and sake educator Elliot Faber, in from Hong Kong with his girlfriend Tiffany Coney Ung, both crouched on the stairwell and looking up

expectantly like two mythical, cornered characters in a game of Pokémon Go. Faber, who has a hand in a growing number of sake-centric food and beverage businesses throughout Asia, is in town to scout a new sake tour concept. As we walk along Sakagura-dori (lit., Sake Brewery Street), Maegaki points out the notable sights. The collection of breweries—designated a historic site—is steeped in sake history. Wooden structures hundreds of years old jostle up against white-walled *kura* (蔵, breweries) from the early twentieth century. Some feature rows of vintage *kame*, or ceramic sake urns, visible at the front or through the windows. From one vantage point, we can see three different tall, narrow, red brick chimneys—two of them belonging to Kamotsuru Brewery. They are picturesque, coal-fired relics that once fueled wooden rice steaming vats, long ago replaced by electric- or gas-powered versions. Maegaki points out the typical Hiroshima *namako-kabe* or "sea-cucumber walls" on some of the brewery buildings, named for their resemblance to the speckled skin of

certain sea-cucumber species. A crosshatched band of dark-colored, diagonally placed ceramic tiles covers the bottom portion of the whitewashed brewery, reinforced by thick white plaster piping. This sturdier portion of the wall protects against flood damage, while the plain white stonework on the walls above it are highly fire resistant.

Today, Saijo possesses all of the qualities needed to brew superior sake: pure water from nearby Mt. Ryuo; rice grown four miles (6 km) to the north, where the 115-foot (35 m) altitude and difference between day and night temperatures (diurnal range) are close to ideal; and a three-hundred-year history of sake-making expertise. But at the beginning of the twentieth century, there were still major hurdles to overcome to allow it to fulfill its potential.

We drop in on the venerable Hakubotan Brewery, which has roots that go back to 1675, housed in two handsome Edo-era wooden brewery buildings. It caters to and is beloved by locals, offering a slightly sweet, umami-forward regular sake. An array of framed, elaborately inked national sake-competition awards covers one wall, proof of the brewery's history of excellence.

At Fukubijin Brewery, Maegaki explains how in 1917 the business became the first cooperative, legally incorporated brewery, a tactic devised to circumvent laws controlling the amount of rice each brewery could buy. By pooling their individual buying power, members of this cooperative collectively became an influential force in the region, even operating a brewing school for aspiring master brewers and fermentation engineers until about 1970. We try some deliciously warming *amazake* (sake's sweet, no- or low-alcohol cousin, made with fermented steamed rice and *koji* mold) and continue our walk.

At nearby Kamotsuru—along with Hakubotan, one of the two largest breweries in town—we stroll through the beautiful new museum opened only four months earlier, filled with historic sake-making tools, exquisite porcelain sake vessels and vintage signage from the Taisho and Showa eras (1912–1989). But wait, what's this? We stop before a dazzling display case lined with row after row of Daiginzo Tokusei Gold Kamotsuru, special-issue bottles that feature flecks of cherry blossom-shaped gold leaf floating within, their caps also wrapped in blinding gold foil. Although it was never presented as a *ginjo* sake since it was released under the old classification system, Kamotsuru released this *tokyu* special-class sake at the very beginning of Japan's rocket-fueled economic expansion back in 1958, two years before Prime Minister Hayato Ikeda promised to double the income of Japan's citizens.

"As life became more affluent," a placard reads, "Kamotsuru offered a sake 'one step higher' in quality and looks." The bottles signaled a new obsession with luxury goods that came to dominate Japan in the postwar era. The brand began to sell in earnest in the mid-1960s, and remains available today, touting a polishing rate of 50 percent. Kamotsuru representative Yumi Shintani tells us the original ratio was likely under 55 percent.

Tokusei Gold might be viewed as a ginjo precursor, pointing the way to a low-polish, premium style that would achieve full expression with the advent of the ginjo era.

Happily, we're in the company of the person best equipped to help us untangle the story, our guide Maegaki, whose cheerful exterior masks a scholar's knowledge of sake history. He's also a born raconteur, a quality which, when combined with the industry-wide famous cooking of his mother Kayo

Kamoizumi president Kazuhiro Maegaki, holding a cup of first press *(arabashiri)* junmai daiginjo.

and wife Miyoko, makes for a long, fascinating, delicious and sake-soaked afternoon. We settle in to a sunny, tatami-matted room overlooking a serene formal rock garden, as Kayo and Miyoko bring out the first courses of a spectacular oyster-themed lunch.

Maegaki launches into the story of Hiroshima ginjo sake. "A long, long, time ago," he begins in a portentous voice, milking it for effect, "a man named Senzaburo Miura was active in sake brewing." Miura was born in 1847 in the nearby port town of Akitsu into a family of general goods wholesalers. More interested in brewing than commerce, a little before his thirtieth birthday he tried his hand at making sake. Repeated failures drove him to subterfuge. "Disguising the fact that he was a sake maker, he traveled to Nada to become a *kurabito*, acting like he knew nothing about brewing," Maegaki continues. Miura learned all that he could there. But when he returned to Hiroshima, his sake-making efforts failed again. Finally, he asked the president of the large Nada sake maker Ozeki to come to Hiroshima to instruct its brewers.

After each long, fluent paragraph of his story, Maegaki turns to Moysset and says, "Gochi-san!" which is his French assistant's cue to translate his boss's Japanese into English. Since neither language is Moysset's mother tongue, we feel for him. Looking like a deer caught in the headlights, he pauses for long moments, but skillfully delivers his translation in French-accented English.

Miura and the baffled Hiroshima brewers learned that their local water was categorized as *nansui*, or soft water. It was completely different from Nada's *kosui*, or extremely hard water. They understood that without the abundance of minerals that sake yeast feast on to fuel fermentation, their brews just weren't mustering the fermentation power they needed. They couldn't simply adopt Nada brewing techniques; they were going to have to figure out a new, Hiroshima-style of brewing.

Miura first decided to try to compensate for his low-mineral water by adjusting the koji-making portion of the process. This is where the koji mold's tentacle-like hyphae burrow into and feed on the starchy grains, their tips unleashing a cascade of enzymes, which in turn break down the starch into glucose and the proteins into amino acids. The newly released glucose in turn becomes food for hungry yeast cells.

But adjusting the koji alone led to a sake that was cloyingly rich and overly concentrated. So he decided to try fermenting at a very low temperature, knowing this would make the yeasts sluggish, slowing down the process to allow maximum fermentation of low-mineral content water.

Low-temperature brewing was a taboo idea at the time, Maegaki explains, because brewers knew it increased the chance of spoilage, which could sicken or possibly even kill customers. Everyone knew that dead customers were bad for business. "Miura challenged orthodoxy and he succeeded, creating a really fine-textured sake." This sake was elegant where his previous effort had been cloying. This is how, in 1898, Miura completed the develop-

Above A tatami-matted sitting room in the Maegaki home. Overlooking the rock garden, it would have been designed for sipping tea while enjoying the view.

Left Designed by Mirei Shigemori in 1955, the garden, with its raked stones, manicured trees and carefully placed jutting rocks, depicts the various islands of the Seto Inland Sea.

A display of Kamotsuru's Tokusei Gold junmai daiginjo at the brewery's museum. The sake was ahead of its time when it was first brewed and bottled in 1958.

ment of the low-temperature fermentation method of brewing, earning him the moniker "the father of ginjo sake."

Maegaki reminds us that brewers at the time did not have detailed scientific knowledge of how yeast works, and mechanical rice-polishing had not yet been popularized. Since both modern aromatic yeast and highly polished rice are today considered part of what makes ginjo sake, Miura's invention was more of a precursor to ginjo.

In 1907, the first national sake competition was held, and Hiroshima breweries, thanks to this groundbreaking new brewing technique, swept first, second and third places. These proto-ginjo sakes were known at the time as *ginzo* (吟造), referring to sake brewed to exhibit a refined fragrance and transparency. Maegaki speculates that the word evolved from the term *ginmi* (吟味), literally "examination brewing," referring to their use as competition sake only.

"But," continues Maegaki, deploying a word that will surface regularly during our session, as he delves deeper into sake lore, "that wasn't even Miura's biggest accomplishment." He excuses himself to fetch what he considers Miura's most enduring legacy.

By this point, we've downed a number of bottles of Kamoizumi, including a just-pressed, crisp apple- and fresh grass–scented junmai daiginjo brewed for competition purposes only, and an intense, honeyed unpasteurized *genshu*, or undiluted sake. The mood is jolly. We've polished off the giant bamboo basket of sake-steamed Hiroshima oysters, and are just finishing our whole, sansho pepper-perfumed head of sea bream. Our table is divided between those who eat the eyeballs (Tiffany among them) and those who don't. "If you have any more eyeballs, you know exactly who to pass them to," jokes Elliot.

Maegaki returns with a reissued edition of the handbook Miura published in 1898, *Kaijoho jissenro* (Practical handbook of the revised brewing method). He notes that although the Hiroshima brewing style has come to be known as the "soft-water brewing method," nowhere in Miura's book is the term "soft water" mentioned.

"Miura's real gift to sake brewing," says Maegaki, "was the way he did his utmost to pass on this new brewing method to everyone." The idea of publishing training materials for future brewers and study groups is hardly standard *shokunin* (craftsperson) culture, he explains. "Usually craftspeople don't reveal their secrets. You can look, but you aren't taught. Apprentices learn by watching." Maegaki notes that Miura's approach was closer to today's open-source technology, and it was that sharing of technology that helped Hiroshima brewers improve their skills. "This material was for the public, not for the individual," he says. A lot like how Nakano of Dewazakura and his circle of friends operated half a century later, inspired by the Hiroshima brewers to share information and goad each other on to perfect modern, mass-market ginjo sake.

"Here, at the end of the book," Maegaki adds, holding it up, "it says *hibaihin*: 'this article is not for sale.' He wasn't thinking about sales or profit. It was truly open source. That's where he was so amazing."

Satake and the Advent of the Rice-polishing Machine

Miura wasn't the only sake legend from Hiroshima. Around the time he wrote his open-source guide to sake brewing, a Saijo-born inventor, Riichi Satake, was coming into his own. Brilliant from birth, by age thirteen, he was employed as a land surveyor for the town. By fifteen he was sketching in his head the machine that would liberate his townspeople from the drudgery of archaic rice-milling methods. By his early twenties, he was a railway engineer.

"At the time, water power, in the form of the waterwheel, was used to polish rice," says Maegaki. But there were no rivers to power the wheels in Saijo. Foot power was obviously limited. Electricity was becoming available. So Satake, bankrolled by Kamotsuru Brewery, invented the first motor-powered rice-polishing machine in 1896. Propelled by its soft-water brewing technique and new rice-polishing technology, Hiroshima became one of the three most famous sake-brewing regions in Japan, alongside Nada in Hyogo and Fushimi in Kyoto.

At this point, Maegaki exclaims, "I've become tired. This talk will cost a lot, and you'll receive the tuition fee at the end. Canadian dollars are okay," he says with a magnanimous grin.

Tomorrow we expect to learn more about this historic sake-making prefecture when we head to the town of Akitsu to meet perhaps Japan's most famous woman *toji*, whose family home and brewery are practically next door to the birthplace of ginjo's folk hero, Senzaburo Miura.

Saijo, Hiroshima Flight

Sake name: Kamoizumi "Shusen"
Sake type: Junmai ginjo
Brewery: Kamoizumi, Hiroshima
A mellow and earthy junmai ginjo redolent of autumn leaves and mushrooms. Play with serving temperatures to explore its unique pairing versatility.

Sake name: Fukubijin "Josen"
Sake type: Junmai
Brewery: Fukubijin, Hiroshima
Like the Shusen, this is more mellow and savory than fruity and floral, with an expert balance of sweetness and acidity, featuring the soft mouthfeel of Saijo water.

Sake name: Kamotsuru "Tokusei Gold"
Sake type: Ginjo
Brewery: Kamotsuru, Hiroshima
A classic. One of the earliest daiginjo sakes on the market, introduced in 1958. Mildly aromatic in the Saijo tradition. Each bottle contains two tiny gold flakes in the shape of cherry blossoms.

Chapter Four

The Polishing Wars

Settling into a cozy sofa-strewn space located just off the entrance to Imada Brewery, we are warming ourselves over hot cups of green tea when president and master brewer Miho Imada appears, cracking her mile-wide smile. The contrast between her diminutive physical stature and her outsized reputation in the sake-brewing industry is striking.

Imada, during her twenty years as *toji* (chief brewer) has set a new standard for innovation in Hiroshima sake by reviving a defunct local heirloom rice, Hattanso, and creating innovative labels like her Seaside sparkling junmai that uses white instead of the usual yellow koji mold. She's also the inventor of a "hybrid" starter technique that combines the fast *sokujo* method with the *kimoto* method's reliance on naturally occurring lactic acid.

Next to us sits Andy Russell, another foreign *kurabito* brewery worker we meet on our travels. He worked at Juhachi Zakari Brewery in Okayama for three years before gravitating to Imada's brewery, attracted by its boundary-pushing approach to brewing. Russell's soft Scottish brogue is one of many international accents heard in breweries around Japan, a sign of sake's growing worldwide appeal. Though we were readers of his blog, *Origin Sake*, it's not until we meet him in person that we connect the dots and put blog and writer together in our heads.

Apart from her university years in Tokyo (studying law at Meiji University) and a decade producing Noh theater events in Tokyo, Imada has spent her life in Akitsu. Her affection for the town, and for the Seto Inland Sea where it is located, runs deep. The essence of the surrounding land and sea, she feels, is encoded in her sake.

The sources of her inspiration are plain to see: facing Akitsu is the calm sea and its scattering of picturesque, tree-covered islands. To its back, there's the protective embrace of the mountains that separate Higashi-Hiroshima from the rest of the city.

"There's the influence of the mild climate and the sea on my sake, and of course food culture is really important," Imada says. "How do we feel the seasons? What are our precious, important flavors? There's a real cultural and geographic aspect to it." Her sparkling junmai is a good example of how sake across Japan reflects the local culture and pairs well with its food. A crisp brew with notes of citrus and apple that relies on the post-bottling fermentation of residual sugars to supply the bubbles), it would have been an ideal companion for the famous Hiroshima oysters we ate at the Maegaki home.

Facing page A statue of Senzaburo Miura, the Akitsu-born, early ginjo sake pioneer who is revered today for his innovation, and his wish for Hiroshima brewers to improve their craft. **Above** Miura's former residence can be seen behind the brewing chimney at Imada Brewery. **Right** Post-brewing morning solitude at Imada Brewery.

A true sake town, Akitsu was home to seven breweries when Imada was a child, and about a third of her classmates were the children of sake-brewery workers. Even the Saijo breweries, located about twelve miles (19 km) away, were staffed by toji from Akitsu. The town's location on the key water-transport route along the Inland Sea made it a thriving port town in feudal Japan. During the Edo period, Akitsu was where the citizenry flocked to pay its annual rice tribute to the Mori clan that ruled Hiroshima. Most of it was shipped on to Kansai, the region to the northeast dominated by Kyoto and Osaka. Its strategic location kept enough of that rice in Akitsu though, giving rise to a growing number of sake breweries from the sixteenth century onwards. Today, there are only

Graphic image of the *henpei* (flat-polishing) and newly developed *genkei* (original shape) styles of rice polishing from the Satake Corporation.

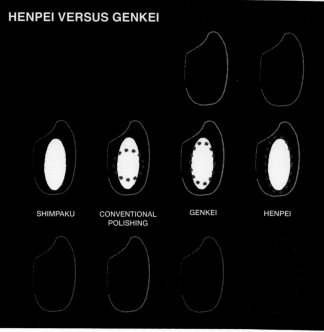

HENPEI VERSUS GENKEI

SHIMPAKU   CONVENTIONAL POLISHING   GENKEI   HENPEI

two left, including Imada's own brewery.

Given this longstanding culture of sake, it's not surprising that native son Senzaburo Miura, "the father of ginjo sake" who grew up in a house practically in the backyard of the Imada household and brewery, fell under its spell. The second-born son of the town's general goods wholesaler, Miura is credited with starting the Hiroshima Toji Guild and later in life serving as mayor of Akitsu.

Like Kamoizumi president Kazuhiro Maegaki who we met in chapter 3, Imada admires Miura, but from the point of view of a fellow townsperson, one whose family got to see firsthand just how much he did for the local sake brewers. It was Miura who—most likely in conversation with Imada's great-grandfather Shinji Imada—conceived the Imada family's brand name Fukucho ("Forever Fortune").

Miura and his fellow brewers worked relentlessly to perfect low-temperature fermentation, paying attention to every small tweak to the koji-making process, and exactly how the *shubo*, or starter, was made. "The man whose motto was 'Try a hundred things, and make a thousand improvements,' thought of these experimentations in a very granular way," says Imada. "When they failed, they all shared the information with each other, 'this works, that doesn't work.' He really believed in the process. He taught his technique to everyone in his circle. He didn't just make his own company and get rich from it; he wanted to make it the whole town's industry, to elevate the town's sake and its craftspeople. That's why even today, he's so well known."

Though it is local hero Miura whom Imada considers her mentor and inspiration, it was through the Satake Corporation—founded by Saijo

rice-polishing machine inventor Riichi Satake—that Imada found her next creative project: a matched pair of bottles simply called Henpei and Genkei, names that refer to the two different styles of rice polishing used. The beautiful and rustic forest green-and-white labels graphically illustrate these styles, with a design of flat shapes for Henpei and round shapes for Genkei.

On one level, the series is liquid catnip for sake aficionados obsessed with rice-polishing technology, rice-polishing ratios and the varying effects these can have on the final result. But on another level, the small-batch new issue, made in collaboration with the Satake Corporation, brings to the fore a conversation that is increasingly taking place in the craft-sake world. Namely, how much do rice-polishing ratios really matter anymore?

The ginjo boom, as we've seen, ushered in an era of premium sake distinguished—among other things—by its high polishing rates, or *seimai buai* (精米歩合). The lower the seimai buai, the more grain has been milled off. Proteins, fats and minerals in the husks can lead to off-flavors; removing them results in a light, clean and elegant drink. To help guide consumers, in 1992, Japan's National Tax Agency created a classification system called the *tokutei meishoshu* (special-designation sake) system. Inherent in these classifications was the judgment that the lower the polishing ratio, the more "premium" the sake.

Over the years a seimai buai arms race has played out, with ratios shrinking from sixty to thirty-five to seven. In 2019, Niizawa's Brewery's Absolute Zero was made by polishing its Kuranohana rice continually for over seven months. Legally, if the ratio dips even a fraction of a percent below one, its seimai buai is deemed zero. Absolute Zero replaced Tatenokawa's one-percent Zenith junmai daiginjo as the sake with the lowest polishing ratio, and sake fans rejoiced in the fact that this was the end of the polishing wars; it was impossible to push rates any lower.

Above Imada Brewery's Henpei and Genkei sakes, brewed with the heirloom rice variety Hattanso that was revived by Imada. **Left** At our tasting of the two sakes, Imada added a third, a *junmai ginjo* made with Hattanso rice, but polished in the usual way.

We say "rejoice," because as brewing techniques have improved, skilled toji have learned that by manipulating the koji-making process, fermentation temperatures, yeasts and rice varieties, they can produce delicious sake that does not rely on low polishing ratios. John Gauntner, the premier non-Japanese sake educator in the world, at one time advised students, "If you remember one word, remember *ginjo*." In today's sake world of category-defying choices, this is less universally true when talking of sake quality. Some of our favorite sakes, in fact, are stellar low-polish labels that under the old system would be considered a lesser sake. And as we'll see in the story of Henpei and Genkei, advancements in polishing techniques alone are disrupting the connection between polishing ratio and sake quality. Before getting into that, though, it's helpful to know a little bit about the Fukushima Prefecture brewery that first perfected the flat-polishing style twenty-five years ago.

Daishichi Brewery and Super-flat Rice Polishing

Tenth-generation Daishichi Brewery owner Hideharu Ohta is descended from a long line of Mie Prefecture samurai. Three brothers from this family migrated north in the early seventeenth century, becoming retainers to a regional ruler, Lord Niwa. The brothers followed him from town to town as he was transferred here and there by the Tokugawa shogunate. Eventually, they settled in Fukushima and it is there that they took on the role of sake brewers and purveyors to the feudal house. Daishichi was founded in 1752 by first-generation owner Saburouemon Ohta.

As it evolved, the brewery flirted a little with postwar sake-making techniques, but always returned to more traditional methods. Eighth-generation president Shichiuemon Ohta was an early adopter of the fast-brewing sokujo starter method when it was introduced in the early 1900s, but quickly decided the kimoto starter method was better; the brewery has not veered from that

Miho Imada (center) and her team at Imada Brewery. From left to right; Andrew Russell; Shinobu Suginishi; Miho Imada; Miho Tanimizu; Hiromasa Sugiura.

traditional style since. During World War II, when the government encouraged dropping *kioke* wooden barrels in favor of what it believed to be more hygienic enamel tanks, Daishichi did so. But when Hideharu Ohta visited Romanée-Conti vineyard in Burgundy in 2001 and saw wine barrels that had been in use for 150 years, it became the catalyst for his return to brewing in the traditional wooden kioke. Ohta also uses old-fashioned iron cauldrons for rice steaming.

Yet for all of his embracing of traditional methods, in the early 1990s, when Ohta read a paper by a technical officer at the National Tax Agency about a new way of rice polishing, he was intrigued. For once, the focus was not just about continually lowering sake rice-polishing ratios, but on improving *efficiency*: how to polish less but obtain better results.

Ohta contacted the researcher, Tomio Saito, and along with Daishichi's head of rice polishing, Yoshio Ogata, began testing the new henpei "flat-polishing" method in 1993. When it was perfected in the spring of 1995, Ohta used the method for Daishichi's silky, layered Minowamon junmai daiginjo sake. Since the Daishichi method went above and beyond even what Saito envisioned, Daishichi dubbed it the "super-flat" polishing method.

The method was considered revolutionary because it could preserve the integrity of the oblong *shinpaku*, or heart, of Yamada Nishiki rice and avoid cracking it, which would result in a less ideal brew.

The polished rice's flat, oblong shape had a higher starch-to-undesirables ratio (undesirables being the proteins, lipids and minerals that can create off-flavors) than rice polished with conventional milling. In other words, you could polish rice to 70 percent using the flat-polishing method, and it would be equivalent to a 51 percent conventional polish. It was both a less wasteful and more energy-efficient method. For his contributions to rice-polishing technique, in 2006 Ogata was named a Contemporary Master Craftsman by the Japanese government.

Daishichi then began working with a researcher at Nodai, the Tokyo University of Agriculture, on furthering the technique. Over the next two decades, Nodai graduates who went to work for the Satake Corporation, maker of rice-milling machinery, took this flat-polishing know-how with them. When Satake came up with its new flat-polishing machine in the fall of 2018, Daishichi was among one of the first to purchase one, since it more fully automated what Daishichi had been doing using old, manually controlled machines. Daishichi's super-flat polishing method required a heavy helping of highly skilled craftsmanship on the part of the rice-mill operator. The reason Daishichi's rice-polishing expert Ogata had been so richly decorated, Ohta explains, was for the way he perfected this hand-crafted aspect of the Daishichi super-flat polishing method.

Satake's new milling machine, thanks to its new, super-abrasive cubic boron nitride grindstone, automated much of that, speeding up the flat-polishing process significantly. The new milling machine also represented Satake's re-entry into a market which had lately lost market share, to rival Shinnakano. In addition to automating the *henpei* method, the Satake machine can also do something completely new: what it calls *genkei* or "original shape" milling. With this method the rice is milled uniformly on all surfaces so it retains its original shape. It's a method more suitable to the popular heirloom rice Omachi or Hiroshima's own Hattanso rice, which have rounder, rather than flatter, hearts.

The Henpei and Genkei Series

In the summer of 2018, Imada attended a seminar for sake makers from five regional prefectures. There, the Satake Corporation—today a multinational manufacturing group—revealed plans for its groundbreaking new sake rice–polishing machine.

Of two hundred attendees at the seminar, Imada was the only one who expressed interest in the new technology. Her curiosity paid off: in January 2020 Imada Brewery and Satake released its Tokunaga Satake series, bottling one tank of sake made with henpei-polished rice and another brewed with rice polished genkei style. Both were made with Hattanso rice polished to 60 percent. The precision of the method means that a 60 percent polish ginjo sake tastes remarkably like a 40 percent daiginjo. "The amino acids on both are really low, so they were a really creamy and pretty sake," says Imada.

The fascination went beyond just a ginjo polishing ratio tasting like a daiginjo; although both types

of polishing reduced the protein content of the rice by about the same amount, the henpei, or flat style, for still-unknown reasons, resulted in a clearer-tasting sake. Yusuke Sato, the president-toji of the cult brewery Aramasa in Akita, was so taken with these results he's purchased his own Satake milling machine and plans from here on to polish all of his rice in the flat style.

Sato points to the high efficiency of the flat-rice polishing machine and notes, "Our brewery uses very good rice cultivated by contract farmers. More than a quarter of it is pesticide-free and it's three times more expensive than regular sake rice, so I don't want to polish off any more than I have to. That's why I've installed the flat-rice polishing machine."

Daishichi Brewery's newest Satake rice-polishing machine can polish sake rice in *genkei* and *henpei* styles, though it is especially valued for its ability to polish in the "super-flat" *henpei* style.

Where Do We Go from Here?

Just as Daishichi did in the mid-90s, Imada Brewery with its Henpei and Genkei series, highlights the shrinking relevance of sake classifications, and their basis in rice-polishing ratios. The special-designation sake classification system, Imada points out, has only been in place for about thirty years, but it will probably disappear within the next decade. The question on her mind is: what will replace it?

"I'm really thinking about this now, as are all of us in the sake world," she says. "For a hundred years, we've been studying and making ginjo. At first, when we polished rice, it was incredibly difficult to control the taste. Whatever bad elements you polished off, whatever perfection you achieved, that was hard won. But now, we've finally mastered that technique. So we ask ourselves what do we want to do with it now? Everyone is thinking really hard about what the next step should be, but we don't know. To figure it out, we're trying all kinds of things, anything that seems possible."

Daishichi's wooden brewing vats range from fifty to one-hundred years old. They require special care to maintain proper hygiene, but are worth the trouble for the way they promote active fermentation and condensed flavors, creating strong and rich sake.

In the coming chapters, we'll be exploring the ways that the sake world is charting its course to post-ginjo sake. Not all believe that in order to survive they have to radically change; there is room for classic sake with impeccable pedigrees and technique, as well as for those whose products challenge conventional tastes.

Hideharu Ohta, for example, would like to see *junmai* sake (pure sake with no added alcohol) considered as a completely separate class than ginjo, a distinction that has become blurred. "The classification of sake is often expressed by a pyramid with junmai daiginjo at the top," he says. "This gives the impression that the closer to the top, the higher the value of the sake. As a result, there is a tendency to make junmai sake like junmai ginjo and junmai ginjo like junmai daiginjo. But that's an attitude that denies all deliciousness except junmai daiginjo—and that's nonsense."

Instead, he'd like to see a system where there are "many pyramids" depending on one's specific preference. "The fruity aroma and refreshing taste of ginjo sake, and the varied, full-bodied taste of junmai sake are not hierarchically related, and should be ranked in their own taste fields," he says.

When he made the conversion to wooden brewing vats in 2001 he experienced this epiphany. "I felt that the sake brewed in the wooden vats possessed a very strong, concentrated feeling and the potential to mature and grow. This experience convinced me it would be possible to make

high-class sake that is not daiginjo, by brewing junmai sake in wooden vats." His hypothetical junmai pyramid would reward sakes with a more powerful taste, "richer in umami."

As we'll see in the coming chapters, Imada's and Ohta's paths are just two brewers' approaches to achieving new levels of sake excellence. Others are experimenting with various aspects of sake making, from rice to yeast to water to koji mold and agricultural practices. All of the makers on our journey—whether in their brewing styles, business practices or simply in where they view their place in the ever-expanding sake world—are, as Miura advised, "trying a hundred things and making a thousand different changes."

Polishing Delirium Flight

Maybe tricky to source, these sakes are worth the hunt. Gather your sake friends and explore the existential sake question: are polishing rates passé?

Sake name: Genkei Hattanso
Sake type: No grade
Brewery: Imada Brewery, Hiroshima Prefecture
Along with Henpei Hattanso, this sake is part of the Satake series which explores the subtle differences between the two sakes, identical except for rice-polishing style. Both are brewed with the heirloom grain Hattanso revived by master brewer Miho Imada.

Sake name: Daishichi "Minowamon"
Sake type: Junmai daiginjo kimoto
Brewery: Daishichi, Fukushima Prefecture
Daishichi is known for crafting solidly built premium sakes in the kimoto style. Minowamon is the pioneering product that launched the brewery's exploration of the super-flat polishing technique.

Sake name: Tatenokawa "18"
Sake type: Junmai daiginjo
Brewery: Tatenokawa, Yamagata Prefecture
Though Niizawa Brewery's Absolute Zero 0 percent polish junmai daiginjo may confer peak polishing-rate bragging rights on those who chase such things, Tatenokawa's 18 amply expresses the effects of highly polished Yamada Nishiki. From the nakadori, or middle pressing, of the tank, which is the most highly prized.

Chapter Five

The New Grains: The Era of the Hybrid

Standing here in this large, brightly lit function room, we could be in Petaluma or Peoria, or any small-town's glitziest downtown hotel. Star-shaped crystal chandeliers shine down on peony-patterned carpeting, and lazy Susans crown tables covered in snowy, lace-trimmed table linens. The first course of our banquet is carefully covered in glassine paper to lock in its freshness.

It's the mid-March timing of the event, the three large sake casks on the stage, the pyramid of square wooden *masu* sake cups and the fridge full of sake—all branded with the swooping calligraphy of the Nanbu Bijin Brewery logo—that mark this as a distinctly sake culture event: the annual *shinshu*, or "new sake" party to celebrate sake made with rice harvested during this brewing year.

Production at this brewery, founded in 1902, in the far northern reaches of Tohoku's Iwate Prefecture has been underway since early October, and the *koshiki daoshi*, or ceremonial tipping over of the wooden rice-steaming vat at the end of the brewing season, is still three months away. But fifth-generation Nanbu Bijin president Kosuke Kuji declares this the optimal time for his party. Tonight he'll thank the community of his hometown, Ninohe, a handful of top employees and his farmers for their support, celebrating with fresh pressings of this year's sake. Shinshu parties are an annual rite at breweries, but they can vary wildly in nature. Michael still remembers the staggering amount of fresh *namazake* (unpasteurized sake) he consumed at Hakkaisan Brewery's raucous party celebrating the completion of the making of the season's tokubetsu daiginjo sake. Tradition dictates if someone comes over to offer you sake, you drink what's left of your current cup and then accept

more. Pretty much every brewer came over to refill his cup, multiple times over. Michael still remembers the hell there was to pay the next morning. We're not sure what to expect here tonight.

We left Tokyo this morning, boarding our teal-and-white Hayabusa bullet train for the under-three-hour trip north. The skies gradually turn slate gray as we speed toward the Kitakami River basin, bordered by the Ou Mountains and the Kitakami range to the west. The latter bisects Iwate, separating Ninohe and the prefectural capital Morioka from the jagged Pacific coastline. The river itself is the longest in Tohoku, and spans most of the length of Iwate.

The tables begin filling with locals, and Kuji, an ebullient man whose thousand-watt smile has electrified countless Instagram posts, makes his way to the podium, champagne glass in hand. "We have all of our new sake here," his voice booms. "But what I really want you to try is this *awa* (sparkling) sake. It's made with new techniques, it's being consumed all over the world, and it's slated to be used to toast the opening of the Tokyo Olympics!"

The audience—shy and a little in awe of this larger-than-life local hero, who now roams the world talking up Ninohe to urban sophisticates—looks up at him, rapt and silent. Kuji barrels ahead. The boy who once had his heart set on becoming a

Kosuke Kuji, the president of Iwate Prefecture's Nanbu Bijin Brewery, has been a booster of local rice and a force in the internationalization of premium sake.

professional baseball player is very much alive here, emoting raw passion and competitive zeal. His talk turns to the brewery's lauded tokubetsu junmai. "The ingredients it's made with, Gin Otome rice, the techniques, *everything* came from Ninohe! Our brewery rep took it to a sake competition and it took number one twice in recent competitions, the only one [in Iwate Prefecture] to have won an international competition. And this is from Ninohe! We're exporting now to forty-five different countries, but the *jimoto* (the hometown) is here in Ninohe. And if we don't all love it here, then it's not *jizake* [locally made sake]. We have the worldwide champion tokubetsu junmai here, *the same one* that's in Tokyo and New York. But it will always be available here. We want to show the world how wonderful Ninohe is—its terroir, its value! Please have fun!" Kuji returns to our table as the head of the local Iwate bank takes over the mic. Kuji beams, noting, "'*Kanpai*' ['cheers': literally, empty the cup] really is a good word, isn't it?"

We are sitting at the most glamorous table in the room, thanks to the presence of Mai Morita, Miss Sake. She emerged victorious from the first annual Miss Sake competition, beating six hundred other contestants by demonstrating poise while wearing a kimono and drinking sake, as well as her ability to convey sake's nuances and charms.

Nanbu Bijin sake barrels adorn the *shinshu* (new sake) party held every March, when community and business leaders, farmers and brewers celebrate the season's first sake pressing.

But Kuji is the focal point of the room. After watching him speak it's easy to see how he became one of the driving forces behind the internationalization of sake. Because Iwate Prefecture has seen its population fall from 1.42 million in 1980 to 1.25 million in 2019, and because domestic sake sales have followed a downward trajectory since the mid-1970s, Kuji knew when he joined the family business in 1990 (and took over as president in 2013) that opening up foreign markets was imperative for the long-term success of the brewery. So he became an active force in the Sake Export Association, which was founded in 1997 and now represents twenty breweries around the country.

"Japan's population is 126 million, and the worldwide population is more than 7.5 billion," he says, noting that the global market is one that has been shown to love Japanese food. If you couldn't sell to that 7.5 billion that would be one thing," Kuji adds. "But most of those countries like and respect

Sake-rice Hybrids in the Past Twenty Years

There have been many advancements in the development of new sake-rice strains in the past two decades. Whether it's an effort to tailor a rice to the unique environments of a region, improve how it behaves during fermentation, or simply to dethrone Yamada Nishiki as the king of rice, it means a lot of choices for brewers and the promise of more diversity in the sake rice we see listed on a label.

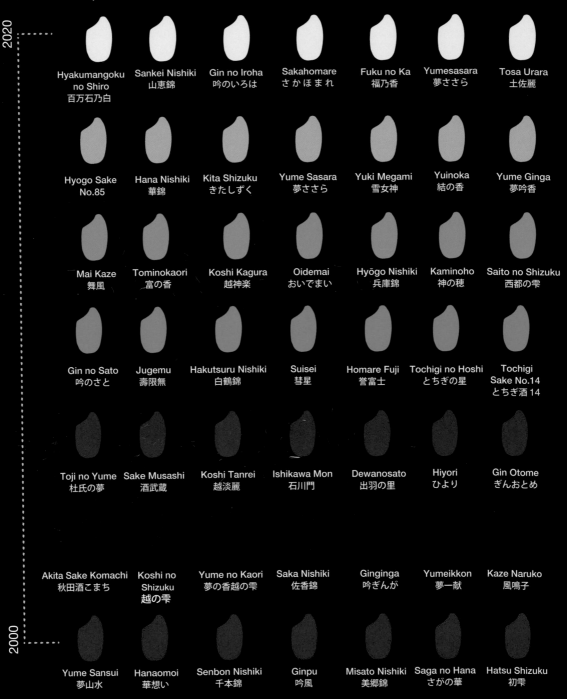

Kosuke Kuji holds up a bottle of his Nanbu Bijin sake.

Japanese food and drink. Japan's food has been accepted more quickly, while sake is a little behind. That's why we have to do something to boost sake sales." Looking abroad also came naturally to him. During a one-month high school homestay in Tulsa, Oklahoma, the father of his host family fell in love with Nanbu Bijin sake. At that moment, Kuji began to appreciate the unique cultural value of sake. "That study-abroad experience changed my heart," he says.

He joined other brewery heirs at the department of fermentation science of Tokyo University of Agriculture (Nodai) in 1991. His record of excelling started there, when he was selected to create and oversee a student brew for Katsuyama Brewery in Miyagi. He also did tours of duty at the Kumamoto Prefecture Sake Institute, and made Okinawa's local drink, awamori, at Yaesen Brewery, Ishigaki Island.

Entering the family business as the manager of sake production in 1995, he took home a gold medal at the US National Sake Appraisal and continued to rack up gold medals. In 2016 and 2017, as Kuji brags to tonight's audience, the brewery took home gold at the International Wine Challenge in London, first for its *honjozo* (alcohol-added sake) and the next year for his tokubetsu junmai label. His pride is justified; taking home back-to-back golds in a field of more than 1,200 breweries each year was a huge accomplishment. Kuji's sake improvement and internationalization efforts continue in the classroom, too; he teaches brewing classes as well as international development and economics at Nodai.

The Return of Sake Regionality through Hybrid Varieties

As brewers like Kuji have become more familiar with the international market, they've recognized the need to make sake more approachable and understandable. One way brewers are now trying to explain sake to Westerners steeped in the language and culture of wine is to embrace the notion of the French term "terroir" which refers to the unique characteristics of a region. Tonight, Kuji uses the term to refer to the soil, the climate and topography of the environment that produces a unique wine or other agricultural product. As they've become more and more familiar with foreign wine and spirits, many brewers have adopted the language of terroir both for marketing purposes and because it reflects their desire to create a more authentic local product.

But this is a contentious topic: many will tell you that sake excellence has more to do with the skill and artistry of the *toji* brewer than where the rice came from or who grew it. One problem with fitting into the Western terroir paradigm is sake rice. Almost since the debut of Yamada Nishiki in 1936, it has been transported from its native Hyogo Prefecture to breweries near and far to satisfy brewers who want to work with the best rice on the market. Increasingly, it is also being cultivated in many prefectures outside Hyogo. But as the cachet of local products has grown, so has the race to develop regional hybrid rice varieties that rival king Yamada Nishiki in taste and aroma but are better suited to local climates. Often these new varieties, like Iwate's Gin Otome, are developed in partnership with prefectural research centers.

Tracking the minor tsunami of new varieties Japan's various prefectures have released is part of the excitement of watching a sense of regionality return to sake. "There's a huge amount of variation now," says Jamie Graves, Japanese portfolio manager at Skurnik Wines in New York. He points to cult Yamagata Prefecture brewer Takagi Brewery (makers of the Juyondai brand) and its eighteen-year effort to breed a successful hybrid of Yamada

Nishiki and Miyama Nishiki rice to create a variety called Sake Mirai ("Sake's Future") in 1999. Since Yamada Nishiki is native to Hyogo Prefecture in the west of Japan, Takagi Brewery wanted to create a local hybrid that retained some of Yamada Nishiki's best characteristics (large, high-starch *shinpaku*, or heart, low protein content) but suited to the local colder climate. Miyama Nishiki, native to Nagano but suited to all the northern prefectures, fit the bill as the best mate with which to cross Yamada Nishiki.

Over the last twenty-five years well over fifty new sake-rice hybrids have emerged. Niigata's fifteen-year effort to develop its own local rice culminated in the triumphant unveiling of Koshi Tanrei back in 2004. It is the rice child of, naturally, Yamada Nishiki and Niigata's own Gohyakumangoku, a stalwart of sake brewing that was developed in 1957 and widely adopted for cultivation from the mid-1970s. Koshi Tanrei was less prone to cracking when polished than Gohyakumangoku (allowing for daiginjo-level polishing), while its shorter ripening time compared to Yamada Nishiki made it much better suited to Niigata's cold climate and shorter growing season. For brewing tastes that were moving away from Niigata's signature "light and dry" style, the new hybrid introduced a little of Yamada Nishiki's richness and umami.

Hybrids gained even more popularity when it became clear that brewing with one's own prefectural rice can lead to a gold-medal-paved future. In 2007, when the first sake made with Koshi Tanrei appeared on the market, fifteen Niigata brewers submitted entries to the annual national competition, and five took home gold.

Tochigi Prefecture's New Hybrid

During our visits to over thirty breweries, the latest local hybrids were frequent topics of conversations.

Master brewer Makoto Ono and president Shigeki Tonoike of Tonoike Brewery, located in Tochigi Prefecture's Mashiko pottery village.

At Tonoike Brewery in Tochigi Prefecture, third-generation president Shigeki Tonoike and master brewer Makoto Ono served us a delicious Sanran junmai ginjo and a junmai daiginjo made with one of the newest sake-rice hybrids, the prefecturally developed Yume Sasara ("Dream of the Bamboo Whisk," an allusion to the trusty brewery tool used to clean wooden tools and receptacles). The rice, released in 2018, is a cross between Yamada Nishiki and the Tochigi rice T-25. (Until a rice is put on the market it goes by its laboratory serial number.) Among Ono's many prizewinning sakes, three are made with Yume Sasara, and are characterized by a spritely balance of umami and acid, with a bit of effervescence on the finish. They are an especially good match with Tochigi's famous winter strawberry, the sweet, juicy and oversized Skyberry.

Yume Sasara is quickly gaining favor in Tochigi over locally grown Gohyakumangoku, and although Ono says it's easy to use and has so far been highly evaluated, it is still "a work in progress." Both farmers and brewers need time to learn how to grow and brew with it. It lacks the depth of flavor of Yamada Nishiki, and the breakage rate when it is polished is still too high. Differences in quality throughout the prefecture still haven't been ironed out. We wonder about the interplay with yeast and ask if the rice has been bred to match well with local prefectural yeasts.

"Yes," replies Ono, "to a degree. But it's best to think about what kind of sake the customer wants to drink most and decide what rice and yeast to use based on that. We also have to decide which brewing method to use, sokujo or kimoto." *(Kimoto takes longer and relies on the development of natural lactic acid.)*

Scenes from Tonoike Brewery: sake barrels welcome visitors at the entrance (top left); *kurabito* prepare *koji* rice in the wood-paneled *koji* room (above); the brewing team (left), helmed by *toji* Makoto Ono.

In Iwate Prefecture, the large-hearted, big umami-producing hybrid rice Gin Otome ("Pure Princess") is sibling to another prefectural original, Ginginga. Nanbu Bijin is now best-known for its Ginginga junmai ginjo and International Wine Challenge award-winning Gin Otome tokubetsu junmai sake, a velvety mix of floral, sweet and umami notes. The brewery's toji, Junji Matsumori, likes it so much he drinks it warm, year round. Back at the Shinsu party Kuji says he will never stop brewing with Yamada Nishiki or Omachi—"they represent this country." He believes to just focus on one or two local varieties results in brewers who are "technically imbalanced." He says, "If you only know how to make *maguro nigiri* (tuna sushi), that's strange, right? You have to think about sushi as an entire category." Even so, 70 percent of the junmai sake he makes now is brewed with Gin Otome.

As Kuji talks rice varieties, Michael is off in a corner, being swept off his feet by a rogue sake that Kosuke Kuji's younger brother, Nanbu Bijin vice president Yuzo Kuji has brewed. Called the Yuzo Special, Michael says, "It's like night and day from Kuji-san's. It's freakin' dry, plus-fifteen Sake Meter Value [see page 21], which is why they have it warm to soften it a little. Kuji-san likes the pretty, aromatic profiles, and his brother is the opposite."

Yuzo's sake is a perfect match for steak, sukiyaki and other meat dishes he favors, and is good warm: his preferred sake serving temperature. "To warm sake is to bring it into the future," he says, conjuring up a time-travelling sake rocketing ahead to an era when sake, and its appreciation, are more advanced. But he means that warming exerts a mellowing influence, drawing out rounder flavors that might take a year or two or even more to develop on their own. Heating it really does seem to speed up time.

The Miyama Nishiki rice used for the Yuzo Special, we learn, was grown outside of Morioka City, about a ninety-minute drive to the south, by a Nanbu Bijin brewer named Apollo, who is also a farmer. The black-and-white graphic novel–style labels are done by local hipster artist and chef Yuta Ishikawa, again the polar opposite of the pretty, refined labels that Kosuke's brews wear.

Yuzo Special, brewed by president Kosuke Kuji's younger brother, Yuzo, is a bone-dry and savory sake, markedly different from the typical fruity and alluring Nanbu Bijin style. The rice for this sake is grown by a Nanbu Bijin brewer/farmer named Apollo.

The two brothers are opposite in appearance as well. Suit-and-tie-clad Kosuke scoots around the room, glad-handing locals and posing for pictures like the captain of the team celebrating a big win, his eyes wide, his huge laugh ricocheting off walls. Yuzo, meanwhile, in black turtleneck and soft russet-colored corduroy jacket, lounges on the sidelines cracking sarcastic jokes and looking like a founding member of the Japanese Rat Pack.

But there's another person we want to meet at the party, the farmer who grows Nanbu Bijin's Gin Otome rice. Shortly after we've expressed this wish, Kosuke Kuji nearly drags over to our table a sheepish, shy-looking gray-haired man in a suit, introducing him as Ryoichi Itsukaichi. "This is the champion farmer!" he booms. "This is the absolute origin of terroir, right here. This man, he's the Terroir King! Please ask him how he grows the rice."

We offer Itsukaichi a seat, pouring him some Gin Otome *nama shiboritate* (unpasteurized, just pressed) ginjo. We all savor it for a moment, saluting him, the farmer who grew the rice. Once dissolved and fermented, it's become this lovely fresh sake, animated by the robust, unbridled energy of the grain. The farmer, bashful about his English, especially when he gets a word slightly wrong, declines to accept more food when it is offered by a server, this time a course of fermented seafood from Iwate's Sanriku coast.

Itsukaichi tells us that he was cultivating table rice when he first met Kuji, who asked him to grow sake rice for him. "We can't grow Yamada Nishiki in Iwate Prefecture because it's not hot enough," he explains. "Table rice has been improved to the point where it can even be grown in Hokkaido, but traditionally, we have just not grown sake rice here." Now he grows about fifty acres (0.5 hectare) of Gin Otome—scattered in postage-stamp-sized parcels around the brewery's northern Iwate location, all

for Nanbu Bijin. Only about three feet (1 m) tall compared to Yamada Nishiki's four-plus feet, it's easier for farmers to grow. Its shortcoming, notes Itsukaichi, is that its heart is not always well centered inside the grain. A well-centered heart is a quality that is prized in sake rice because it results in less breakage during polishing and allows for higher polishing ratios and thus more daiginjo-style brews. It is also the main criterion by which sake rices are evaluated and graded each year. Still, Itsukaichi proudly reports that this year his Gin Otome received its highest rating to date, a sign of his skill as a farmer.

Although Nanbu Bijin is almost single-handedly boosting demand for sake rice in the Ninohe region, where farmers receive no government subsidies and rice farming is a barely sustainable practice, Kuji acknowledges, "Rice farming is in bad shape. Farmers are quitting, and then there's the problem of *kokeisha* (successors). When sons hear their fathers talk about how difficult rice farming is these days, they don't want to follow in their footsteps."

Even though Itsukaichi is one of the lucky ones, he says it's still a struggle to pay his young farmers, motioning to them sitting at a table nearby. "But," he adds, "Nanbu Bijin is making global sake, and we take a lot of pride in that and in our own production. We'd like to grow as much rice as we can."

Apparently, we are such celebrities among the farmer's family and staff that they are gawking at us and trying to surreptitiously take pictures. Itsukaichi's wife Yoshiko and her sister Kazuko Nishizato hang back, at first too bashful to introduce themselves. When they do, Kazuko steps forward and says, "I'm the *younger* sister," an unexpected display of sibling rivalry.

The emcee announces the raffle draw: "Table seven, guest number five, congratulations!" This is the farmers' signal to retreat. As we say goodbye Michael comments, "When Itsukaichi-san brought his wife over I felt like Tom Cruise—she looked like she was going to cry! It's really humbling."

The party fades to an end as guests file out, holding raffle prizes and a renewed sense of pride knowing their local sake is making an impact on global sake culture.

During the taxi ride back to our hot springs inn, snow begins to fall, first softly, then peltingly, soon turning to a blinding curtain of white. In minutes, the ground is covered with several inches of white fluff and we get a sense of what it must feel like here in mid-winter, with deep drifts forming overnight.

Ninohe feels small and remote. Yet it's the source of some of the best sake in Tohoku, and that added sense of identity and pride that Kuji and Nanbu Bijin have conferred on the town are priceless. Kuji's advice to young brewers returns to mind: "I tell them that skills, techniques, all that will follow. Your feelings and attitudes are the most important thing. Among all the beverages of the world, ours is the only one with the name of the country attached to it: *nihonshu* (literally, "the alcohol of Japan"). It's our national drink. That's why I want us to take pride in it. Pride is the most important thing."

Hybrid Rice Flight

Sake name (Japan): Nanbu Bijin
Sake name (US): Southern Beauty
Sake type: Tokubetsu junmai
Brewery: Nanbu Bijin, Iwate Prefecture
The 2017 Grand Prize winner at the International Wine Challenge, made with Iwate's own Gin Otome rice polished to 55 percent.

Sake name: Sanran
Sake type: Junmai ginjo
Brewery: Tonoike, Tochigi Prefecture
Brewed with one of the newest and most promising hybrid ginjo rice strains, Yume Sasara. Tonoike is located in the Mashiko pottery village, so this one calls for your favorite ceramic ochoko or guinomi style of sake cup.

Sake name: Juyondai "Sake Mirai"
Sake type: Junmai ginjo
Brewery: Takagi, Yamagata Prefecture
Made with Sake Mirai rice, a Miyama Nishiki hybrid that the brewery had a hand in developing. This one is worth the hunt for that knee-wobbling first sip.

Chapter Six

The Heirloom Rice Hunters

In 1970, thirty-three-year-old Tadayoshi Toshimori was a brewery president-in-training, learning the business from the ground up, in preparation to become the fourth-generation head of his family's Okayama Prefecture brewery. Among his duties was delivering sake to customers in his small town of Karube. Part of present-day Akaiwa City, it lies about a thirty-minute drive north of Okayama City, west of the Yoshii River. The temperate effects of the Seto Inland Sea to the south can be seen in the sunny, warm climate and fertile fruit orchards.

One day, in 1970, Toshimori dropped by the home of farmer Kiyono Migimasa to make a delivery. In the barn he spotted dried samples of Omachi rice plants hanging in the order of the year of their harvest, a time period spanning ten years. "I was shocked," Toshimori recalls, "because I'd never seen rice plants that tall. I'd read that there was once a rice called Omachi, but it was the first time I had actually seen it." One of the features of Omachi is its remarkable height; averaging five feet (1.5 m) tall, it's been known to reach nearly six feet, compared to roughly three feet for other sake-rice varieties. In the barn the stalks were so long that the tangled, dried remains of their grain-bearing heads, panicles and husks looked disproportionately small in comparison. "No one was making sake with Omachi at the time," says Toshimori, and so no one was growing it. Migimasa was the exception, producing the rice solely for the local Shinto shrine's sake offering to the gods and for purification rites.

In Japan, sake has always connected gods and mortals. In the country's earliest texts, sake is referred to as *miki*, written with the characters for "god" and "sake." Today the word *miki* or *omiki* is reserved for sake used in Shinto rites and festivals; sipping it is a reverential act of communion with the gods. So sake breweries have historically had close, symbiotic relationships with Shinto shrines. The

shrines conduct rites seeking prosperity for brewers, and brewers in turn supply local shrines with sake for rituals, ceremonies and festivals, as well as the decorative *kazaridaru* barrels that are stacked in rows on shrine grounds.

To this day, every brewery has a wooden shrine, or *kamidana*, mounted on the wall somewhere on its premises where the god of sake is enshrined and honored with sake-filled flasks. In varying degrees of regularity, brewers stand in front of the shrine, clap twice, lower their heads and pray for a successful brewing season. So it seemed fitting that Shinto priests in a small local town like Karube would be the last to let go of brewing with this old, nearly forgotten variety of rice.

But Toshimori's first thought upon spying the dried rice plants had nothing to do with the local shrine and Shintoism. It was much more practical: "I want to see what kind of sake this rice makes."

Visiting the Birthplace of Omachi Rice

Our conversation with Toshimori comes during an immersive trip to Okayama to see the birthplace of Omachi (雄町) rice, a variety today known to stir cult-like devotion among its many brewer and sake-drinking fans. Among the fifty to one hundred or so different heirloom sake-rice strains that have been identified (the number varies depending on

Tadayoshi Toshimori (left) and advising *toji* Toyokazu Tamura (right) hold harvested Omachi rice. Tamura is retired, but is still an abiding influence at the brewery.

which expert you ask), Omachi is perhaps the most widely adopted and universally beloved. Typically these rice varieties were replaced with higher-yield, easier-to-grow varieties that could withstand the rigors of mechanization and chemical inputs. Among the heirlooms, Omachi—which yields sake with a round, rich mouthfeel and an earthy, spicy and herbal backbone—is one of our favorites, making Okayama a must-visit on our brewery itinerary. Karube, where Toshimori discovered Omachi, is in the heart of Okayama Prefecture's Akaiwa district, and this is where it grows best. We want to meet a few of the only brewers in Japan who are making truly local Omachi sake, and the highly skilled farmers who cultivate it here.

On this brilliantly sunny and hot July day, settled in the comfortable sitting room at Toshimori Brewery, we feel like wide-eyed children listening to the Omachi origin story unspooling directly from the mouth of its discoverer. Established in 1868, the first year of the Meiji era, Toshimori Brewery made formal what the family had been doing since pre-Edo-era feudal times: brewing sake as well as soy sauce and growing rice, peppermint and Chinese sugarcane for the local daimyo lord.

Toshimori, silver-haired, leonine (though still youthful, he tells us, because of all the junmai sake and sake lees he ingests), sifts through his memory, recalling that landmark moment in sake history in which he played a starring role. But first, he wants to give us a little background.

His entry into his family's business, he explains, coincided with the *jizake* local sake boom of the 1970s, which began after Japan had experienced its first burst of rapid economic expansion. Japanese who were familiar with the big national sake brands began to take an interest in the quirks and special merits of sake from overlooked rural areas. They were also looking for a drink that tasted better than the sweet, syrupy, highly adulterated *sanzo-shu* sake that had satisfied their parents and grandparents.

In Okayama, Toshimori was ahead of his peers in recognizing this trend. "How could we make our

Heirloom Sake Rice

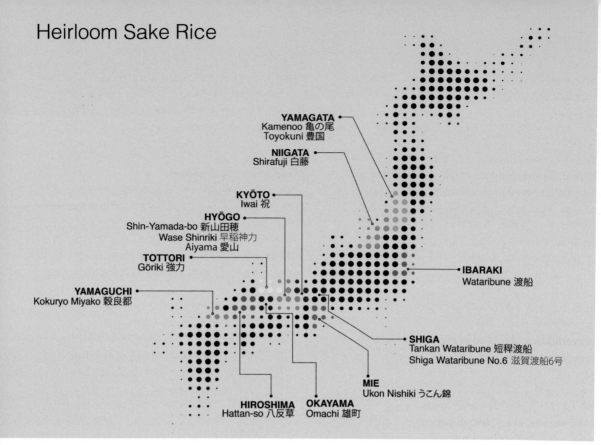

YAMAGATA
Kamenoo 亀の尾
Toyokuni 豊国

NIIGATA
Shirafuji 白藤

KYŌTO
Iwai 祝

HYŌGO
Shin-Yamada-bo 新山田穂
Wase Shinriki 早稲神力
Aiyama 愛山

TOTTORI
Gōriki 強力

YAMAGUCHI
Kokuryo Miyako 穀良都

IBARAKI
Wataribune 渡船

SHIGA
Tankan Wataribune 短稈渡船
Shiga Wataribune No.6 滋賀渡船6号

MIE
Ukon Nishiki うこん錦

HIROSHIMA
Hattan-so 八反草

OKAYAMA
Omachi 雄町

Above Heirloom rice varieties can be found in many different parts of Japan, each carrying its own origin story. **Right** A flowering Omachi plant in the heart of premium Omachi country, Akaiwa.

local sake stand out, how could we keep jizake alive here?" he wondered. "Tokyo had its own regional sake (although, it should be noted, not its own regional rice), as did Osaka. I wanted to have a local product, but in order to have your own jizake, the first thing you need is your own rice—local rice— your own local water and your own techniques. If you have those three things, you have jizake."

When he met farmer Kiyono in 1970 and spied those shockingly long stalks, Toshimori recognized it for the true "local" rice that would make the region stand out. The farmer had no stored seeds, so he gave Toshimori a few heads of unhulled rice grains. It was the beginning of Toshimori's ten-year, uphill mission to revive the rice. He could not have foreseen that in forty-five years his rediscovered grain would be second only to Yamada Nishiki in popularity.

Omachi is said to have first been discovered in 1859, when a man named Jinzo Kishimoto was returning to Okayama from a pilgrimage to the

shrine at Mt. Daisen in Tottori Prefecture. He spotted two unusual ears of rice, which he brought back home and began to cultivate. Eventually the rice variety spread through the region and became known as Omachi, after Kishimoto's village. Under the Meiji government's agricultural subsidy system, Omachi was adopted as the prefecture's premium agricultural product. In the early twentieth century Okayama's agricultural experiment station succeeded in isolating the pure strain of this ancient native grass. Today Omachi is considered the godparent of all Japanese sake rice, progenitor of more than 60 percent of current sake rice.

By the early 1930s, Omachi was thought to be so superior to other sake-rice varieties that brewers believed the only way to win the country's top sake prizes was with Omachi junmai ginjo. Remember that first prizewinning 1934 junmai daiginjo from Kodama Brewery that we mentioned on page 50? It was made with 100 percent Omachi rice. Omachi, in other words, was the Yamada Nishiki of its day. But all of that changed with the arrival of World War II. Drastic food shortages led to a drop in low-yield Omachi cultivation in favor of table rice, and, in the chaos of that period, it nearly disappeared. By the time Toshimori rediscovered it, it had become known as a "phantom sake rice."

Toshimori became a one-man proselytizer for Omachi, seeing it as his prefecture's chance to challenge the supremacy of Yamada Nishiki and the country's regional sake powerhouses. "I looked at my own feet, here, on this land, and realized that like wine in France, sake made from Omachi could reflect this place," Toshimori says. "At one time, every sake in Japan was jizake. But we became disconnected from that." His son and future fifth-generation president Hiromitsu Toshimori's goal for the brewery is for it to be the equivalent of "a first-class chateau in the wine world, where rice is grown, harvested and brewed in-house."

After receiving that handful of unhusked rice in 1970, Toshimori started by working with the rice farmers under contract with his family brewery. First they were reluctant to switch from more lucrative Yamada Nishiki to a rice that was more difficult to grow and lower in yield. "I had to offer inducements," says Toshimori. He put a premium on Omachi that strained the company's finances.

Why did he pour his energies into what must have seemed a quixotic pursuit at the time? "Well, it was an *otoko no roman*," he answers simply, using the Japanese phrase for a man's epic adventure, a heroic undertaking tinged with romance. Toshimori, like other brewers passionate about conveying the primal allure that rice and sake hold for Japanese, are romantics and storytellers. To borrow the phrase favored by another fan of jizake—Banjo Brewery's Kuno Kuheiji—they want to capture lightning, or in their case "the drama of the field," in their bottles. So Toshimori began growing his own Omachi rice, which he soon supplemented with rice grown by contract farmers.

Gradually the farmers came to see the value of having a noted local rice. They began to understand that Toshimori wanted to do the opposite of what the big makers were doing: brew with rice grown without pesticides and processed by hand. He wanted to prioritize quality over quantity, and rescue Okayama sake from what he calls the postwar "fall of sake" into mass-market monotony. Over a decade, the revived Akaiwa Omachi began to make its mark. In 1983 the first Omachi sake of the modern age (brewed by Toshimori Brewery *toji* Toyokazu Tamura) took gold at the National New Sake Appraisal, Japan's most prestigious contest, alerting the sake world that a new rice had arrived on the scene.

Another way Toshimori has tried to return to ancient jizake customs is to brew sake in massive earthenware jars known as *ogame*, which date back five-hundred years. "It's sake that gives you a taste of the earth," he says. Since the late 1980s, the brewery has worked with local master craftsman Togaku Mori, who uses a 300-foot (90 m) long *noborikama*, or multi-chambered "step-climbing kiln." The kiln fires glowing ceramic pots over four-and-a-half feet tall and four feet in diameter (just over a meter tall and wide) in the ancient Bizen style of pottery. Bizen is the old name of the province that once included present-day Okayama City and Akaiwa, a geographic designation that dates back to the eighth century; the association between Omachi sake and Bizenware is strong in this southeastern portion of Okayama Prefecture.

aforementioned Banjo Brewery in Nagoya and Mitobe Brewery in Yamagata, would like to grow their own Omachi, Toshimori asserts that that's not possible yet, since Omachi grows best in the sunny, clear climate of Okayama. The fact that most Omachi sake is today brewed outside of Okayama is a testament to the deep allure of this rice; it's strong enough for far-flung brewers to forfeit any claims that their Omachi sake is *jizake*, or expresses the local geography. Instead, they tout its provenance, proud to share their own expressions of Akaiwa Omachi.

Yamagata Returns to Its Own Heirloom Sake Rice

Less than a decade after Toshimori's eureka moment in farmer Kiyono's Akaiwa barn, two sake brewers in the Tohoku region, Norimichi Kusumi and Kazuyoshi Sato, began wondering about a vanished heirloom rice that originated in their very own prefecture's rice basket, the Shonai Plain. This grain had been discovered in 1893 by a brilliant self-taught farmer named Kameji Abe. The year of Abe's discovery had been a cold one, and rice crops had suffered extensively. On a trip to visit Kuma-gawa Shrine (another heirloom rice discovered during a shrine visit—coincidence?), among a paddy filled with the table rice Sobee Wase, he spotted three golden ears of rice. They had somehow, miraculously, survived the widespread crop damage.

Abe asked the owner of the field for the ears, took them home and began his growing experiment. For two years he had no luck; the stalks were too tall and toppled over. In the third season he tried growing them in a paddy near the low-temperature

Today, top Akaiwa Omachi ranks among the most expensive sake rices in Japan. Okayama Prefecture now produces 94 percent of the 2,700 tons of Omachi grown annually, yet much to Toshimori's chagrin, the prefecture only brews a fraction of that amount—85 percent goes to breweries outside the prefecture willing to pay top yen for it. As much as some of them, like the

mouth of his water source. Only one root stalk survived during this trial. It was with this one hardy plant that he coaxed out what was to become Kame no O ("Tail of the Turtle"), a play on his first name, which includes the kanji character for "turtle."

By 1920, Kame no O was considered a versatile and superior rice; it made excellent table rice, sake rice and sushi rice. Close to 500,000 acres (200,000 hectares) of the grain rippled across the fields of Tohoku and Hokuriku (the northwestern region of Japan's main island Honshu). It was also grown on the Korean peninsula and in Taiwan. The ideal rice for its time, Kame no O did not, however, survive the advent of mechanized rice production. Its strong resistance to cold was offset by susceptibility to insect pests, it did not tolerate chemical fertilizers well, and its low yields were no match for higher-producing hybrids. Gradually, it was outstripped by its industrially better-suited descendants, including Gohyakumangoku, Sasa Nishiki and Koshi Hikari. By the 1970s Kame no O was all but forgotten.

Partially under the influence of the jizake boom of the 1970s, but also because the toji who had mastered the nuances of brewing with Yamada Nishiki were looking for new taste profiles and new challenges, the two brewers, Kusumi and Sato of Koikawa Brewery in Yamagata and Kusumi from Kusumi Brewery in Niigata, separately began plotting the return of Kame no O. (The two brewers have historically disagreed over whose Kame no O is the authentic heirloom but that has not diminished the revival's appeal.) Kusumi was able to get 1,500 seeds of the heirloom grain from his prefecture's agricultural experiment station, debuting his Kame no O ginjo sake in 1983. The revival captured the public's imagination as well. A popular manga comic book titled *Natsuko no sake* (Natsuko's Sake), based on the story of Kame no O, became even more of a sensation when it was turned into a nationally televised drama. Today there are roughly thirty-three breweries across Japan producing Kame no O sake.

Kameji Abe, the farmer who possessed only a temple elementary school education, was widely

Stalks of heirloom Kame no O rice, a variety used since the 1980s at Koikawa Brewery. The brewery is located on Yamagata Prefecture's Shonan Plain, long the site of rice cultivation.

admired for other farming innovations as well, including his experiments with dry-paddy horse tilling. In 1927 he was awarded with a prestigious imperial Medal of Honor. Another of his passions was writing haiku poetry under his literary pen name Kasui. This poem marries his two loves, farming and haiku writing, and illuminates the humble patience and passion of a true rice farmer:

思うまま／道はかどらぬ／稲見かな
omou mama/ michi hakadoranu/ inami kana

Progress on this path
is slower than expected
—observing rice plants

One more poetic rice-farming digression: Abe refers to his rice plant observations along the roadside as *inami* (稲見), literally "looking at rice plants." The same characters appear in the world *inamiboshi* (稲見星), the Japanese term for the Ox house of the Chinese constellation system. Literally

Miho Imada of Imada Brewery, pictured with one of the brewery's *jikagumi* (direct from the press) sakes.

translated, though, it means "the star that appears around the time rice shoots start to be seen." In ancient Japan, even the heavens revolved around the central act of growing rice.

Miho Imada and the Revival of Hattanso Rice

Twenty years after Tohoku brewers began eyeing a revival of Kame no O, another rice comeback began in Hiroshima to the southwest. Miho Imada—third-generation heir of her family's Imada Brewery—had just taken over as toji in 2000, after a grueling eight-year apprenticeship under previous toji Yasuhiro Kiyotaka. She, too, had heard stories about an ancient local sake-rice grain called Hattanso (八反草, meaning "twilled fabric grass"), a forebear to Hattan Nishiki, the hybrid that has defined Hiroshima sake since its introduction in 1983. But as far as she knew, there were no Hattanso seeds left.

In late 2001 the news broke that the Hiroshima Gene Bank, which collects and preserves the prefecture's genetic resources, in fact did have some seeds, and had begun trials on Hattanso. Just as

Toshimori had been, Imada was eager to try brewing a good sake with truly local rice. The institute had a surplus of unhulled Hattanso seeds that year, and divided it among interested Hiroshima growers. Imada convinced three contract farmers to grow the handful of seeds she received. By the spring of 2004, with the cooperation of the farmer's association in the ancient northern Hiroshima rice-growing region of Takamiya, she launched larger-scale cultivation of the rice.

For the first few years it was tough going. Though Takamiya farmers are highly skilled and their fields are favored with the expansive diurnal temperature swings and pristine mountain water needed to produce top-quality rice, Hattanso poses unique challenges. Water and fertilizer management is tricky, and because of Hattanso's height, there is greater risk of crop damage when typhoons sweep through their paddies. Like Kame no O, Hattanso is not even considered a sake rice, but a table rice for eating. Was it really worth all the trouble? Like Toshimori before her, Imada had to make an offer worth the farmers' while. "I buy it at the same price as Yamada Nishiki, which is the most expensive sake rice in Hiroshima Prefecture," she says.

By 2006 the farmers' yield was large enough for Imada to begin brewing with Hattanso. Here, too, the learning curve was a steep one, complicated by the fact that it took several more years for her contract farmers to learn how to turn out a uniformly good crop every year. High crop variability made it difficult to brew with the rice. What level of polishing would the rice tolerate? What was the breakage rate of its starchy heart, or *shinpaku*? How fast would it absorb water when soaking? How fast would it "melt" in the starter and main mash? All of these are variables that can change from year to year, even when dealing with the best and most familiar of sake rices. With a newly revived, not yet stabilized strain, the challenges seemed Sisyphean.

Hattanso's beginnings are slightly murkier than

Omachi's or Kame no O's. In the second half of the nineteenth century, private breeders began improving sake rice, says Imada. Hattanso's origin in 1875 is credited to a certain Ryusuke Otawa. Imada is not sure, but believes that Otawa discovered an heirloom grain and then stabilized it, rather than producing it from a cross-breeding experiment. In any case, it is the oldest of the Hattan family of Hiroshima rices. As rice farming became increasingly mechanized and productivity was prioritized, old strains that were challenging to grow were gradually abandoned for shorter, higher-yielding hybrids better suited to the machine age.

The Hattanso sake Imada has perfected over the past fifteen years is mellow, balanced and gentle, compared to Yamada Nishiki's more muscular and showy power. It has a softness and lovely finish well suited to Hiroshima's mild climate and its fish- and shellfish-based cuisine. Today about 30 percent of Imada's sake is brewed with Hattanso, and she still remains the only brewer in Hiroshima and the country brewing with it, probably, she says, because newer varieties have been designed for ease of brewing, and are therefore more appealing.

Like Toshimori, Imada was captivated by the romance of the story, and the purity and pre-industrial integrity of all heirloom plants. Hattanso had not been miniaturized or bred to be a commodity crop that sacrificed flavor for ease of processing and transport. As she wrote on her website, for her Hattanso represents the "roots" of all newer Hiroshima varieties, the soil of her home prefecture, and the "tender, big-heartedness" they have nurtured in her people.

Heirloom Rice Flight

Sake name (Japan): Kumamoto Shinriki
Sake name (US): Sacred Power
Sake type: Junmai ginjo
Brewery: Chiyonosono, Kumamoto Prefecture
The brewery behind the revival of the Kumamoto strain of Shinriki, a rice widely used in the late 1800s before falling into near extinction.

Sake name:
Chiyomusubi Goriki 50
Sake type: Junmai ginjo
Brewery: Chiyomusubi, Tottori Prefecture
Revived in the late 80s in Tottori, Goriki rice has defined Tottori sake. As the name "Goriki" (strong power) suggests, you'll find a muscular profile rich with good acidity and savory umami notes.

Sake name: Koikawa
Sake type: Junmai daiginjo
Brewery: Koikwawa, Yamagata Prefecture
One of the breweries behind the revival of Kame no O, the heirloom rice here has been polished to 40 percent yet still makes an impact with its savory charms

Chapter Seven

Crazy for Omachi

Our plan was to wrap up our July trip at the Omachi Summit, a gathering of fanatic sake lovers who identify as *Omachisuto* after the heirloom grain they adore. Where Yamada Nishiki might be the *yokozuna*, or sumo grand champion of sake rice, Omachi is the Obi-Wan Kenobi, with mystical powers rooted in the electric green rice paddies of Okayama Prefecture. Our visits to Toshimori Brewery and a second Omachi-centered brewery, Muromachi, showed us just why it is so famously difficult to grow, and nearly equally as tricky to brew. Omachi offers the antithesis of the light, fruity and floral Yamada Nishiki sakes that had set the standard for premium brews for the past forty years, instead providing a rich, deep, sweet and savory hit of umami and a long, satisfying finish. If you're looking for a sake to pair with meat, dairy or fried foods, Omachi is never the wrong choice. And if ever there was a rice that fits into the revived fashion for sake food-friendliness, this is it.

So on the morning of a sweltering late-July day in Tokyo we took the two-and-a-half hour shinkansen bullet train trip from Kanazawa to Tokyo. Hungry, we stop at a branch of the Hawaiian Host chain, a kind of Japanese-Hawaiian Denny's where the only kale salad we see in Japan appears on the menu. Why is it, we wonder, that in Japan, where one can eat so well and, on the whole, so nutritiously, a North American can feel starved of fresh vegetables? To quell our craving, we both start with the salad, a petite plate of baby kale and a few pine-nuts, about a quarter the size of the jumbo salads North Americans regularly consume.

At the summit's trade-only tasting at the Hotel Grand Palace in Chiyoda Ward, it is all business. The tasters are impressive in their speed and focus. A couple of squirts from a dropper into their tasting glass, a sniff, taste and spit, and then it's on to the next, systematically working their way through the 215 entries from thirty-four different prefectures. British-born Philip Harper, the most famous non-Japanese brewer in the country, who plies his trade at Kyoto's Kinoshita Brewery, is there. Impressively, he's taking notes in Japanese. On one side of the room, a stout, dandyish fellow in a blue-and-white pinstripe summer suit and sunflower yellow shirt, wearing heavy, dark horn-rimmed glasses and shiny white shoes, makes his way through the lineup. On the other, a tall, thin man in a white designer T-shirt that looks like it was woven and folded by fairies practiced in the art of origami floats down each row

Above Clay soil from an Akaiwa Omachi field. The importance of the sticky soil lies in the way it enhances the fertilizer that farmer Hajime Sakon applies.
Right An Akaiwa Omachi rice paddy in the late summer.

of tables bearing sake-tasting samples—your typical Tokyo fashion parade.

Then there's the more down-to-earth Omachisuto fanatic Yukihide Morikami, an Okayama-born engineer who lives in Tokyo. Toting a backpack, he shows us around the room to some of his favorites: Toraya Honten's Shichisui junmai daiginjo, Kumaya Shuzo's junmai ginjo and the widely admired Isojiman Brewery's junmai daiginjo and tokubetsu junmai. Not surprisingly, the two bottles of Isojiman have been drained by the time we get there. This is the brand that convinced owner-*toji* Yusuke Sato of Aramasa Brewery in Akita to give up journalism, join the family business and remake it into a highly coveted brand: it's convincing stuff.

"A lot of these Omachi sakes are not well-known," Morikami tells me, "because they're small production, they're consumed in Okayama and they never make it out of the prefecture to Tokyo." As the vast majority of Omachi sake produced comes from outside Okayama where the rice is grown, one of the pleasures of the summit is getting to taste

Okayama Omachi *jizake* from just such small, lesser-known producers.

In the hallway outside the tasting room, Harper, a curly haired, bearded man who looks like he could be a member of a touring 1980s classic rock band, gives us his thoughts on Omachi. They are many and also considered—honed over decades of brewing. "It's all about the umami, he says, "There's a story about it being from the gods. That's nice, but if it didn't taste good it wouldn't matter." He motions reverentially to a group of kibitzing, suntanned men standing a short distance away—the farmers from Akaiwa in Okayama who supply him with high-quality Omachi—and says, "We're lucky to get our rice from those guys." He's been in the business long enough to not have to go through the JA, or Japan Agricultural Cooperative, the powerful network of nearly seven-hundred regional co-ops that operate throughout the country. But asked how he gets his Omachi, he demurs, saying, "There's the brewer's union route, but we're lucky to have more direct connections."

Harper has described Yamada Nishiki as being Windows and Omachi as the charismatic contender Macintosh. Sake expert Haruo Matsuzaki uses the analogy of baseball. "Some people love Omachi because Yamada Nishiki has become too popular," he says, "It's like in baseball most people love the [Yomiuri] Giants, but I love the [Hanshin] Tigers."

Where Apple conquered the world in large part thanks to the designers and engineers who came up with its streamlined design and intuitive user interface, premium Omachi sake is revered by Omachisuto as being the product of ace farmers and brewers. Its *shinpaku*, or starchy heart is so soft that the rice has to be polished much more slowly and carefully than Yamada Nishiki, and brewed much more precisely since the heart melts faster during fermentation. And while Yamada Nishiki has

Large, golden ears of Omachi rice ready for harvest. Known for producing sakes that are rich, savory and sometimes with a bit of spice, it is also a challenging rice to grow and brew with because of its tall height and delicate *shinpaku*, or heart.

President Mitsuru Hanfusa and his son Masataka of Muromachi Brewery in Okayama Prefecture, pictured above one of the brewery's *moromi* tanks.

been grown for years outside of its native Hyogo Prefecture, Harper notes, "Omachi presents another level of difficulty for farmers. You don't find Omachi away from Okayama . . . you have to be that much more serious about it as a farmer to undertake all that extra work and heartbreak."

While there is a well-defined hierarchy of Yamada Nishiki growing in areas in Hyogo, from *Toku-A* on down, Omachi rice is harder to assess on the same scale because it is so hard to grow. Yet no one disputes where the best growing area is in Okayama: Akaiwa, the less-than-a-square-mile-large (2.5 km²) area that is home to Harper's farmers. He's brewed with Omachi from a number of different paddies, but admits, "There is a real sense of power about the rice from that region." Both Toshimori Brewery and Muromachi Brewery, which we include in this chapter, are located in Akaiwa.

At a panel discussion after the tasting, experts agreed that the level of brewing displayed at the summit has risen continuously in recent years. As competition judges, they've been tasked with evaluating the entries based on three main criteria, umami, *fukurami* (depth, or roundness) and *namerakasa* (smoothness, softness). This year's entrants mirror trends that are taking off in the rest of the sake world: showy, gorgeous sake yeasts; various levels of effervescence; soft, flavorful prettiness. On the other end, the judges find

impressive richness and balance, especially in the *kimoto* and aged kimoto sakes. The ability to age well is one of Omachi's unique attributes. Sake journalist Atsuko Sando notes that in addition to Omachi's characteristic umami and balance of sweetness and acidity, the best entries also exhibit refreshing, sometimes even slightly wild, or natural qualities—again reflecting both different facets of Omachi and evolving preferences we've seen rippling throughout the world of craft sake.

Muromachi Brewer and Its Master Farmer

Just a week earlier, we'd seen for ourselves the variegated, vivid shades of green that seemed painted onto the lush, hot, southern Okayama valley where Akaiwa Grand Cru Omachi is grown.

Heading east from Okayama City, we enter a long, verdant valley. First, you notice the neon green of the young rice plants, and the tiny clover-like weeds that dot the paddies like a scattering of confetti, then the more muted green of the fringe of trees above them, and finally the hazy dark green of the distant mountains. The valley is almost entirely surrounded by the foothills that protect it from inclement weather, one reason it produces such high-quality Omachi.

Our day starts with a visit to Muromachi Brewery, where president Mitsuru Hanafusa and his son Masataka, president and senior managing director, are on hand to greet us. The brewery, founded in 1688, is the oldest in Okayama. All of its *tokutei meishoshu* (ginjo and junmai sakes) are made exclusively with Omachi rice. In the early eighteenth century, the family owned large tracts of lands and acted as a money lender to the local daimyo, Lord Ikeda, brewing sake with the excess rice that they received in return. The elder Hanafusa shows us a large drawing from the early 1920s of the sprawling facility, which included two separate breweries dotted with four chimneys.

During our tour of the current fifty-year-old brewery, we stop before a tank with a single stalk of Omachi rice hanging from its top, an astonishing and record-setting roughly six feet (2 m) in length. We pass a towering rice-milling machine and enter another room, where a heady and gorgeous peach scent wafts up. Workers are washing and peeling the famous Shimizu Hakuto peaches that the Hanafusas grow on their property, which will be transmuted into the brewery's peach-flavored sake.

Entering the family's elegant, tatami-matted home built in the early 1900s, we spot a gilt-framed early-Showa-era painting bearing landscape motifs, Buddhist imagery and bold kanji strokes that read "Muromachi." It's the logo of the brewery's private brand, which has been sold at Mitsukoshi's Nihonbashi department store since 1925. Our whirlwind sampling of the brewery's sake includes its prize-winning 40 percent polish Muromachi Jidai junmai daiginjo, several Omachi junmai sakes and the wine-like, export-only Sakon sake, named for the farmer that grew the rice. Not many farmers get a sake named after them, but eighty-five-year-old Hajime Sakon is legendary in these parts.

After a rendezvous at the local JA office, the Hanafusas drive us, along with Sakon, to see three of his rice paddies near Seto City. Sakon, who still works the fields with the help of his son, is such a wisp of a man—his trousers are cinched high at his waist to keep them from dropping, and his JA baseball cap is several sizes too big for his head—

Left to right Esteemed Omachi farmer, Hajime Sakon; Japan Agricultural Cooperative farm-management agent Takaomi Nukata; President Mitsuru Hanafusa of Muromachi Brewery.

Omachi farmers in Akaiwa, Okayama, show off their rice, which is among the most costly of all Japanese sake rice varieties.

that it's hard to believe he's the most revered of the thirty-four Omachi eco-farmers in Seto, a man whose reputation spans the prefecture and beyond. A sixth-generation farmer, Sakon inaugurated the farming of Omachi in 1989 with a handful of seeds that a local farmer had saved—a story similar to that of Tadayoshi Toshimori's in nearby Karube. He has farmed it ever since. He's also truly a man of this land; he grew up in Seto and his home is just steps from the fields in which we are standing.

This is a good place to test the theory that nutrient-dense, rich clay is one reason for Akaiwa's superior Omachi and find out if it is the same clay used to fire the local Bizen pottery.

With us is Takaomi Nukata, a wiry, sneaker-clad man with salt-and-pepper hair and a weather-lined face, a farm-management agent with the local branch of the JA farmers' cooperative. It's close to 90°F (32°C) and the humidity is oppressive. Nukata and Sakon are slightly apologetic about the current condition of Sakon's rice paddies; they are apparently on the weedy side now, though if they hadn't pointed it out, we would not have thought it an eyesore. The senior Hanafusa explains what makes this location ideal for growing Omachi, pointing to the low mountains both to the north and to the south, which protect the fields from wind and

typhoons. They also create the fog, mist and temperature variability that are crucial for producing high-quality rice, the same factors that benefit grape vines in wine regions.

The strong, nearly ever-present sun is also a key factor, and one that makes this an ideal region to grow both Okayama's fragrant *hakuto* (white peaches) and Muscat grapes. Plentiful water from the mountains is captured in a network of lakes, some of them man-made; water from them runs down to the fields along narrow watercourses by the side of the road. Locals believe the *Momotaro* (Peach Boy) fairy tale originated in this region: the Ogre Island of the fairy tale *Onigashima*, where Momotaro travels to battle demons, Masataka tells us, is based on a real Okayama island called Megijima. And the prince upon whom Momotaro is based is enshrined in two different Okayama shrines.

The field we are gazing at was planted only a month before, so the two-and-a-half-foot (80 cm) high shoots are at their most *iroaza*, or vivid, Masataka points out. "These three fields are Sakon-san's. They're planted well, aren't they?" he asks appreciatively. What makes a superior farmer is not entirely visible to the untrained eye surveying his fields. Why do people nod admiringly at the mention of Sakon, and murmur, *ude ga ii* (literally, "his arm is good," meaning "highly skilled")? To ask Sakon directly is not, we learn, the way to go, since he'll credit the local climate and topography.

Farmer Sakon kneels over boxes of his home-grown peaches, selecting the best to give to us.

Prompted by Michael, Nukata thrusts a hand into the water and lifts up a fistful of sticky, greenish-gray sludge, clay-like in appearance. Instead of focusing on the nutrient content of the soil, though, Nukata explains that its strength is the way it enhances the organic fertilizer that Sakon applies, its density allowing the nutrients to feed the rice plants over a long period of time. Mitsuru Hanafusa tells us that although we are within the ancient region of Bizen, the clay used for Bizenware is not the same as that of Sakon's soil.

Further confounding our attempts to pin down a single, ideal, Omachi-nurturing soil, is the fact that Toshimori Brewery, just a fifteen-minute drive away, draws from a completely different soil type. Tadayoshi Toshimori, we recall, told us that the secret to his soil is that it is sandy, pebbly and granite based. The excellent drainage it allows, and of course the southern Okayama climate, he added, are what makes the rice from Karube's Akasaka region (a micro-region inside the larger grand-cru Akaiwa area) so good. Two neighboring rice growing areas, two different soil types and two fine sake products. Quality sake, we are reminded, is not something that can be reduced to variables on a spreadsheet, but like any artisanal beverage, it is the complex admixture of soil, sun, rain and the intuitive crafts of both farmer and brewer. The brewers themselves can tell the differences in taste, they assure us, but the price set by the JA for the Omachi of the two neighboring areas are the same.

One tidbit Nukata offers is the way that Sakon elects to plant his Omachi. While most farmers begin with plantings of potted bunches of three or four small seedlings that are de-potted and trans-ferred by machine into the soil, Sakon starts with root stalks of only two or three much larger and more delicate unpotted seedlings. Taller and spindlier than Yamada Nishiki, shoots need to each be given more space, bringing down the yield of one field of Omachi to about 70 percent of that of Yamada Nishiki. In a month, the cluster will have grown to yield about twenty to thirty shoots. Although also done by machine, this method requires a high degree of patience and skill, yet pays off in the end in the quality and flavor of the grain.

The paddies have not yet been drained, some-thing that will occur in the second half of July, and are several months from the majestic golden colors of mid-October harvest time. Massive white herons swoop down now and then to feast on the bugs, tadpoles and finger-sized frogs that help enrich the soil. The tinkling, nostalgic sound of a vending truck recording sounds plays in the distance.

At first, we thought the emphatic assertion that Omachi should be grown in an agroecological, if not organic, manner was down to principle—un-usual for Japan, where organics are less prevalent than in North America. But the truth is less about ideals and more about practicality: Omachi grows best under conditions closest to organic. Chemical amendments make it grow too rapidly, toppling the ungainly stalks. That rapid growth can result in off-center shinpaku, or hearts, which will crack more easily during polishing.

Sakon's organic fertilizer is composed mostly of rice straw, cattle manure compost, rice bran and oyster shells. Again, we ask: what makes Sakon a master farmer? One reason he offers up to us in his soft, whisper of a voice is his intuitive application of this fertilizer: a little more when the seedlings are young and growing rapidly, much less when the grains are developing, "so that they can become more refined in taste," he explains.

Our short time with him reveals little glimmers of insight into his technique, but how can you in one visit comprehend the wisdom gained over a lifetime of daily toil, close observation of nature unfolding in three small fields and ceaseless trial and error?

The rushing of water through the miniature canals along the fields has served as a constant, soothing backdrop to our conversation. Next, we make a brief stop at its source, a man-made lake that feeds Sakon's fields. The lake grasses that dot its surface help purify the water, Hanafusa explains. By now, we're nearly at Sakon's house, where we will drop him off on our way back to the brewery. But before we leave he insists on gathering a box of his giant, luxuriantly fragrant and downy peaches for us to take with us.

Squatting over boxes of fruit on the floor of his garage, he carefully makes his selections and places them in a cardboard box. It is a touching sight, the farmer, bent over the literal fruits of his labor, putting together a gift for strangers from far away. As we pull away in the Hanafusas' car, we look back to see Sakon waving, and notice he has taken a seat on a small brick. He grows smaller and smaller, receding into the green distance.

Omachi Flight

Sake name: Sakehitosuji
Sake type: Junmai ginjo
Brewery: Toshimori, Okayama Prefecture
From the brewery behind Omachi's revival.

Sake name: Miyoshikiku
Sake type: Junmai ginjo origarami nama
Brewery: Miyoshikiku, Tokushima Prefecture
A sake that harmonizes acid, alcohol, umami and sweetness. Myoshikiku's sake has the reputation of walking the sweet line, but with Omachi as the prime ingredient, that sweetness is transformed into added dimensions of taste.

Sake name: Sakura Muromachi "Sakon"
Sake type: Junmai ginjo
Brewery: Muromachi, Okayama Prefecture
You may not be able to find master farmer Hajime Sakon's peaches, but this sake brewed with Akaiwa Omachi rice from his own fields is well worth seeking out.

Water: Hard or Soft?

It's a chilly, gray January day in Suwa, located in the middle of mountainous Nagano Prefecture. Though abundant sunshine has made the town a hot spot for solar energy investment, we won't see many rays during our two-day visit to this ancient place. Five thousand years ago the area was home to a thriving, prehistoric Jomon period (14,000–1,000 BC) culture; today it's become a haven for urban refugees attracted by the two-and-a-half hour train ride from Tokyo, third-wave coffee, crisp mountain air, plus good hiking and dining scenes. Alighting at Kami-Suwa Station and seeing a charming hot-spring foot bath right on the train platform itself instantly resets the body from stressed-out city mode to blissed-out mountain mode.

Keith Norum, International Sales Director of Miyasaka Brewery, the maker of the Masumi brand of sake, has brought us to the ideal vantage point to view the five-square-mile (13 km²) Lake Suwa. Since time immemorial, locals have witnessed the freezing over of the lake. When the ice warms slightly, you can hear the rumbling sounds of sheets cracking, canting upward and over each other like nature's lesson in plate tectonics. The sound has been likened to that of distant drums or a caged lion, and the result is a raised, jagged-toothed path of ice across the lake.

Known as *omiwatari*, or the "gods' crossing," locals have interpreted these tracks as being left by Takeminakata, the god of Upper Suwa Taisha Shrine, as he traversed the frozen lake to visit his wife Yasakatome, goddess of Lower Suwa Taisha Shrine. It was also a sign that the lake was safe for mortals to cross, and the event was marked by a Shinto purification process. At one local shrine, Shinto priests have kept records of the omiwatari for six hundred years—more than fifteen generations. Climate scientists have mined this treasure trove of data to help show that climate change is driving long-term change in seasonal ice formation around the world.

Some years, the ice has been rock solid enough to allow army tanks to make the crossing. Today, the lake looks decidedly un-frozen; Norum tells us that during the thirty years he's lived in Suwa, omiwatari appear less and less frequently, the last one in 2018.

On this gray day, we're standing at Tateishi Park on the eastern shore of Lake Suwa to get the lay of the land, and to try to understand the complex web of geographic and geologic forces that give Masumi sake its mineralogical backbone. To our left, Norum points out the Southern Alps of Japan, and to the southwest, the main

Left The *omiwatari* (gods' crossing) on Lake Suwa. **Right** Medium-hard water from the nearby Ou Mountains is boiled to sterilize sake-making tools at Mitobe Brewery (see page 99).

Climate Change and Sake

Climate change has been a persistent, thrumming threat in the background of each of our brewery visits, a lurking danger that is exacting a gradual toll on Japan as it is around the world. Tomonobu Mitobe, owner-*toji* at Mitobe Brewery in Yamagata Prefecture, advises visitors not to travel to his corner of Japan in the summer any more. For the past five years or so, temperatures have been unbearably hot, and lashing rains more characteristic of Southeast Asia's rainy season have become frequent. Yamagata and the whole country have become much more humid overall, he adds.

In 2020, one brewery, Michikazu, announced its plan to relocate from Gifu Prefecture to far northern Hokkaido in part to escape the worsening effects of climate change. In Okayama Prefecture, home to the best Omachi rice, extreme heat in 2019 led to a very poor crop. Many farmers there, in anticipation of a typhoon, will drain the water from their rice field to prevent overflow. But that summer the typhoon never arrived, and the period of dryness before the fields were re-flooded stressed the plants, explains Mitobe, who buys Akaiwa Omachi for one of his sakes.

Okayama farmers' co-op agent Takaomi Nukata says climate change is something that farmers there worry about. But he notes, "Weather is something you can't really take countermeasures against. So instead, we're working on the technology of growing," meaning selectively breeding for climate hardiness.

Mitobe agrees. Where up until now, the focus on rice breeding was to foster cold-resistant rice, he says breeding heat-resistant rice is going to become equally important as temperatures continue to rise.

Mitobe has also been farming his own rice under a separate company, Mitobe Inazo, which he founded in 2018. To counter extreme heat, he says plants must be given the coldest water possible, and harvest is adjusted according to seasonal temperatures and growth rates. As the winter brewing season becomes warmer due to climate change, adequate cooling equipment and ice supplies help protect against damage to the fermenting starter and main mash.

In Hokkaido, Japan's northernmost prefecture Otokoyama Brewery master brewer Hidefumi Kitayama sees climate change as "a blessing" because a warming climate means a wider variety of sake rice can be cultivated. Yet he notes that the rice he's been getting from the main island Honshu has been too hard, a result of hotter temperatures. This can result in weak-flavored sake, he notes, adding, "Honshu is in trouble."

building of Suwa Grand Shrine. To the north is Akimiya Shrine, behind which the old Koshu Kaido road from Tokyo ends and the Nakasendo road begins. These seventeenth-century highways were part of a five-road network over which daimyo lords and their ostentatious retinues traveled back and forth from Edo to their home castles in a carefully choreographed ritual. Known as *sankin kotai*, or "alternate resident duty," the system was a canny way for the Tokugawa shogunate to keep tabs on its retainers (when they were not in Edo their family had to be, and vice versa) and deplete their coffers to prevent them from becoming too powerful.

Behind us, to the northeast, is the horseshoe-shaped Kirigamine Highland, an extension of the Yatsugatake range and a geologic crossroads, where, over eons, two smaller islands fused to form this part of Japan's main Honshu island. The three fault lines that run beneath the town are testament to those movements. Temblors are not uncommon, but locals like to think the land is constantly blowing off steam, perhaps forestalling the big one. All of this, plus remnants of the Jomon culture and Suwa's historical importance as one of the country's oldest Shinto religious centers, adds Norum, lends "a weird, mystical element" to Suwa.

Above Water is a crucial factor in shaping a sake's quality. **Below** The Miyasaka family, left to right, matriarch Kumi, brewery president Naotaka Miyasaka, and son Katsuhiko.

"Because the geology here is so complex, you can get pretty interesting differences in the mineralogy of water over very short distances, just from the crinkling of the land," he says. Miyasaka operates two breweries, Suwa and Fujimi, only fifteen miles (24 km) apart from each other, yet each draws water from a different source. The original Suwa brewery, which the family has run since 1662, draws soft water from the Kirigamine Highland to make a sake that's gentle, round and with a hint of sweetness. Its bigger, higher-elevation Fujimi counterpart was designed to handle increased demand and to take advantage of the pure mountain environment, abundant water and long, cold winters—all ideal for high-quality sake brewing. It went into operation in 1982, drawing harder water from the Southern Alps' Nyukasa Mountain and yielding a drier, more angular sake.

An Abundance of Micro-Terroirs

Other examples of water variability, even among sites in close proximity to each other,

abound. This, we learned, was the case between Akitsu and Saijo in Hiroshima, and it is so in the small town of Tendo, Yamagata Prefecture. There, two well-known breweries, Dewazakura, headed by the Nakano family, and Mitobe, are only a fifteen-minute walk away from each other. Yet Dewazakura's local spring water has a soft profile, while Mitobe draws a much harder water from the temple Risshakuji in the nearby Ou Mountains (which the poet Basho immortalized in haiku).

In part because he had high-quality water flowing underneath his property, Yasaku Mitobe dug a well there in 1898 and began brewing sake. Fifth-generation president Tomonobu Mitobe attributes this stark difference in water type from the surrounding area to the mysteries of the temple's micro-terroir, noting that without a detailed geological analysis, it's hard to understand the underlying cause of the difference. His water shapes sakes with a crisp, sharp finish, a "cut" quality that inspired the name "Masamune" after the great priest and swordsmith Goro Masamune (for more, see page 109). Dewazakura's manager of export development Naoki Kamoto says he, too, is not privy to the geological features that shape the brewery's water. It is simply, he says, "a gift given by the sake-brewing god."

During the early nineteenth century, there were three Nakano (of Dewazakura fame) family branches that operated sake breweries in Tendo. The main branch of the family owned extensive rice fields, but only the first-born son would inherit these. Other family members branched out into

miso and soy sauce making. Staff from each brewery formed long lines at the local well, awaiting their turn to haul water back by cart to their respective breweries in 36-liter (10-gallon) wooden barrels. The benefit of digging a well right on one's property, as Yasaku Mitobe did, is the quick commute to the brewery where the washing and steaming and brewing process can begin.

Pristine as they are, brewery water sources are susceptible to activities on the land that surrounds them. Over thirty years ago, as the nitrogen content in fertilizer used in nearby fruit orchards increased, Mitobe Brewery dug a deeper well in order to access an even purer source of water. Today, most sake water in Japan goes through some sort of filtration process.

One Brewery, Four Different Brewing Waters

A good illustration of how different waters can shape different experiences, like the fabric used in a bespoke suit, can be found at Kodama Brewery in Akita Prefecture, the makers of the Taiheizan and Tenko lines of sake. Alcohol comprises 16 percent of his Tenko sake, says president Shin'ichiro Kodama, which means that the remaining 84 percent is water. "You can imagine," he notes, "how different types of water can influence the freshness, taste and texture of sake."

He uses four different types of water, two of which—Shirasuno well water and the high-quality filtered public water supply of the neighboring town of Showa—originate from the Taiheizan Mountains. "So you could say our regionality, or 'terroir,' in a sense, is the forests, earth and water of Mt. Taihei," Kodama adds. The soft Shirasuno well water is a key

ingredient in all of Kodama's competition sake as well as the Tenko junmai daiginjo series the brewery makes, resulting in its smooth, full-bodied texture. Kodama transports this water via stainless steel tanks in 1,300 liter (350 gallon) batches.

Because of slight variations in water softness from well to well, the Showa town water is slightly harder than the Shirasuno well water even though both are from Mt. Taihei. So Kodama uses this water for

Above Taiheizan: one brewery, four waters—Akita's Kodama Brewery uses four different water sources to make its sakes. Left The water ionizing machine at Miyasaka Brewery's Fujimi facility helps bring the waters of its two brewery sites into accord for a more uniform brewery style. Facing page Shin'ichi and Eiko Kodama, owner and Head of International Sales and Marketing respectively.

most of his junmai, junmai ginjo, honjozo and futsu (regular) sake. All of the Kodama sakes made with Mt. Taihei-sourced water share the same foundation, so to speak: softer water that made its slow passage through the geological strata of Mt. Taihei, lighter on minerals such as calcium and potassium than you would find from mineral-rich volcanic soil. As we've mentioned, sake making requires an abundance of good, fresh water. Mt. Taihei, like so much of the mountainous, sometimes volcanic Japanese landscape, provides generously.

The Kodamas had heard about the extreme softness and mild taste of water from the Shirakami Mountains in the northwestern corner of Akita and southern Aomori Prefecture. Dotted with deep, clear blue lakes and beech tree forests, the area was declared a World Heritage site in 1993. A pristine water source like this will trigger a Pavlovian response in any brewer. Kodama was no exception. He hatched a plan to launch a new line of junmai sake using Shirakami water. The result was his Shingetsu junmai kimoto series. While Shirakami water is smooth, light and refreshing, when combined with the slower, natural lactic acid-producing kimoto brewing style it becomes rich in umami, earthy, with hints of grass and mushroom.

The experiment led to an interesting finding: the super-soft Shirakami water was resistant to dimethyl sulfide, a precursor compound to the dreaded *hineka*, or stinky off-flavors that result in immediate disqualification in tasting competitions. This congenial quality allows Shingetsu to stay fresh for a longer period of time, which would make it a great export sake. There is just one drawback: the mountain spring is a two-hour drive away, a barrier large enough to make the label only available in limited quantities.

The fourth type of water that Kodama Brewery uses is from a well on the Oga Peninsula, commissioned by a sake retailer on the peninsula who was a die-hard John Lennon fan. It was once his custom to release this sake at his shop on the anniversary of Lennon's death. It's not uncommon for well-known sake makers to produce limited-edition private brands to shops, distributors and hotels, just as an actor or sports star might want to have their private label wine or spirit. Kodama produces more than ten such labels. Delightful as the image is of a bunch of Akita Beatles fans sipping on this sake and singing along to John Lennon songs, this particular shop eventually closed. Luckily for the Lennon fans, another distributor took up the line, so the brand, and the tribute, continue.

But there are other factors beyond hardness and softness in how water shapes sake taste. Eiko Kodama, Shin'ichiro's wife and Kodama's Head of International Sales and Marketing, explains that while numerically Shirakami water is similar to the softest water of Fushimi in Kyoto, geographical differences and the microbiome of the Shirakami forests will also subtly affect taste. The interactions between fungus, yeasts and other microbes contained in both the terrestrial and human microbiome are still uncharted territory, and no doubt we will learn more about how they affect fermented beverages, food and health. Shin'ichiro's great uncle, the same curious biochemist who invented the Akita Kimoto method (see page 15), discovered a yeast in the Shirakami forest. Named Shirakami Kodama Kobo, it has gained a following among bakers. "There are still so many wonders in untouched forests there," says Eiko Kodama.

One-Hundred-Year Water

To the southwest, along the Sea of Japan coast, is Mt. Haku, revered as a holy site since ancient times, on the border between Ishikawa and Gifu prefectures. Actually a three-peaked range, the copious snowfall it receives in winter, and its rain and

snowmelt in summer, are the sources of four river systems that have provided bountifully for the surrounding land and its people. The oldest brewery in Ishikawa, Fukumitsuya, has been brewing with Hakusan water since 1625, which the brewery credits for giving its sake body and sharpness. Run-off from the volcanic mountain is rapid; the character of local water is influenced by the deep layers of fossilized shell at the base of the mountains, which endow it with high levels of magnesium and calcium. Fukumitsuya's fourteenth-generation heir, Taichiro Fukumitsu, notes that this water quality brings out a beautiful mineral, iodine quality in the brewery's aged or vintage line, Mizuho.

But it wasn't until 1980, when researchers at Kanazawa University calculated Hakusan water took one hundred years to run off the dormant volcano and pass through strata of fossilized shell before finding its way to the groundwater, that the name *hyakunensui*, ("one-hundred-year water") was coined. In 1986 Fukumitsuya built a 500-foot (150- meter)-deep well to access it closer to its source. Like Otokoyama Brewery in Hokkaido, Fukumitsuya has diverted some of its water to a well on the property, open to the public for personal use. Its hyakunensui particularly shines, Fukumitsu says, in making dashi stock, coffee or tea.

The Character of Water, the Skill of the Brewer
While brewers will go on extolling the virtues of their water, the line between where the influence of

water type and quality over the final product ends and where technology and the master brewer's skill begins is blurry.

Back in Suwa, Nagano, for example, Miyasaka Brewery noticed that its sake brewed at its Suwa branch performed better at competitions than sake made at its Fujimi branch. In order to make this the standard for the entire brewery, in 2014 the company purchased a large, futuristic-looking ion-exchange water-conditioning system that can adjust the mineral balance of Fujimi water to match that of Suwa's. Made by a company called Organo that was founded in Suwa in the 1940s, both the machine and the brewery's investment in it are in keeping with the area's long history of technical innovation. Suwa was the center of the silk-weaving industry in the nineteenth century, and in the twentieth century came to be known for fine tooling, watches, optics and high-tech industries. In the spirit of Suwa, brewery president Naotaka Miyasaka says he's less interested in expressing any subtle differences in the water of local micro-terroirs and more in fine-tuning to make the best-tasting sake possible.

In Nara Prefecture, the talented owner-*toji* of Yucho Brewery, Yoshihiko Yamamoto, uses the extreme hardness of his water as one tool in his brewing toolkit. The mineral hardness of water, he explains, expresses "the energy of the earth." So does unpolished or only very lightly polished rice. "I use these two earth energies to control fermentation," he says. Until fairly recently, brewers lacked sufficient cooling capacity to expertly control fermentation as they can now. "It was believed to be difficult to brew sake with very hard water," says Yamamoto. "But you can make various sakes with any water because of technology." Many say that hard water is not suited to unpasteurized sake, yet Yucho's entire Kaze no Mori line is unpasteurized.

The key is knowing how to fine-tune the fermentation of sake mash. High levels of calcium and magnesium present in the pristine, hard well water that Yamamoto sources from the base of Mt. Kongo make for what he calls "happy water" and "happy yeast," since the latter feed on minerals that the *koji-kin* fungus spores have turned into sugar. Yamamoto's *sumato kura* (smart brewery) is equipped with a monitor that checks the temperature of the fermenting mash every minute. If fermentation activity drops too low, he gives it a shot of hard water, which, he says "is like adding Red Bull—it makes the yeast cells start moving again." If the fermentation activity is too high, he lowers the temperature of the mash to slow it.

While Yamamoto the brewer uses the language of control and mastery to describe his process, the toji's job is also that of an orchestra conductor: coaxing out different tonalities of water, rice and yeast, lowering or raising the volume to achieve varying emotional responses. The notes he strikes range from rich, sweet and sour for his Takacho bodaimoto, to crushably light, creamy and effervescent in his Kaze no Mori Alpha 3 junmai daiginjo. Integrating the components of sake into an energetic, harmonious whole is where the creativity of the toji, as it has done for centuries, still shines.

Water Flight

Sake name: Isojiman
Sake type: Junmai ginjo
Brewery: Isojiman, Shizuoka Prefecture
Soft. *The water from the Akaishi range in Japan's Southern Alps plays a major role in shaping the Isojiman profile. A quintessential, easy-to-drink Shizuoka sake.*

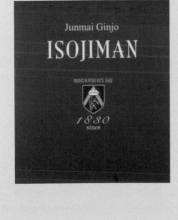

Sake name: Yamagata Masamune "1898"
Sake type: Junmai kimoto
Brewery: Mitobe, Yamagata Prefecture
Medium hard. *While this brewery utilizes the many Yamagata rice varieties cultivated in the prefecture, Mitobe is also a master at working with Akaiwa Omachi. This example will knock your socks off. Full and juicy, with a sharp finish provided by the brewery's Ou Mountain water, which flows through limestone pockets.*

Sake name: Kuroobi Do-Do
Sake type: Yamahai junmai ginjo
Brewery: Fukumitsuya, Ishikawa Prefecture
Hard. *Hard water defines many Ishikawa breweries, and Fukumitsuya's ranks among the hardest. Intense and powerful, made with Yamada Nishiki and Kinmon Nishiki rices, and matured about two years. This is a connoisseur's sake.*

Chapter Nine

Amazing Shrine Water

Our destination today is the coastal Nada area of Hyogo Prefecture, a place that, as the seat of sake-brewing power from the mid-nineteenth century on, looms large in the history of sake making. It was here, in the waning years of the Tokugawa shogunate, that sixth-generation brewer Tazaemon Yamamura made a startling discovery that forever changed and elevated brewers' notions of water.

In 1840, puzzled as to why the sake at his brewery in Nishinomiya consistently produced superior sake to that of his brewery in Uozaki (now part of Kobe), Yamamura went about systematically eliminating all possible variables. He used the same rice and polishing ratio for both. He tried using the same brewery workers at each brewery. He tried brewing at the exact same time, with the same method at both breweries. Yet his Nishinomiya sake was consistently better. Finally, he had the water from his Nishinomiya brewery—which filters down through Mt. Rokko to be drawn up from underground wells—ferried by oxen the five-and-a-half miles (9 km) to Uozaki, and found his answer. Although Nishinomiya had been known for sake excellence since the early fifteenth century, for the first time people understood that its magical ingredient was Nishinomiya water. From then on, Yamamura had Nishinomiya water transported to Uozaki, and brewers have touted their water as a key to their great-tasting sake. His discovery was to play a key role in Nada's assumption of sake dominance over its northern neighbor and erstwhile powerhouse, Itami.

Miyamizu Mania

Drawn from the merger of three different underground currents near Nishinomiya Shrine, Yamamura's Nishinomiya water became known as *miyamizu*, or "the water from Nishinomiya." The shrine itself was a favorite of aristocrats during the Heian era (794–1185); the literal translation of "Nishinomiya" is "Kyoto's western shrine." Underground rivers from the north and east pass through what was once seabed, and thus are rich in phosphorus, calcium and potassium. The speed with which the waters from a third source tumble underground from Mt. Rokko ensures that they are very well aerated. Their abundant oxygen stores serve to cleanse the water of iron oxide, sake's known nemesis because of its way of discoloring sake and infusing it with off-flavor and fragrance. The confluence of these three water sources creates a truly magical brewing water that gives Nada-Gogo sake its edge. ("Gogo" means "five villages" and is a reference to the five sake-brewing villages in and around Kobe and Nishinomiya that are wedged between Osaka Bay and Mt. Rokko.) The sake their combined powers yielded, it was said, tasted crystalline and crisp, like the clear sky of autumn.

Although brewers at the time did not understand the geography or hydrology behind why miyamizu was better, its fame spread, making it the most coveted brewery water of the day. Businesses known as *mizuya*, or water vendors, formed to cater to the water needs of less hydrologically endowed brewers. When brewing season approached, well owners filled cedar barrels with water then gave them to third-party carriers to be delivered to brewery customers.

Bottles of Sakura Masamune Yakimare Ki-ippon junmai.

A Sake-rice Bento

Our journey to Nada begins at a hot springs inn in Ninohe, Iwate Prefecture. Several dips in the Obonai hot-spring baths have rejuvenated us after the Nanbu Bijin *shinshu* "new rice" party of the night before (see chapter 5). Momoko, the inn's kimono-clad, merry-eyed receptionist, a bundle of cuteness ripped straight from the pages of a manga series, has sent us off with bento boxes for the train. The flat field of snowy rice with a pickled plum at its center is an edible representation of Japan's national flag, rendered in two of its most representative foods. It has special significance for us, too: the rice is Gin Otome, grown by Ryoichi Itsukaichi, the bashful farmer from the shinshu party.

   One of the pleasures of our odyssey has been sampling regional rices in our *ekiben* (short for *eki bento* or "station boxed lunch") by day, and their sake counterparts by night. This bento flips the pattern, putting sake rice in our lunch. The Gin Otome sake rice is not as sticky as the usual bento table rice. But there's a milky sweetness to it that makes it a nice foil to the salty pickled umeboshi plum, soy-sauce glazed broiled white fish, and the soy- and mirin-simmered daikon strips that accompany it. The small bottle of Yakult, a popular fermented yogurt drink, completes this festival of fermentation, a showcase for the national mold of Japan, *Aspergillus oryzae*.

Yamamura's discovery was just one of a number of reasons the Nada region catapulted ahead of Itami. All of them involved taking advantage of harnessing water. A little background is helpful. By the early 1600s, sake was being transported via pack animal from Kansai to Edo, the capital. But the demands of rapidly growing Edo became too much for this overland supply route. Entrepreneurial wholesalers began sending sake to the capital by merchant sailboat, alongside a variety of other daily necessities, on boats called *higaki kaisen*, which bore decorative woven bamboo lattices attached to their gunwales. These boats were fast but not the most reliable, and the frequency of shipwrecks gave rise to a genre of Edo-era insurance fraud: wholesalers reported fictional shipwrecks then illegally sold their "lost" cargo.

   Shipbuilding concerns (some of them backed by Nada-Gogo sake brewers) and Osaka-based

shipping agents flourished. By 1730, the *taru kaisen*, a much speedier boat, began competing with the higaki kaisen. By the late 1700s these elegant craft were devoted solely to the transport of sake barrels.

   At its 1804 peak, Itami was shipping more than twenty million liters (5.3 million gallons) of sake to the capital via taru kaisen. But Nada—directly fronting Osaka Bay—was simply better located for efficient transport to Edo. Water mills, meanwhile, had proliferated on the six rivers that ran down the slopes of Mt. Rokko behind Nada, dramatically increasing the amount of milled sake rice available for brewing. Inland, Itami's foot-powered mills were no match for such a competitor. And Nada's unique style of sake making, which used a much higher ratio of water to rice than makers in other regions, made high quality water even more of an important factor in the final quality of the brew. As shipbuilding concerns and a bustling harbor rapidly materialized in Nada, Itami's dominance started to fade.

Large breweries that catered to the demands of the capital grew more powerful, and Nada's sake-making expertise continued to expand. One of the most famous master brewer guilds in the country, the Tanba Toji, emerged from Nada-Gogo, and Nada was on its way to becoming the most powerful sake-making region of its time.

A Visit to Sakura Masamune Brewery

The story of Tazaemon Yamamura has become one of the most oft-told tales of sake brewing; today a monument marks the location of the first miyamizu well. To get the story of miyamizu and the brewing culture it spawned from the source, we make our way to Sakura Masamune Brewery, the family brewery of Tazaemon Yamamura.

The family began brewing in 1625 about fifteen miles (24 km) to the northwest in Itami, moving to its present location in Uozaki in 1717. Sakura Masamune is one of a number of breweries that relocated from Itami to Nada-Gogo for its water and the other benefits we've outlined. Uozaki-go, like nearby Nishinomiya-go, is one of the five villages of Nada-Gogo.

Today eleventh-generation Tazaemon Yamamura is at the helm of the brewery. The "eleventh-generation" part is somewhat deceptive. He is what is known as a *mukoyoshi*, or son-in-law, who has been adopted into the family. When there is no male heir to carry on the business or family line, or no male heir deemed capable to do so, the family may seek a suitable match for a daughter. The mukoyoshi is officially adopted, taking on the daughter's family name. It's a tradition that lives on today; Japan has one of the highest adoption rates in the world but this is due to the fact that the majority of adoptees are men in their twenties and thirties.

Like Kabuki actors' stage names, some brewing families still adhere to the tradition of handing down the founder's first name as well. So the current eleventh-generation head became Tazaemon Yamamura, just like his wife's famous ancestor. At Yucho Brewery in Nara Prefecture, when Yoshihiko Yamamoto became the thirteenth-

Eleventh-generation president of Sakura Masamune, Tazaemon Yamamura.

generation president of the brewery after the death of his father, he took on the ceremonial brewing name Chobei. He signs off on emails with the electronic signature Chobei (Yoshihiko) Yamamoto.

It's late in the afternoon when we finally exit the commuter train we've taken from Kobe and begin walking downhill toward the water. The looming, tightly packed buildings that darken the sky are the modern descendants of the dozens of breweries that once crowded the landscape. Hakutsuru and Kikumasamune breweries are just around the corner, continuing Nada-Gogo's dynastic domination of the *ote*, or largest brewers in the sake trade.

The five-story modern concrete building that houses Sakura Masamune was built just a year before the devastating magnitude 7.3 Kobe earthquake and fire of 1995, which destroyed all the wooden structures next to it. Inside, we're greeted briefly by Yamamura, then sit down for a chat with master brewer Norihide Harada. With his slow, deliberate manner and precise way of answering us, Harada, a member of the Tanba Toji Guild, is the embodiment of the technical side of brewing. Trained as an engineer, he didn't join Sakura Masamune until he was thirty-two, rising to the rank of *toji* in fifteen years.

Harada explains how, in addition to his discovery of miyamizu, the persistent and imaginative sixth-generation Yamamura also pushed the boundaries of hydro-powered rice milling to produce a markedly more delicious and profitable sake. The master brewer, we notice, calls the past and present Yamamuras by their generation number, Sixth Generation and Eleventh Generation, like the Forty-One and Forty-Three nicknames applied to the presidents Bush.

But here's how Sixth Generation advanced water milling techniques. Thanks to the half-dozen swiftly flowing rivers that empty into Osaka Bay, water wheels had, during his time, already replaced human-leg-powered mills. It was Sixth Generation's idea, Harada tells us, to push water-wheel polishing to new extremes. Until 1843, breweries polished brown rice on the water wheel for a day to achieve about a 95 percent polishing rate. The rice was still brown in color, yielding a golden sake described as *yamabuki iro no sake*, or "butterbur-colored sake." It was thick and strong. Sixth Generation lengthened the polishing time to three entire days on the water wheel to get a smaller, whiter grain.

The more refined, elegant sake it yielded (probably still only about an 85 percent or higher polish) fetched the highest possible price in Edo. With this one advancement—creating a more delicious sake through available technology and higher polishing rate—Yamamura became yet another brewer who could legitimately claim to have helped pave the way for the birth of ginjo more than a century later.

Sakura Masamune's master brewer Norihide Harada displays the *koji* for the next day's sake. Along with excellent *koji*, the hard water of Nada is a key contributor to its rich, full and crisp sake.

At its peak in 1913, there were 277 water wheel facilities for rice polishing in Nada. In the village of Sumiyoshi alone, just west of the Sakura Masamune Brewery site on the Sumiyoshi River, there were eighty mills operated by over one thousand laborers. As water-wheel rice polishing advanced to the point where large volumes of rice could be polished much more rapidly, brewery coffers swelled. In 1906, Sakura Masamune's name gained even more luster when the brewery's native yeast was deemed to be the best of all the samples that the Brewing Society of Japan collected throughout Japan. Its Yeast No. 1 became the first commercial sake yeast sold by the society.

At this point, we're curious to know more about Sixth Generation, his personality and what drove his restlessly inventive mind. But Harada's polite answer is, "Please ask Eleventh Generation that question tonight. I can answer technical questions."

Ancient bottles of Sakura Masamune on display at the brewery's museum, which celebrates its four centuries of sake making.

Why So Many "Masamune" Sakes?

Although today there are dozens of breweries that have incorporated the word "Masamune" into their names, Sakura Masamune was the first. During the Edo period (1603–1868), Nada brewers liked to name their brews after popular Kabuki actors. The Yamamura family was no exception. It named its brewery after a famous actor of the day, Shinsui. Several hundred years later, sixth-generation Tazaemon Yamamura decided he'd like a more masculine name.

On a visit to Zuikoji Temple in Kyoto, he spotted a scroll bearing the name Rinzai Seishu (臨済正宗), referring to one of the three main sects of Buddhism. He was struck by the word *seishu* (正宗, "righteous sect") and how it was a homophone for *seishu* (清酒 "clear sake") —meaning it had the same pronunciation but was spelled with different kanji characters. But there was also a third possible reading of 正宗: *masamune*. Masamune was the surname of Japan's most famous swordsmith, the priest Goro Masamune (c. 1264–1343). This allusion dovetailed nicely into Yamamura's plan to masculinize the name of the brewery. Typically Japanese in his love of kanji character wordplay, Yamamura adopted the name Masamune.

Others loved the Masamune name—with its spiritual, sake and martial references—so much so that it was widely adopted. By the time the Yamamura family got around to trying to trademark the name in 1844, it had been claimed by another brewery. So they affixed the name of Japan's national flower, *sakura* (cherry blossom), and their new name was born. To date, there are dozens of breweries in Japan that incorporate the name Masamune.

We shelve our family queries, saving them for dinner, when Eleven has promised to join us.

But first we tour the massive seventy thousand-square-foot (6,500 m²) brewery with Yamamura and Harada. Its high ceilings are needed to accommodate its sake-brewing equipment in an ergonomic manner. Yamamura points out the brewery's very tall five stories are the same height as the eight-story apartment building across the road.

Harada, who is one of an impressive seven licensed toji working at the brewery, takes us to a large, north-facing window on the third floor, where Mt. Rokko looms in the near distance like a gentle giant buttressing Kobe's backside. This north-facing window was a standard fixture in Nada-Gogo breweries, he explains. Brewers would throw open their windows to let the *rokko-oroshi*, the frigid Rokko winds, sweep in off the mountaintops, rapidly cooling just-steamed rice. "We're harnessing nature to help do our work," Harada adds.

Over the years, due to typhoons, wars and environmental degradation, brewers have had to relocate some miyamizu wells, but Yamamura says that there are still about one hundred wells in Nada supplying thirty to forty breweries. While Sakura Masamune is famous for the discovery of miyamizu, today the brewery uses this water for its *shikomi mizu*, or brewing water only. The water is transported by tank truck from its three miyamizu wells in Nishinomiya to its Uozaki brewery. For

Straw-mat-wrapped *komodaru* sake barrels adorn the entrance of Sakura Masamune.

washing and steaming, it relies on softer local Kobe ground water from the Mt. Rokko aquifer, which it fortifies to adjust mineral levels.

Our tour complete, we take off the de rigueur hygienic shower caps—guaranteed to make anyone look foolish—that we've donned for the tour. Like cheesemaking facilities and meat-processing plants, sake making requires a pristine environment to prevent contamination. Some breweries even warn visitors not to consume yogurt or *natto* (fermented soybeans) the day of their visit for fear of foreign mold contamination.

Yamamura leads us across the street to Sakuraen, a beautiful memorial hall that was constructed on the site of the old wooden brewery buildings. It houses an exhibit space, bar, restaurant and shop. In the front courtyard of the building, there's a giant iron cauldron or *kama* tipped on its side, which once was used for steaming rice. Inside we find a handsome museum filled with sake-making artifacts and art. There's a tall, time-worn cedar barrel, its iron bands rusted, a spigot thrust into its stout waist. Such barrels, explains Yamamura, were used for carrying miyamizu to customers, usually by horse- or ox-drawn wagons. On the second floor, we examine an exquisite set of woodblock prints, all depicting scenes of sake making or sake commerce. One is of a bustling port scene, in another, workers wearing wooden *geta* clogs roll casks of sake to the dock to be loaded onto *taru kaisen* boats.

A quick stop in the shop follows, where Michael falls for the beautifully labeled and boxed Yomigaeri Hyakunen, which he snaps up for tasting in his sake regionality class. The sake is crafted using Yeast No. 1, the historic first commercial yeast, revived here in a sake brewed exactly as it was a hundred years

ago, with miyamizu water. Later, Michael will discover that it is full of umami and acidity and wafting notes of toasted nutmeg and burnt orange peel. Nancy opts for the flagship dry and clean 70 percent polish Yakimare Ki-ippon junmai and a Miyamizu Hana tokubetsu junmai. And she can't resist the all-Hyogo Prefecture special-issue Kit-Kats, made with the powdered essence of Sakura Masamune Yamada Nishiki daiginjo. Old Japan has been repackaged for a new generation, in the bright pink colors of the cherry blossom-viewing season.

Seated on tatami mats at the building's second-floor restaurant we grill strips of generously marbled Hyogo beef in our cast-iron pots, along with cabbage, shiitake and enoki mushrooms (see recipe on page 214). Our sukiyaki is paired with a Sakura Masamune junmai ginjo, which, true to the label on the bottle, "Bonds Well With Beef." Eleventh Generation (Yamamura) explains that his goal is not to chase trends, but to make sake that helps food taste better, not overpower it. "I'm in Nada," he says, "so I want to continue to make futsu-shu [regular, rather than ginjo sake]." Referring to the elite ginjos, daiginjos and the cult brewers who have gained fanatical followings for their aromatic, wine-like sake, he adds, "Not everything has to be *tokubetsu* (special, extraordinary) and handmade. We've been making regular sake for ages. That's what Nada is about, and it's all good." Slurping our caramelized slabs of beef and savory mushrooms along with the warm junmai, there's no way to disagree. This is satisfying food and drink, the culinary equivalent of wrapping ourselves in a soft wool blanket on a snowy night. We nod in assent.

But we're still hoping for that insight into Sixth Generation's mind. "Well, Ten, Nine and Eight were all very quiet," Eleventh Generation says. "Six was very energetic. He would try anything, and Seven was that way, too. Number Eight went through World War I and a lot of hardship, but he was quiet. It was his wife who was really scary."

Not quite going in the direction we'd hoped for, we follow along. Eighth Generation's determined wife commissioned Frank Lloyd Wright to build the family a vacation home in the wealthy town of Ashiya. "It was a huge undertaking, cost a bundle of money during World War I, and shocked everyone," says Eleventh Generation. "At the time, the brewery had very few employees, because all of them had joined the army, while she was having this extravagant house built. In the end, they only used the home—now open to tourists as the Yodoko Guest House— occasionally to drink tea."

Besides being the source of some frustration for the family, the story illustrates the magnitude of the wealth that large Nada sake-brewing families like the Yamamuras amassed. It was not just spent on expensive follies, either: Eighth Generation's family was also responsible for spearheading the construction of Nada Junior High School.

Our evening over, Eleventh Generation walks us to the station as the moon shines on Osaka Bay. Reflecting on the millions of gallons of water that have flowed down the Rokko Mountains over generations, to be brewed into sake that made its way across Japan and later the world, it's easy to imagine why, during the ascendancy of Nada brewing, a poet of the day wrote, "If you look at the twilight sea, it smells like a tasteful sake."

Nada Flight

Sake name: Yamadaho
Sake type: Junmai daiginjo
Brewery: Hakutsuru, Hyogo Prefecture
Made with Yamadaho (also known as Yamadabo), an old rice and parent of Yamada Nishiki; Nada water; and the brewery's proprietary yeast.

Sake name: Yakimare Kyokai Ichigo Kobo
Sake type: Junmai
Brewery: Sakura Masamune, Hyogo Prefecture
Made with the defunct Yeast No. 1, which was first isolated at this brewery, and Nada's famous miyamizu water.

Sake name: Mizuho Kuromatsu
Sake type: Junmai yamahai
Brewery: Kenbishi, Hyogo Prefecture.
From one of Japan's oldest sake breweries, established in 1505. Full-bodied, savory and complex. Drink it now or put it in the cellar (that's right, this sake would be fun to try in a decade or more).

Chapter Ten

Snow Country

Yukiguni, or "snow country," is the evocative label that covers large swaths of northern and northwestern Japan that lie along the Sea of Japan, from Hokkaido, Aomori, Akita and Niigata prefectures, down to Fukui. The heavy snowfall of the region provides the backdrop and soundtrack for sake's creation.

Listening to the snow, falling and accumulating without pause, sake is brewed, little by little. In the silence and tension of the cold, crisp air the sound of falling snow can be heard. Inside the kura, its outside wrapped in a white world, the toji's voice flies, and the sake—into which he has poured his heart and soul—is born.

Kotaro Saito, president of Saiya Brewery in Akita, based the name of his prestige junmai daiginjo label Chosetsu ("Listening to Snow") on these words written by his mother Momoko.

Lonely images of remote, isolated snow country hold an especially romantic appeal for the hemmed-in city dweller, who might think of Yasunari Kawabata's bittersweet novel, *Snow Country*. It tells the story of a wealthy Tokyo dance critic who enters an ambivalent relationship with a geisha who lives in a small snow-country town. But it was another writer who, after visiting Saiya Brewery from Tokyo to research the climate and topography of the area, suggested the name Yuki no Bosha, meaning "Thatch-roofed Cottage in the Snow," for the brewery's best-known brand. "He was in a car on the way back to the airport and gazed out at the snowy landscape dotted with thatched-roofed buildings buried in snow," explains Saito. The name stuck, and Saiya has used it ever since.

In addition to its romantic image, the heavy snowfall of this region confers many practical benefits on the sake maker. Falling snow purifies the air, then melts into water that runs off mountain peaks, soaks through layers of earth and rock and provides pristine groundwater for brewing. It also nourishes some of the best rice in Japan.

Kamikawa Taisetsu Sake Brewery

緑丘蔵

Facing page The logo on the main brewing building of Kamikawa Taisetsu symbolizes Hokkaido's wintery climate, Ainu design and the five tastes. **Left** The *yukimuro* (snow room) at Hakkaisan Brewery in Niigata Prefecture. **Below** A view of snow-laden trees from the *koji* room of Kamikawa Taisetsu.

"One characteristic of having so much snow is that there is little temperature difference between day and night in winter," explains Rumiko Obata, fifth-generation head of Obata Brewery on Sado Island. Although the island gets less snow than the mainland, she notes that for Niigata Prefecture as a whole, uniformly low temperatures are ideal for slowly fermented ginjo sake. "It's a good environment for maximizing the power of yeast, and at the same time prevents bacterial growth," she says.

Hakkaisan Brewery's *Yukimuro* Snow Room

The *yukimuro*, or "snow room" for fermenting and aging sake is seen throughout the snow country. In Niigata, rooms constructed of snow (salted to melt and then solidify it) and then covered in layers of straw were used to preserve and gently age everything from fish and rice to sake and vegetables. In the snow room, sake, miso and other fermented products mellowed and ripened, developing more rounded flavors. The low-temperature, high-humidity environment kept meat and fish from drying out and retained freshness. In summer, restaurants and inn workers would fetch snow from the yukimuro to use as a natural refrigerant.

Hakkaisan Brewery, located in the inland region of Uonuma, Niigata, built a modern yukimuro in 2013, where it ages its super-premium Yukimuro sake for three years, chilled by a one-thousand-ton pile of snow. The brewery is divided into two parts, with the giant mound of snow on one side, and sake tanks in the other. Hakkaisan brand ambassador Timothy Sullivan explains that the snow cleanses the air of dirt and dust particles and makes for a cleaner brewing environment. It's so cold that year round, no electricity is needed for refrigeration. The room stays chilled at a steady 37°F (3°C), which, he adds, gives the sake a deeper, richer flavor. Sullivan, who grew up in the snowbelt city of Syracuse, New York, says yukimuro and snow-country customs in general "use snow as a natural resource," rather than treating it as an obstacle and a nuisance as it is in upstate New York.

One beautiful example of the resourceful use of snow is Niigata's textile tradition *Echigo jofu*, a hand-loomed luxury fabric with a 1,200-year-old history. (Echigo is the ancient provincial name of today's mainland Niigata.) Still practiced by an aging group of artisans, it is one of many crafts that occupied villagers during the half year when they could be snowed in by as much as nine feet (2.5 m) of snow. The process involves twisting *ramie* hemp fibers into thread, dyeing and then weaving it with a hand loom into fabric. Rooms are kept at an unheated 40°F (5°C) since dry heat will cause the thread to snap. The woven cloth is then washed, and the men of the village tread on it with their bare feet in wooden barrels to soften it. A process known as "snow bleaching" follows, in which the ozone of melting snow vapor "bleaches" the fibers, making its colors more vivid.

For young men though, the harsh winters of snow country historically made finding work in winter difficult, giving rise to the tradition of men heading to sake breweries for the brewing season, an alternative to the fields and fisheries that occupied them during the summer months.

Hokkaido Road Trip

Neon blue sky, snow-fringed spruce trees drooping under the weight of their frosting of white powder, thick quilts of snow spread across the surrounding landscape. We've parachuted into snow country and on this late January morning, we're headed from Sapporo, the prefectural capital of Hokkaido, to two breweries, one old and venerable, the other young and up-and-coming. It's our first time on Japan's northernmost island, roughly the size of Ireland and a prefecture unto itself.

Our traveling companion today is Carlin Kumada, a tall, gentle northern Californian who happened to be backpacking through Hokkaido in the summer of 2006, and met a woman named Rie Kumada. He ended up marrying her, taking on her family name and becoming vice president at her family's sake store, Meishu no Yutaka. In addition to overseeing all electronic and operational aspects of the business, he's also an international sake competition judge and now, after over a dozen years living here, an ideal guide to the prefecture and its sake.

We're only four days into this research trip and have visited as many breweries. Today will be

Kamikawa Taisetsu's *tokubetsu junmai* is made with 100 percent Hokkaido-grown Suisei rice.

numbers five and six. After traveling by shinkansen through the flat, almost suburban-feeling Tochigi, there was a detour to the port town of Hachinohe, near the very northern tip of Aomori Prefecture, then it was back on the shinkansen and through the Seikan Tunnel, which connects Japan's main island of Honshu to snow-covered Hokkaido. At a train transfer stop in Hokuto City, we're both fascinated and slightly disturbed by the local mascot, Sushi Hokki, a poseable, anthropomorphic Sakhalin surf clam sushi with a snow white head that bleeds into a bright red curved tail, and a pebbly stomach made of individual plastic grains of rice. We briefly consider getting one as an *omiyage* (souvenir) but worry that non-Japanese friends won't quite get it.

All our trips are intensely scheduled, so spending several hours on a scenic drive with a local is a nice way to decompress and survey the land. Last night's dining adventure with Kumada was a trip to the branch of the Genghis Khan *yakiniku* (grilled meat) restaurant housed in the old Sapporo beer brewery. An institution in the city, the restaurant's name is a reference to the nomadic mongol leader, whose troops lived off the meat of their herds; the round, individual cast-iron grills at each table replicate the helmets the warriors reputedly repurposed as griddles. Guests are ushered into a cavernous room and immediately given large plastic bags into which we stuff all of our outerwear. We're also suited up in protective plastic aprons. The live charcoal fires harnessed to char massive amounts of hand-cut lamb (every part of the animal imaginable, it seems, is on offer), can leave people smelling like yakiniku for days; wrapping up our outerwear helps mitigate the olfactory aftereffects. It's a good thing too: if there's one thing that can mar a brewery visit it's bringing strong perfume or other foreign aromas in with you.

This morning, our dinner an aromatic, lingering memory, we head north on the Hokkaido Express-

Master brewer Shinji Kawabata's signature style is characterized by a brilliant and balanced counterpoint of bitterness, crisp flavors and an extremely fresh palate.

way as Kumada shows us some of the many adaptations residents have made to the weather. When snowfall (sixteen feet [5 m] on average annually in Sapporo and about twenty-two feet [8 m] in mountainous areas) is at its heaviest, drivers equip their cars with snow tires plus chains. Snow breaks, or steel racks have been inserted into the sides of the mountains we are winding our way through, to catch snow cascading off the mountains and keep cars safe. In some parts of the prefecture, solar power–heated hot water pipes under the roads melt snow and sprinklers spray warm groundwater onto streets.

As climate change advances, weather patterns are changing (see page 98). "It's a little scary," says Kumada, "because we're not getting the snow we used to. Summers are hotter and rainier, and there are more typhoons." These typhoon storm systems usually come up from the southeast and make landfall between Kyushu and Tokyo. As they curl up the Japan sea coast, the frigid winds that pass between Honshu and Hokkaido normally push the typhoons to Korea or off the Pacific coast. "But with rising temperatures, that wind is disturbed, and we lose our guard," Kumada explains.

Kamikawa Taisetsu Brewery

Today, at least, it's all too easy to forget about climate change and revel in the bright blue skies, deep green forests and snowy whiteness all around us. At Kamikawa Taisetsu, a small-batch brewery that opened in 2017 in a resort area just north of Mt. Taisetsu National Park, we're greeted by a round snowman likeness of master brewer Shinji Kawabata, complete with wire-framed glasses and a bottle of his own sake at his side. This is Japan's second-northern-most brewery, and only about a 125-mile (200 km)

hop away from Russia's Sakhalin island, for many years disputed territory claimed by both Japan and Russia.

Kawabata guides us through his ergonomic, spotless and compact brewery, explaining his process in a rich, booming baritone. Compared to many *kura* that we've visited, his feels like a minimalist dollhouse version: stark white, small tanks, the distance from the steaming and cooling room to the fermenting mash just a few steps down a short metal stairway. As we peer into a tank, we need to be mindful of the *kurabito* that come, one after another down the stairs carrying batches of steamed rice to add to the mash.

A Hokkaido native, Kawabata studied information and electrical engineering at Kanazawa University in Ishikawa Prefecture but says, "It was difficult to keep up with my studies, so I dropped out and focused on part-time work instead." Working at breweries in Ishikawa, Fukuoka, Iwate, Yamagata and Gunma prefectures, he adds, "I learned that there are various brewing methods depending on the climate, scale of the brewery, equipment, and so on. That helped in building this new brewery."

The air is a brisk 14°F (-10°C) outside, but in the rice-steaming room, the windows are open to speed the cooling of just-steamed rice. A fan connected to the bottom of each tank pulls cool air through the batch, just one of Kawabata's clever hacks to make his sake production more efficient, though he's not sure of its effect on final quality. "There are people who break down rice temperature, water tempera-ture, all that in a very detailed way, but I'm not sure it makes that much difference," he says.

The casualness of this statement is not the kind of granular and precise *toji*-speak we might have expected. On the drive up, Kumada had told us, "Kawabata-toji is very much a *shokunin* [craftsman]. He's passionate about sake and bringing the overall level of Hokkaido sake up. He'll tell you his secrets.

He doesn't keep them to himself because he wants everyone to make sake as good as his."

The brewery's location was selected for its abundant, high-quality ground water, which bubbles up from Hokkaido's largest river, the Ishikari. It runs close by the brewery and is fed by snowmelt off of the Taisetsu volcanic range. Kumada credits Kawabata for "more or less single-handedly saving the Hokkaido sake industry," and it seems he's still on this crusade. Two more offshoots of the brewery—each headed by its own toji— will be open by the time this book is published, part of his long-term plan to revive the local Hokkaido sake-brewing industry.

Kawabata returned to Hokkaido after his tour of duty brewing around the country in 2010. His first post was at Kinteki Brewery, where he brought home gold for a sake made with all-Hokkaido rice, something that was a revelation to locals. When Kawabata left the brewery five years later fans were so unhappy they launched a petition begging for his return. Their wish was granted two years later when he signed on with the boutique Kamikawa Taisetsu Brewery. Here, he brews with several local rice varieties—Ginpu, Kita Shizuku and Suisei—and turns out sakes that are light, velvety, juicy and gentle on the nose. "I like sake that you can drink a lot of," he explains. "This way you can taste more varieties, compare, and continue to drink."

Although things have loosened up a bit since 2017, at the time, the government seldom issued new sake-brewing licenses, in theory to protect existing makers during a period of declining domestic sales. Kawabata managed to find a Mie Prefecture business that held a license but no longer owned a brewery, and had it transferred to Hokkaido, which made opening Kamikawa Taisetsu possible. His fan base followed him, forming a booster club that at first helped out with brewing and now holds various brewery-related events. Although the brewery is too tiny to allow for any tours, a walkway around the second floor allows visitors to peer in from the frigid cold to watch the koji-making and brewing processes in action. Kawabata has rewarded his fans with more gold

President Goro Yamazaki of Otokoyama Brewery. The brewery takes advantage of the fresh cold winter air, medium-hard waters that flow from the volcanic Taisetsu range and local rice such as Ginpu to brew its sake.

medals and a growing international reputation. Thanks to Kawabata and his star power, Kumada tells us, Hokkaido residents "are paying 20 percent more for sake compared to the rest of the country."

Tasting and Describing Sake

Over lunch at a small ramen restaurant, we discuss cultural difference in Japanese and Western approaches to tasting and describing sake. If you have read Japanese sake descriptions on bottle labels, you'll know that they are usually couched in terms that are vague, emotion-based and very different from the concrete descriptors borrowed from the Western wine tasting lexicon. Adjectives like "gentle," "soft," "generous" and "bountiful" are used alongside "fruity," "ginjo-aroma-ed" and "elegant." Kumada explains that in judging competitions, the differences between Western and Japanese judges stem in part from the fact that many Japanese judges are brewing scientists whose job is to focus on and eliminate flaws and imperfections, not to extol the burnt marshmallow and candy-cane aromas of the sake they are tasting. Western sake experts, meanwhile, want to make sake more relatable to non-Japanese. Both Western wine-tasting terms and the notion of terroir, are in part an effort to bridge that knowledge gap and make sake more understandable.

But is this really desirable? Monica Samuels, a Sake Samurai who is in charge of sake and spirits for the US boutique import agency Vine Connections, believes it is. "In general, it's not the Japanese way to be really detailed and descriptive about sake," she says, "but rather to be always very humble. They'll say, 'The sake doesn't get in the way of the food.' But to a Westerner, that's so obvious." When she advises Japanese on how to market sake to Westerners, she'll explain that Americans like a lot of detailed tasting and pairing advice. "Saying a sake has a tropical fruit aroma is not as impressive as saying it's got the aroma of super-juicy, over-ripe pineapple.'" Japanese will chuckle at such American foibles, Samuels adds, yet she believes there is a purpose to descriptive tasting notes. "They bring sake to life for people not confident in their own palates," she explains. "If you offer enough descriptors, people are able to pick out one of them and it makes them feel less in the dark."

Otokoyama Brewery and a Storied Brand Name

Our next stop is Otokoyama Brewery in Asahikawa, a forty-five minute easterly drive from Kamikawa, headed by fifth-generation president Goro Yamazaki. As we pull into the large brewery complex situated on a main thoroughfare, Yamazaki and toji Hidefumi Kitamura are there to greet us, even though the brewery is in a flurry of activity preparing for its annual snow festival. This weekend close to ten thousand visitors will be deposited by the

busload to tour the brewery and museum and visit the small playground with its giant snowman and tobogganing hill. As at Fukumitsuya Brewery in Ishikawa Prefecture, visitors can bring their own containers, up to twenty liters (5.3 gallons) in capacity, to fill up with clear water that flows off of Mt. Taisetsu. In addition to using it to brew tea and coffee, for many locals, it is their water of choice for *mizuwari* (when water and spirits are mixed together), or mixing with shochu or other spirits.

Yamazaki's brewery was founded in Sapporo in 1887 by Niigata transplant Yokichi Yamazaki, who moved it to Asahikawa in 1899. The army's Seventh Division had moved there not too long before, and the railway extended to accommodate it. Many businesses picked up stakes to cater to the swelling population of this frontier town.

In the 1960s, through a clever bit of brand-name resuscitation, the brewery forever linked its name to the storied brand, Otokoyama ("Man's Mountain") and a history that stretches back over 450 years. The original Otokoyama Brewery was located in Hyogo Prefecture. Launched in 1661 under the patronage of the lord of Itami, it reached its apex in 1733, when it was selected by the eighth Tokugawa shogunate, Yoshimune, to be *gozenshu*, or his designated drink—something like getting a royal warrant of appointment from the British monarchy to prove you've supplied the royal house with goods or services. A favorite of the samurai class and kabuki actors, Otokoyama's logo was a familiar sight in ukiyo-e woodblock prints of the era. And like the name Masamune, many other breweries adopted the brand's name.

Two hundred years later, up in Hokkaido, Yamazaki Brewery, like all breweries in the area, found it hard to compete with the sakes of Nada, where the country's best brewers had access to the country's best sake rice

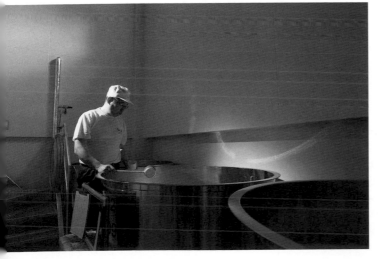

Toji Shinji Kawabata checks the flavor and balance of the main mash at Kamikawa Taisetsu.

and its magical *miyamizu* water. Sometime during the 1960s, the Yamazakis broached the subject of succession with the descendants of the Yama-moto family, founders of the original Otokoyama brand. The brewery itself had long since closed. In 1968, third-generation Yamazaki Brewery president Yokichi and his younger brother Shiro traveled to Hyogo Prefecture to continue the talks, procuring both the official Otokoyama trademark seal, or stamp, and seal bag—the equivalent of the keys to the Otokoyama brand and kingdom. The Yamazakis also received the Yamamoto family's holding of antique sake-brewing tools and artifacts. No money changed hands, says Goro Yamazaki, who adds that in this day and age of large breweries buying out small ones, such a free exchange would be highly unlikely. The Yamamoto family does get the satisfaction of its famous brewery name living on, and its memora-bilia and artifacts displayed for the public rather than collecting dust or being broken up and sold off.

Today in Asahikawa, above the brewery gift shop, is the museum's collection, dating from Otokoya-ma's Edo-period heyday: woodblock prints by Kitagawa Utamaro, a hanging scroll by Katsushika Hokusai, vintage sake mash paddles, barrels and other tools of the trade. Across the hallway from the museum, visitors can peer down through large glass panels to see the brewers in action.

As early as the 1960s, the Yamazakis became exporters of premium sake to the West, an effort led by current president Goro Yamazaki's uncle, Shiro. In the same way that brewing know-how is passed on through networks of brewing-school classmates, Shiro Yamazaki's conduit to Western export opportunities was his classmate from the National Research Institute of Brewing (NRIB), the brilliant brewmaster Takao Nihei. Nihei was dispatched to Hawaii in 1954 when he was twenty-eight, to aid

Drip-pressing competition daiginjo at Otokoyama Brewery.

the struggling Honolulu Sake Brewery. Despite a stellar career that beckoned back in Japan, he ended up settling there for life and raising a family. Late in life, he told World Sake Imports founder Chris Pearce that he stayed on in part because of his attachment to the first-generation Japanese American community. They told him the delicious and affordable glass of sake that he had made possible for them was what made their difficult lives as sugar-plantation laborers bearable.

In 1977, Otokoyama debuted at the Brussels-based juried food and wine show, Monde Selection, and took the first international gold medal in sake in 1984. The story may be apocryphal, but our friend, the San Francisco sake retailer Beau Timken, recalls a time when Otokoyama junmai daiginjo made with Hyogo Yamada Nishiki was the sake presented as in-room hotel gifts for high-rolling Japanese "whales" who jetted into Las Vegas to gamble.

On a tour of the brewery, Yamazaki and Kitamura show us new equipment they've installed. Smaller *koji* tables have replaced larger ones for better maneuverability and finer temperature control, each equipped with a fan. Kitamura has a room in a nearby building where he sleeps during brewing season, when two people at a time take on the night shift. "I was in this room at one o'clock this morn-ing, mixing koji," he tells us. Today the brewery is pressing its competition sake, made with Yamada Nishiki rice polished to 48 percent and yeast No. 1801, a high-aroma variety only available to breweries that have entered into a special contract with the Brewers Association of Japan.

In the main mash room, the strong, sweet, alcoholic smell of fermenting rice hits our noses. We see today's batch of steamed rice, the last of three batches of rice that are added to the mash before it is left to its approximately month-long fermentation. "If you immediately cool it, it will dissolve too easily, the rice remains in a gelatinized state, and it doesn't return to form," Kitamura says. "This results in an overabundance of flavor. So we want to cool it slowly." The door that will let in fresh air is not opened immediately, only after some slow cooling has occurred. This technique, we notice, is the opposite approach to rice cooling that both Kawabata and Sakura Masamune's master brewer Harada described to us.

Such discrepancies in brewing processes and techniques are widespread. Kawabata's casual, yet confident mastery of his brewing process, and the hard-won conviction of the other two master brewers reinforces what we've learned on our travels: the paths to excellence are legion, unique to each brewer, as well as to his or her location, training and years of hands-on brewing practice. And one method, or even scale of brewing, is not necessarily superior. Later, Kawabata of Kamikawa Taisetsu will say how impressed he is with the high quality of Otokoyama's sake, given its much larger production size of seven thousand *koku* (about 334,000 gallons) a year, compared to his own five hundred koku (about 2,400 gallons) yearly production. (One koku is 180 liters, or in the era when rice was paid in tribute to feudal lords, 150 kilograms/ 330 pounds of rice—the amount considered sufficient enough to feed a peasant for a year.)

On the drive back, night is approaching fast. Our car is wrapped in a cold, white world, and our minds are ruminating in its warm interior, replaying the events of the day. Across the snow country, sake is quietly fermenting. We imagine the noise of the voices of the master brewers flying through the cool, crisp air, the rhythmic soothing sound of snow falling gently outside, and the slow birth of this season's fresh sake.

Snow Country Flight

Sake name: Yukimuro
Sake type: Junmai daiginjo
Brewery: Hakkaisan Brewery, Niigata Prefecture
Smooth, rounded and creamy, this sake is beautifully packaged in a snow-white bottle, made with local Gohyakumangoku rice and aged for three years in the brewery's own snow room.

Sake name: Kamikawa Taisetsu "Suisei"
Sake type: Tokubetsu junmai
Brewery: Kamikawa Taisetsu, Hokkaido
Ethereally light and delicately aromatic, this sake finishes with a pleasing shibumi astringency.

Sake name: Otokoyama "Kita no Inaho"
Sake type: Daiginjo
Brewery: Otokoyama Brewery, Hokkaido
Made with local Ginpu rice polished to 40 percent. Its name means "rice of the north" and it shows off Hokkaido's high quality rice, pure surroundings and pristine water.

Chapter Eleven

Perfumed Water from the Palace

The showpiece of Matsumoto Brewery in Fushimi, Kyoto is a sitting room that is ravishing in its understated elegance, decorated with tatami mats, *fusuma* sliding doors, carved wooden *ranma* transoms and a folding screen featuring an idealized landscape of mountains and mists.

From here, visitors can gaze out onto a manicured traditional Japanese garden. Former master brewer Hidehiko Matsumoto liked to show this room off as the source of his minimalist aesthetic and the traditionalism embedded in his old-meets-new Shuhari sake label. (Sadly, in 2020, after we wrote this chapter he and his father Yasuhiro, the former brewery president, stepped down from their positions after a board shake-up.)

A key term in any form of Japanese craft or martial arts practice, *shuhari* refers to the three stages of mastery: conquering the fundamentals, breaking with tradition, and finally forging one's own original and unique techniques. If the traditional sitting room represented the fundamentals on which his sake was built, Matsumoto's brewing philosophy and techniques put him in the company of a band of young brewers pushing the boundaries of craft sake and exploring notions of terroir (see chapter 12 for more on this). One of the bedrock elements of his sake was the soft Fushimi water that he used for Shuhari's smooth, crisp, slightly effervescent and transporting sakes, which Matsumoto said provided a roundness in the mouth and a slight viscosity.

During our tour of the brewery complex, which included a brand-new rice-polishing facility, Matsumoto led us to a small well and fountain. Its granite base was shaped like an urn and around its foot, flat black polished stones were arranged in a circle. Above the urn, a steady trickle of water

streamed from a delicate green-hued bamboo pipe known as a *sozu*.

In the large courtyard, the well was dwarfed by the hulking nineteenth-century wood-and-brick-clad brewery warehouses surrounding it. But what it symbolized—like the *miyamizu* wells of Nada—was the foundation on which brewing dynasties have been built. We reached for the long, bamboo-handled cup and took deep draughts of one of the most celebrated waters in the country. It was clear and cool, and so clean it was almost sweet.

At the Crossroads of Commerce

Fushimi water has long been the yin to miyamizu's yang, or, in the outmoded parlance of gender stereotypes, the "feminine" counterpart to the Nada region's full, cutting and dry, or "masculine" miyamizu. Made silky by its relative lack of minerals, it yields a softer, more delicate mouthfeel, a smooth consistency that sake expert Haruo Matsuzaki says is well suited to expressing umami. Hidehiko Matsumoto looked at his prized Fushimi water as the "plate, or vessel" onto or into which the flavors of the rice dissolve; his role, he told us, was to fine-tune his sake to draw out or mute those flavors to achieve the expression he was looking for.

Fushimi water's renown started much earlier than Nada's miyamizu water. In 863, Emperor Seiwa gave the name *gokosui* to the pure, soft and flavorful water that began to gush from the ground at Kyoto's Goko Shrine, a term that translates as "perfumed

Above *Moromi* tanks in the main fermentation room of Matsumoto Brewery. **Above right** The worn wooden facade of the brewery, which was established in 1791.

water from the palace." Wider commercial exploitation of this precious commodity came during that brief window of history at the end of the sixteenth century known as the Azuchi-Momoyama period, which bridged the chaotic and bloody Warring States era and the long, prosperous Edo period.

Feudal lord Toyotomi Hideyoshi, along with his boss Oda Nobunaga, had united the country by this point in history. After Nobunaga's death, Hideyoshi succeeded him, building a castle in Fushimi strategically located between Kyoto, Osaka and Nara. A hurly-burly economy sprang up around his castle, as well as along the land and water routes that connected the three key cities. Inns, shops and restaurants catered to tradespeople and travelers,

while the growing number of breweries took advantage of Fushimi's copious supplies of excellent water.

Not long after Hideyoshi's installation at Fushimi, Tokugawa Ieyasu seized power and set up his capital in Edo. The astounding growth of this new boom town led to skyrocketing consumer demand. To strengthen supply chains, the shogunate increased spending on infrastructure and transportation routes. This only enhanced Fushimi's importance as a *shukuba*, or way station town, on the Takasegawa Canal. The shogunate's imposition of the *sankin kotai* or alternative residence duty in 1635 meant that feudal lords and their extensive retinues were almost constantly on the road and in need of food, lodging and of course, sake.

Today Fushimi is home to close to twenty sake breweries, some of which date from the Edo period, including Gekkeikan, founded as Kasagiya in 1637, Kitagawa Honke, founded in 1657 as Funaya, and Matsumoto, which was founded in 1791. But that pales in comparison to what was once here. Sake writer Ayuko Yamaguchi noted in *Sake Today* magazine that Fushimi supported 83 breweries in 1657, producing 15,000 koku (more than 700,000

The traditional sitting room and garden at the Matsumoto Brewery.

gallons/2.7 million liters) of sake every year.

Those were the days when a steady flow of boat traffic along the Yodo River ferried sake from the port town Fushimi to Kyoto and Osaka via flat-bottomed *sanjukkoku-bune*, or "boats with a capacity for thirty koku (1,430 gallons/5,400 liters)." Yamaguchi tells us that when the boats of Kasagiya (modern-day Gekkeikan) and Funaya (Kitagawa-honke) docked, thirsty customers thronged to surrounding taverns to drink their fill of sake.

Geographic Blessings

One of the eleven wards of Kyoto, Fushimi rests on the southern end of the Kyoto basin, directly above an almost unimaginably large underground aquifer. Water has accumulated here in part thanks to gravity: Kyoto is surrounded on three sides by low mountains, which capture rainfall that then filters through these forested hills and into the city's Kamo and Katsura rivers. The southern portion of the city is more than 160 feet (50 m) lower in elevation than the northern part, so water flows to the south, both

above and below ground. The Kyoto water basin is estimated to contain more than twenty billion tons of water, stretching roughly seven-and-a-half miles (12 km) long east-west and more than twenty miles (32 km) north–south. Its deepest point—roughly half a mile (1 km) underground— lies directly to the south of Fushimi. Matsumoto told us that one can dig a hole pretty much anywhere in Fushimi and strike water. Fushimi's name itself is a reference to its hydrological blessings, meaning "hidden underground water."

While all of its water is considered superior, Matsumoto noted that its hardness and quality can vary depending on where the well is located, and how deep it is. Location can also be a source of one-upmanship. The Matsumoto family relocated its brewery here from the Higashiyama district of Kyoto in 1922 for its superior water. The small Fujioka Brewery (maker of the Sooku brand), is only about a three-minute drive east of Matsumoto. Yet owner-*toji* Masaaki Fujioka told Ry Beville of *Sake Today* magazine, "Of the twenty breweries here in Fushimi, we are the farthest east and upstream. I think our water is the highest quality. It's rich in certain minerals, but still very soft."

The Tsuki no Katsura Brand

Another Fushimi brewery that launched during the bustling economic expansion of the Edo period and still survives today is Masuda Tokubee Shoten, founded in 1675 and known for its Tsuki no Katsura brand. We have difficulty locating the brewery on the day of our visit, frustrated by conflicting GPS directives—not unusual in Japan when one is using a non-Japanese phone. Stumbling across Gekkeikan Brewery, we're awed by its massive sake tanks and the way the complex forms an entire neighborhood unto itself. By comparison, the traditional architecture of Masuda Tokubee Shoten, located on a quiet street, is a study in *shibumi*, or unobtrusive, deceptively simple beauty.

Before brewing sake, the Masuda family for generations sold rice and ran a guest house. As a merchant house, the family was granted freedom of entry and exit at the Imperial Palace until it moved from Kyoto to Tokyo in 1868.

One of its prized mementos is the remnant of a bombshell launched during the famous Toba-Fushimi Battle of 1868. Part of the civil war that ended the Edo era and restored power to the imperial court, the fight took place in the heart of Fushimi. Most of the breweries in Fushimi burned to the ground, the notable exception being Gekkeikan. Only about half of them, including Masuda Tokubee Shoten, managed to rebuild. Throughout these reversals of fortune, the vast, seemingly unending supply of underground Fushimi water remained a constant, continuing to lure brewers throughout the Edo and Meiji periods. Matsumoto Brewery relocated to Fushimi, Matsumoto told us, not just because the water was better and the brewery had outgrown its Higashiyama space, but

One of two Fushimi springs found at the Matsumoto Brewery gushes forth in this courtyard.

because "everything had been wiped out from the big battle, so there was this big, open area."

Today the brewery is headed by fourteenth-generation owner Tokubee Masuda (Tokubee is his preferred romanization, pronounced *toku-bay*), a slender gray-haired, mustached and relentlessly dapper man. His studies in Germany and France have made him, like Matsumoto, interested in expressing the character of his chosen rice and Fushimi water. One of the first things he did when he took over the family business in the early 1990s was acquire land and grow his own sake rice. Today he works with about ten different contract farmers.

On the day of our visit, we are ushered past the two *sugidama* cedar balls hanging beneath the brewery's eaves into the brewery building which is suffused with the faded elegance of old Kyoto. In a tatami-matted room, a graceful black vase holding a single red camellia is displayed on an antique slab of wood in front of an equally antique folding screen.

Masuda has not arrived, so we're guided through the brewery by French *kurabito* Guillaume Ozanne. His first portal into Japanese culture was bonsai, the art of growing and shaping ornamental dwarf trees. From there he entered the world of sake brewing. Deciding that his first brewery workplace was too automated for his tastes, he arrived at Masuda Tokubee Shoten in 2016, searching for something more handcrafted. Today he serves as the second in command to toji Satoshi Watanabe.

During the Edo period, the Masuda family made *doburoku*, a thick, sweet, unfiltered home brew. Tokubee's father, Keiichi Masuda, hoped to revive that style, using an old family recipe. But since doburoku was forbidden at the time because sake by law had to be filtered, in 1964 he became the first to bottle and sell what was known as *han seihin*, or a "semi-processed product." It was more filtered than doburoku but still textured and milky. Masuda cleverly re-named and marketed a product people considered half-baked and therefore unsellable, dubbing it *nigori*, or "cloudy," sake. Nigori went on to spark the Tsuki no Katsura brand's rise to national prominence. Masuda père began brewing in this style exclusively and aging his sake as well.

sake brewers and a sommelier joined forces to create Toki Sake, a group promoting aged and blended sake as a separate, luxury category of sake. They believe that aged sake should be appreciated the way great aged sherry and vintage port are in the West. To promote koshu as a category they developed certification standards that require koshu to be aged at least ten years and brewed with sake rice grown in Japan. And they'll be blending their own koshu under the Toki sake brand, for the first time creating a true "vintage" sake.

By now, Masuda himself has joined us in time for a tasting, which is held in a traditional wood-beamed room with a beautifully lit bar. Dressed in a smart white shirt, black trousers and an indigo Masuda Tokubee Shoten *haori* traditional jacket, he looks like the sake diplomat he is, as former chair of the Japan Sake and Shochu Makers Association's Global Strategy Commission and current audit and supervisory board member.

Masuda Tokubee Shoten itself has long cultivated a sophisticated, cosmopolitan culture, and perhaps as a result, has been a firm favorite of writers and artists. Film directors Akira Kurosawa and Yasujiro

Ozanne shows us the worn, metal *koshiki* rice steamer with its old-fashioned cedar lid and false-bottom heat diffuser. Like the large moromi filter that Masuda's father developed to strain out the larger lees from his nigori sake, it is an ingenious old adaptation still in use today. Everything in the room is diminutive, including the green *moromi* (mash) tanks; the brewery's total production is only eight hundred to nine hundred koku, about 4,000 gallons (18,000 liters).

Upstairs, under the massive, rough-hewn wooden eaves, Ozanne shows us stacks of ceramic jugs filled with fifty years' worth of *koshu*, or aged sake. Keiichi Masuda based his aging practices on information he gleaned from a seventeenth-century book, using earthenware casks with lacquer-covered paulownia-wood stoppers. For sake that is destined to be aged for decades in earthenware jars, Masuda says he eschews brilliantly scented yeasts, using Yamada Nishiki rice to brew a strong, undiluted junmai daiginjo.

In 2019, Masuda, six other

Ozu were habitués of the brewery's tasting room, and Ozu recreated Masuda's brewery for his 1961 film *The End of Summer*, a drama centered on the family of a sake brewery owner.

Masuda's own literary style has an impish element to it, which finds an outlet in his sake labels: his drip-pressed junmai daiginjo, elegant and laced with notes of lily and honeysuckle, is named Ha-wa-yu, which is "How are you?" in a Japanese accent. His Bikkuri Gyoten means "Totally Shocked," and Hofuku Zetto means "Rolling with Laughter." Other labels he's commissioned are more art-oriented, such as a sophisticated graphic series by noted French street artist Philippe Baudelocque.

Among the many literary testimonials the brewery has collected and placed on its website over time is this one, from the postwar Osaka-born novelist Ken Kaiko. It seems a fitting way to sum up not just Tsuki no Katsura, but the water of Fushimi itself—lithe, fresh and shimmering with purity:

"Most of today's sake is sticky and sweet, as if one's mouth has been drenched with honey. It has no backbone, no honor, and I hate it. It's not a man's drink. The only exception is the nigori sake of Mr. Tokubee Masuda, which unlike his modest, unaffected face, is well polished, and in spite of its strong character, flows down your throat like a rippling stream and makes your eyes open wide. On ice, there's that freshness. That integrity. It reminds me of when I go deep into the mountains to fish for char, that drink of water from my hand that trickles down from the rocks. And then, it's as if a small rainbow is shimmering in there, don't you think? Let's shake off the dust, and drink."

Fushimi Tasting Flight

Sake name: Tsuki no Katsura "Iwai"
Sake type: Junmai
Brewery: Masuda Tokubee, Kyoto Prefecture
One of two local Kyoto sake rice varieties, the brewery grows Iwai in the northern Tanba region for this sake. Expect delicate fruit aromas and a moderately savory backbone from 80 percent polished Iwai.

Sake name: Sooku "Tankan Wataribune"
Sake type: Junmai
Brewery: Fujioka Brewery, Kyoto Prefecture
Toji Masaaki Fujioka enlists only one brewery worker in the brewing season and makes only 200 koku (9,500 gallons/3,600 liters), so this may be hard to find. A herbal backbone and bright acidity, perfect with charcuterie.

Sake name: Iwai
Sake type: Junmai ginjo
Brewery: Tamanohikari, Kyoto Prefecture
Tamanohikari helped lead the 1960s junmai sake revival and today maintains an all-junmai product list. This sake is in the classic Fushimi style, informed by the local soft water, and is elegant and crisp on the palate.

Chapter Twelve

Mountains and Terroir

Japan consists of close to seven thousand tree-covered islands scattered along the Pacific rim of east Asia like a moss-beaded necklace. The great cities of Tokyo or Osaka may dominate our imagination, but in fact most of the country—70 percent—is covered by sparsely inhabited mountainous areas. And a mere 11 percent of the country's land is suitable for farming.

In sake, the image of a mountain or the character for mountain (山, pronounced *yama, san* or *zan*) appears in countless sake brands and brewery names. Hidehiko Matsumoto, former master brewer of Matsumoto Brewery in Kyoto, says, "the only breweries that have survived in Japan are breweries with great water." And that water has most likely originated on the slopes of a revered mountain or mountain range.

The mountain that supplies water to Hiroshima's Kamoizumi Brewery is one example. Its name Ryuozan ("Dragon Mountain") alludes to the Chinese belief that the dragon god controls both water and weather. The livelihoods of all villagers, especially farmers, were inextricably linked to the mountain and its waters. Local Hiroshima lore describes the farmers' custom of praying to the dragon god enshrined in Ryuozan for bountiful water and good weather: supplicants would climb the mountain with five-nights' worth of firewood strapped to their backs, then camp there, conducting a fire-lit prayer vigil until they ran out of wood.

At the Foot of Tenzan Mountain

The day of our visit to Tenzan Brewery in Saga Prefecture on the island of Kyushu, we have time for a rushed chicken-and-egg *oyako-don* rice bowl at Fukuoka's Hakata Station. Nancy is cotton-headed from a night in a stuffy smoking-allowed room at our business hotel (a rare booking mishap) while Michael, clear-headed and sake rice–obsessed, locks on to his target for the day, Saga no Hana ("Flower of Saga") rice. It's Saga Prefecture's first sake rice, another Yamada Nishiki cross-breed and the second-most cultivated rice in the prefecture after Yamada Nishiki. Nancy makes note of this while marveling at how, even at a fast-casual place like this, care is taken to provide two perfect rectangles of fluffy *tamagoyaki* rolled omelet as a starter.

Located in the small former castle town of Ogi in Saga Prefecture, Tenzan Brewery takes its name from the 3,400-foot (1,000 m) mountain that rises above it. Written with the kanji 天山, the literal meaning of the name is "Heaven Mountain" or "Sky Mountain," carrying with it religious and imperial overtones. Tenzan's granite and serpentine slopes are the source of the brewery's clear spring water, some of which crashes down as part of the 246-foot (75 m) high Kiyomizu waterfall. The fall feeds a spring close by the Gion River, on the banks of which the brewery is sited. These abundant waters,

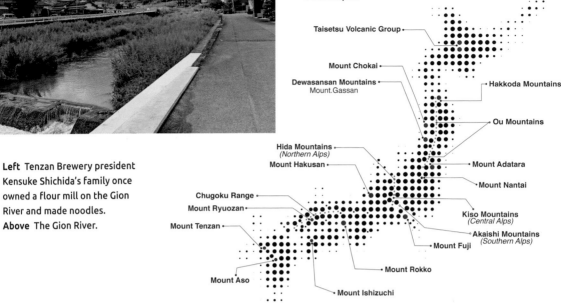

Mountains and Sake

Mountains have long been connected with sake. Here are the some of the mountains and ranges that help shape sake profiles across Japan.

- Taisetsu Volcanic Group
- Mount Chokai
- Dewasansan Mountains
- Mount.Gassan
- Hakkoda Mountains
- Ou Mountains
- Hida Mountains (Northern Alps)
- Mount Hakusan
- Mount Adatara
- Mount Nantai
- Chugoku Range
- Mount Ryuozan
- Kiso Mountains (Central Alps)
- Mount Tenzan
- Akaishi Mountains (Southern Alps)
- Mount Fuji
- Mount Rokko
- Mount Aso
- Mount Ishizuchi

Left Tenzan Brewery president Kensuke Shichida's family once owned a flour mill on the Gion River and made noodles.
Above The Gion River.

rich in calcium and magnesium, are the key ingredient in Tenzan's robust sake. In acknowledgment of both the mountain and its water, each brewing year begins and ends with a pilgrimage to Kiyomizu waterfall where *toji* Jun Goto, staff brewers and—at the end of the season—owner Kensuke Shichida, pray to the god of Tenzan for its continued blessings.

For the Shichida family, which has operated the brewery for six generations, linking its sake with this revered mountain underscores its "masculine" sake taste profile while also evoking the strength and spiritual purity of Japan's famous mountains.

At Saga Station we transfer from our shinkansen bullet train to a bright yellow commuter train that looks slightly Hogwarts Express in its quaintness, especially as it is filled with uniformed school kids returning home after a short Saturday school day. The rice fields of the Saga Plain that we pass look steamy under the searing Kyushu sun, the high heat enhanced by off-the-charts humidity. Saga is believed to be the point of earliest contact between

Japan and the Asian continent, and one of the first areas to pick up China's wet rice cultivation, sometime around 300 BC. The fertile Saga Plain is the rice-producing center of Kyushu. Emerging onto the platform, we see Shichida awaiting our arrival.

Unlike the plain we've traveled through to get here, the microclimate surrounding the brewery, thanks in part to the rushing Gion River—one of three that fan down off of Tenzan and drain into the Saga Plain— feels lush, almost tropical. To the northwest sits the mountain, blue-green in the clouds and mists that hover near its peak. Inside the brewery offices we meet Shichida's father Toshihide. Although the building's exterior has been modernized, this room feels like a nineteenth-century gentleman's study, lined with bookshelves, old photographs and a globe. Only the flat-screen television seems out of place. As is typical in the Japanese countryside, it doesn't have air-conditioning. We're served green tea and the traditional azuki-bean jelly confection *yokan*. Ogi is famous for this product; there are more than twenty specialty shops that sell it, one of which belongs to an arm of the Shichida family.

Kensuke and Toshihide's branch of the family began as operators of a water mill on the Gion, serving as flour millers and noodle makers for high-end restaurants. They also milled rice. When an ancient local sake brewery went under in 1875, its owner made a strong plea to then-president Toshizo Shichida and his wife Tsuki to buy the brewery and all its tools. Reluctantly, the couple found themselves pulled into a new business.

Their architect son, Shuichi, was involved in the construction of three different warehouses in the style of three different eras: Meiji (1868–1912), Taisho (1912–1926) and Showa (1926–1989) all of which are still in use. By 1960, sake making was Tenzan's one and only pursuit. Today it's best known for a rich and juicy style of sake that can compete with the copious amount of shochu liquor that flows in Kyushu.

It was during a trip to visit wineries in France about fifteen years ago, Shichida says, that he began to understand the concept of terroir. "We saw how wine was being made from grapes grown right there in front of us. It was so simple and easy to understand, so natural. It made a huge impression."

His interest in wine and terroir has also involved Shichida in the movement to develop a premium sparkling sake (*awazake*), which he hopes will one day rival champagne in taste, effervescence and as an expression of terroir. It's still a developing craft, Shichida admits, but there are now twenty-five breweries that belong to an association that promotes awa sparkling sake. Since there is no dosage (the addition of sugar to balance out acidity), sparkling sake tends to be drier than some champagnes but still not overly dry. And Shichida would like to craft a drink with finer, longer-lasting bubbles. In

sparkling sake's favor, he points out that it is much easier to pair with food than wine or champagne.

"You think that wine goes with cheese," Shichida continues, but suggests comparing a wine and cheese pairing to a sake and cheese pairing. "Pairing wine with cheese is like karate—one of them has to 'win,' while with sake—not just sparkling, but sake in general—it's more like the martial art aikido," he says. "Each uses the other to its advantage."

After his trip to France, to emphasize the characteristics of the Saga soil in his sakes, Shichida began cultivating relationships with ten local contract farmers. With the help of the Saga Prefectural Agricultural Research Laboratory he formed a rice cultivation study group. Master brewer Goto and other brewery workers collaborate with farmers to improve their Saga Yamada Nishiki harvests, gathering regularly for study sessions and field visits. "The idea is to give feedback to farmers and establish traceability," Shichida explains. "That allows them to promote the sake made from their own rice, which is also very motivating." And, with sake brewed using rice grown in his own prefecture, using water that flows down from the mountain visible from his brewery, he too, hopes to express the local terroir.

Michael, however, is foiled in his quest to learn more about the prefectural hybrid rice Saga no Hana. It is handled by the JA farmer's cooperative so isn't prioritized by Shichida in the way his contract-grown Yamada Nishiki is, although it is

The award-winning band of brewers at Tenzan Sake Brewery, Saga Prefecture.

Kuheiji Kuno assessing sake in his brewery. Kuno is influenced by the wines of Burgundy and its tradition of terroir.

used in Tenzan's sake, along with other local sake rices. But how much does it really matter whether the locally grown rice Shichida brews with is a Saga hybrid like Saga no Hana, or one native to a different part of Japan, like Yamada Nishiki, but grown locally? This is the kind of question that arises often when one culture tries to apply another culture's organizing principles to their own: it's an imperfect fit.

Another example of this imperfect fit is the fact that strictly speaking, sake rice lacks the "vintage" aspect of wine grapes. Sake retailer and Sake Samurai Beau Timken points out that while certain wines are celebrated for their standout vintages, there are no such distinctions in the sake world. "Farmers and brewers only recall the bad years, not the good years," he says.

One brewer who would like to change this is fifteenth-generation Banjo Brewery owner-toji Kuno Kuheiji. His goal is not only to educate sake drinkers to know the different sake-rice varieties "the way wine drinkers know the difference between a chardonnay and a pinot noir," but to pay attention to rice vintages as well. He prints the rice production year on every bottle of his Kamoshibito Kuheiji line. We've also mentioned Sohomare's blending of different vintages of aged kimoto sake, and the Toki group of brewers who are setting the standard for sherry-like aged vintage sake. The word "vintage" has crept into the language of sake, but it means different things to different people.

At Tenzan, Shichida points out that although forging close ties between brewer and farmer might seem novel in postwar Japan, it isn't the first time a

progressive brewer has tried to revive old ways. His grandfather, the third-generation president, was a passionate believer in the importance of increasing agricultural knowledge and nurturing farm leaders, especially after the devastation wrought by World War II. He launched an agricultural university in 1946, which even oversaw the cultivation of Omachi rice, unheard of in the early 1950s. But just a little over three years after it had been launched, a massive flood and typhoon struck Kyushu, killing over one thousand people. "Everything was washed away, the school, our brewery, the entire campus," says Shichida. "Our dreams were washed away, too. There just wasn't enough money to rebuild the university."

During the short cab ride back to Ogi Station we see preparations underway for the evening's big shrine festival, which this year marks its 703rd anniversary. We lean back against the white-doily covered seat, enjoying a brief respite of air conditioning while, incongruously, country music streams from the radio. Each of us has a slight regret: Michael over the dearth of Saga no Hana intel, and Nancy over the lack of time to visit at least one of Ogi's twenty yokan shops.

Dinner with the Miyasaka Family

One of the best demonstrations of the synergy between mountains, sake and food culture happens in Nagano Prefecture during our visit to Miyasaka Brewery. Nagano is home to three large mountain ranges that are known collectively as the Japanese Alps, which provide a playground for winter sports and served as the backdrop for the 1998 Nagano Winter Olympics. Foraged mountain greens and the tradition of pickling to keep food stores available through the winter months gave rise to

Left Kumi Miyasaka's sake lees hot pot (recipe on page 214), meshes seamlessly with the freshly brewed Masumi sakes on the table. **Right** Bottles of Domaine Senkin sake, with Nature pictured in the foreground.

sakes that go well with this robust, flavorful cuisine.

Our first night in Suwa, where Miyasaka Brewery is based, we're invited to the Miyasaka family home for a dinner that pairs local ingredients and the house ingredient, sake lees, with various Masumi sakes. Four generations of Miyasakas are in attendance: company advisor Kazuhiro, age ninety-one, formerly dressed and proper; his genial son, president Naotaka; grandson Katsuhiko, who now serves as the president's office manager for the brewery; and Katsuhiko and his wife Mana's son, Issei, age five. The atmosphere is relaxed, as though we've been drawn into an inner circle of family warmth. Naotaka's wife Kumi, a small, cheerful woman and a highly skilled cook, assisted by Mana, flits back and forth from the partially open kitchen to serve course after course, joining us at the table to offer detailed explanations of each dish. One of them is a just-harvested stir-fry of meaty shiitake mushrooms, still-crunchy medallions of *nagaimo* yam and mild, long green peppers. It is both earthy and umami-rich, especially paired with Masumi's slightly cloudy sparkling Origarami junmai ginjo, which combines the juicy, cider-like qualities of a pet-nat wine and the umami undertow of sake.

The warm days and cold nights of the Nagano highlands produce some of the most intensely flavored vegetables we've tasted during our travels; Kumi tells us about the tradition of "snow cabbage," in which the brassica is left unharvested in the cold until the sugars concentrate to keep the cabbage from freezing. Local TV stations provide updates on the annual snow-cabbage harvest, like an avidly followed winter sport. Many Nagano residents keep root cellars for overwintering vegetables.

While we can pick up on the intense flavors and sweetness that are common characteristics of Nagano vegetables, it's harder to generalize about a specific prefectural sake profile, despite our earlier description of how Nagano sake used to be characterized. Such blanket generalizations are no longer true, not just in Nagano, but throughout Japan, as advances in brewing techniques and shifting consumer tastes are shaping sake in similar ways across the country. Not every sake in Niigata is going to be crisp and dry just as not every sake in Kyushu is going to be rich and sweet, as older stereotypes dictated. But what still exists is the individual mark of the master brewer, his or her influences, tastes and goals on making sake.

Kumi has just arrived from the kitchen, bearing a silver *nabe*, or hot-pot dish, containing pork simmered in a rich broth of sake lees with thin strips of daikon. It gives up a sharp fermented flavor that's cut by the fattiness of the pork, and the sweetness of the winter daikon, perfect with an undiluted Miyasaka Aiyama junmai ginjo. Aiyama rice, like Omachi, has generated an avid fan base because of its ability to express a complex balance of sweetness and umami. Next, Kumi whips up a creamy blender dessert of sake lees with milk and apricot jam, while Katsuhiko plies us with next-level sake concoctions: a warmed Masumi *usunigori* (slightly cloudy) sake spiked with cinnamon, and a fresh *arabashiri* (first-run) sake with yuzu and black pepper. The evening ends late, with the entire group gathered around the piano as Michael improvises, his rhythmic chord progressions swelling and diminishing like ocean waves.

The Advocates (and Skeptics) of Sake Terroir

Just as Shichida has developed close relationships with local rice farmers to strengthen his sake's expression of regionality, so has Miyasaka Brewery. Most of the rice it brews with is grown by local Nagano farmers, and most of it is Nagano's own Miyama Nishiki. Every year, selected Masumi staff and Miyasaka family members join rice farmers in the fields to help plant in the spring and harvest rice in the fall. The farmers, in turn, visit the brewery to witness their product being transformed into sake.

Not only does the sake makers' embrace of the concept of terroir usually lead back to France, it also takes many different forms. Kuno Kuheiji, owner-toji of Banjo Brewery, was so smitten with the wines of Burgundy that he established his own winery, Domaine Kuheiji, in Morey-St. Denis, a Côte de Nuits sub-region. He wants his sake, like his wine, to be an expression of place, and for consumers to appreciate the Yamada Nishiki of Hyogo and the Omachi of Okayama the way wine drinkers seek out the best pinot noir from Vosne Romanée or chardonnay from Montrachet. Although his Omachi sake is not domaine grown, he has bought land in Hyogo to farm his own Yamada Nishiki, and has recently begun brewing there as well.

Kyoto brewer Hidehiko Matsumoto, who earlier in his career worked at Banjo Brewery, also believes that sake should be an expression of land and water. "The water of Fushimi is our terroir," he told us before he departed Matsumoto Brewery.

During our visit with Matsumoto, over green tea poured from a glass teapot, the brewer, dressed in a luxurious cashmere suit and black sweater, talked about his terroir-focused ID series: three bottles brewed from three different parcels of Toku-A rice fields in Hyogo Prefecture. The series grew out of the process of trying to understand why the Yamada Nishiki of one year brewed a better sake than others, and realizing that his investigations led back to the fields and to the farmers. Six years earlier, Matsumoto had begun visiting Hyogo rice fields, linking what was happening there to the moods and feelings expressed in his bottles. Although he admitted that the ideal expression of terroir would be the combination of his Fushimi water and Yamada Nishiki grown on his own domaine, he opted for the best Yamada Nishiki available—from the Toku-A farmers of Tojo who had supplied the brewery for the last thirty years. And, he pointed out, Hyogo is a close neighbor of Fushimi.

Matsumoto went into detail on how the three different parcel locations of the ID series affect their flavor, tone, balance and expressiveness, as well as different rice-field plowing methods, representing the new breed of owner-toji who thinks more attention should be paid to farming to make better sake.

In Yamagata Prefecture, president-toji Tomonobu Mitobe has, like a growing number of his peers, expanded his own rice-growing program, launching a new business called Mitobe Inazo. The name is a pun, he explains. Just before entering junior high school in 1985, a new five-thousand yen note was issued by the Bank of Japan with the likeness of Inazo Nitobe, a famous agricultural economist, educator and diplomat. Based on the similarity of the names Nitobe and Mitobe, Mitobe's classmates gave him the nickname Inazo. "It sounded uncool at the time because agriculture was not cool for junior high school kids," Mitobe says. "It literally means 'the rice maker.' But it seems so cool to me now."

Mitobe Inazo is mostly devoted to growing the prefectural hybrid rices Dewasansan and Yuki

Tasting the Sohomare lineup with president Jun Kono at Sohomare Brewery, Tochigi. The sakes feature *Toku-A* Yamada Nishiki crafted using the *kimoto* method.

Megami as well as the Yamagata heirloom rice Kame no O. In the three years since founding the company, Mitobe has increased the domaine rice content of his sake to about 40 percent. "I want to make it 80 percent in ten years," he says.

Not everyone is convinced by this obsession with terroir—which one might view as a foreign gloss on brewer Tadayoshi Toshimori's passionate call for sake makers to return to making local *jizake*, "using your own rice—specifically local rice—your own local water and your own techniques." For many brewers, one of the appeals of the terroir concept is that it is a way of making sake more relatable to Westerners. This is not insignificant. Though sake is becoming more commonplace in global restaurants, for most Westerners it's still a mystery veiled behind an unreadable language and opaque classifications.

During our visit with Sohomare Brewery's Jun Kono and his son Michihiro, they make the case against "local." "Yes, brewers are increasingly interested in buying local rice," says Jun. "But we want to buy rice from the best in

Sohomare's main building, designed by Hidetoshi Ohno, the Tokyo University architecture professor of Kono's wife Junko.

Japan." Michiro points out that ultimately, unlike wine grapes, rice is a dried ingredient, so it can be transported easily, with little loss of freshness or quality. "In the Nara or Heian eras [710–1185] people would bring good quality rice to the metropolis to make sake." Viewed in this historical context, the Konos see nothing wrong with continuing the tradition of transporting the best rice from its place of origin. The proof, they would say, is in the refined, elegant sake they are known for.

We think about the great sakes we've tasted on our travels. Classic brews—rich, layered, complex—like those made by Sohomare or Kikuhime, are Japan's equivalent of old-world French Bordeaux wines. Yet increasingly, the younger, sometimes cult brewers, obsessed with expressing terroir in their sakes, are grabbing the spotlight. Still, most will tell you that although rice is important, it's really water more than anything else that defines terroir in sake.

Not far from Sohomare, in the town of Sakura, two brothers, Kazuki and Masato Usui, are applying the domaine-style concept of growing and fermenting on the same land at Senkin Brewery, or as they call it, Domaine Senkin. The first brewery to make high-acid, sweet, tart and fruity white-wine-like sakes in Japan, their interest in terroir is a natural by-product of Kazuki's background as a wine sommelier. Their *shikomi mizu* (brewing water) and the water that nourishes their rice is one and the same. All their rice—Yamada Nishiki, Kame no O and Omachi, is grown by local farmers.

"Until about five years ago,

we did use Hyogo Yamada Nishiki or Okayama Omachi," admits master brewer Masato Usui. "Then we began to ask the local farmers to grow these rice varieties for us. It was initially hard for them, but they are highly skilled, and they went to Hyogo and Okayama to study with farmers there."

He thinks that as the farmers' knowledge and comfort with growing these rice varieties has grown, the local rice they use to brew for their Senkin label has gradually reached a quality equal to the Hyogo Yamada Nishiki and Okayama Omachi they use for their Usui label. Although the rice varieties are the same, and comparable in quality, Usui stresses that the products from two different regions are completely different—in the hardness of the rice, the speed of water absorption and aroma.

His preference is to brew with rice "made by a farmer whose face I know, compared to a rice grown in far-off Kansai." There's not only the natural affinity of rice with the local water it has been grown with, he adds, but also an emotional affinity. "To drink together at a party with the farmers of our home area, to talk about how their sons are doing, it's a really special and intimate relationship," he says. "To touch Yamada Nishiki grown here in Sakura motivates you; it's like watering a long-neglected garden, or like a chef knowing the farmers who grow his vegetables."

Yet for all this talk about rice, Usui, like Matsumoto, agrees that ultimately "terroir" resides not in the rice, but in the water. The value of his water is like the value of a winery's grapes, which locate the wine in a specific place. "Senkin sake," he says, "can only be made here, not anywhere else."

Terroir Flight

Sake name: Tenzan "Jizake"
Sake type: Tokubetsu junmai genshu
Brewery: Tenzan Brewery, Saga Prefecture
Made with local Sagan no Hana and Reiho rice, left undiluted to bring out its inherent rice flavors. Full, rich and earthy.

Sake name: Nature
Sake type: Kimoto junmai
Brewery: Domaine Senkin, Tochigi Prefecture
Water is the terroir of brothers and owner-toji Kazuki and Masato Usui. Made with proprietary yeasts, Kame no O rice, and fermented in wooden kioke tanks.

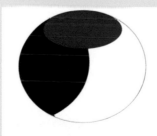

SENKIN **NATURE 2021** Nouveau 2020 Rice Vintage

Sake name: Domain Taka
Sake type: Junmai daiginjo
Brewery: Nagayama Honke Brewery, Yamaguchi Prefecture
Takahiro Nagayama is the mastermind behind this brilliant attempt at defining his terroir. Structure and concentration are the key words for this sake. Made with Yamada Nishiki rice grown outside the brewery's doors and medium-hard water from the Akiyoshidai karst plateau, this is balanced with subtle aromas; a versatile sake that matches a wide array of dishes (or just sip and enjoy on its own).

Chapter Thirteen

Going Organic

At the sun-filled noisy Vin Mon Lapin, one of Montreal's best natural wine bars, a lone sake jumps out on a wine list filled with spontaneously fermented pet-nats from France, low-intervention chenin blancs from South Africa and orange wines from Friuli. We have to try it, of course. It's an organic Katori 90 Namagen (unpasteurized and undiluted) from Terada Honke Brewery in Chiba Prefecture, described on the importer's label as a "rare pre-modern sake." We learn that the sommelier here, Vanya Filipovic, met Terada Honke's master brewer Masaru Terada on a winemaker's tour of the Republic of Georgia and they bonded over their love of drink made with minimal intervention. The sake, made with rice polished to a rustic 90 percent, is rich, savory and complex and it partners seamlessly with a dish of tagliatelle napped with a ragu of whelks and sautéed ramp pesto.

The presence of this sake on this menu makes complete sense once we visit Terada Honke and meet Terada, its twenty-fourth-generation owner-*toji*. The visit to Chiba has personal significance for Nancy; her maternal grandmother Tomiko was born and raised a few hours south of here. Her family sold fishing nets and brewed both sake and soy sauce. Tomiko recalled her longed-for Chiba peninsula homeland in nostalgic *tanka* poems.

Tall, lightly bearded and soft spoken, Terada is dressed in the *kurabito* outfit of indigo *haori* jacket, brewing apron and patterned cotton *tenugui* head scarf. He greets us on this hot July afternoon in an ascetically furnished, cavernous wood-beamed room. A former nature-documentary cameraman, he met his future wife Satomi, the middle of three Terada sisters, at a Tokyo event for the macrobiotic restaurant she worked for. Before the two had any plans to marry, he visited her family's Terada Honke brewery to help out with rice harvesting and sake making. He and Satomi

married in 2004, and the new husband took on the Terada name and head-of-family duties.

Terada Honke is part of a small offshoot of sake making known as *shizen-ha*, or "the natural clique," brewers who, as well as brewing with local rice and water, add another element: low- or no-pesticide or chemical fertilize. Like other breweries in this group, Terada is pushing sake into more wine-like directions. But he's blazing his own trail into truly sweet, sour and wild territory, making sake with barely polished germinated brown rice, wild yeast and his own house-cultivated *koji* mold.

The secret to that rich and complex Katori 90, for example, in addition to the wild yeast and koji, is its *kimoto* starter method and extremely long fermentation: fifty days for the starter, and another thirty for the main mash, made possible by low-temperature winter fermentation, which keeps yeast activity reined in.

Another thing that makes Terada Honke unique is that its main focus is on glorifying the process of

Left A dragonfly perches on a rice stalk in Akita Prefecture, one sign of a healthy ecosystem. **Right** Akita Prefecture is one of the biggest rice producers in the country. **Below** Wooden *kioke* fermentation tanks at Aramasa Brewery, a company that embraces strict organic practices, eschewing any type of additive.

fermentation itself as much as its final products, especially the mighty microbes that can create both rot and the most elixir-like sakes. The Teradas tout the health benefits of fermentation through various channels: the brewery's sake; its fermented-food-heavy, plant-based café; a nationally marketed fermented yogurt product; and product lines based on sake lees and koji molds. Their book, *Koji, amazake, sake kasu no hakko gohan* (Koji, amazake and sake-lees fermented foods), extols the ancient wisdom and virtue of the "fermentation life," noting that throughout history the Japanese have used the magical powers of fermentation not just for food and drink, but for clothing and shelter as well.

Fermented leaves produced indigo dyes for textiles, while aged and fermented soil was used as a plaster for dirt walls.

The brewery's embrace of all things fermented happened relatively recently, during the tenure of its twenty-third-generation president and Masaru's father-in-law, Keisuke Terada. Descended from the Shiga Prefecture Omi merchants (see page 44), Keisuke began suffering from gastrointestinal troubles in the early 1980s, undergoing a number of hospitalizations and surgeries. He changed his diet, discovered the healing power of natural and fermented foods and grew stronger. Natural fermentation in sake making had largely disappeared, but Keisuke decided he would return to the pre-industrialized ways of doing it.

In his 2007 book *Hakko-do: sakagura no biseibutsu ga oshiete kureta ningen no ikikata* (The fermentation way of life), Keisuke described the teeming world of microbial fermentation as though it were a selfless, utopian society. He explained that looking at fermentation means looking at life—a life in which microbes co-exist in diverse ways, support each other and make use of each other. "When their work is done," he says, "they give up their place to the next microorganism and disappear."

Keisuke's influence on the course of the brewery and his beloved status in the family is apparent in the framed photograph of him that sits on an antique wooden chest, next to a framed calligraphic work that reads "Thank you very much!" over and over. His fermentation diet did help him recover from his ailments, but he finally succumbed to pneumonia in 2012.

Masaru Terada continues Keisuke's natural brewing practices, making even more strongly flavored and wild sakes than those produced during Keisuke's time. But he continues to make Gonin Musume, the first sake Keisuke produced after recovering from his long illness. Determined to use organic rice, Keisuke located an organic farmer in Yamagata Prefecture through an agricultural magazine and created the brewery's first organic, yamahai-style sake. Another Terada Honke label is Daigo no Shizuku sake, made with the *bodaimoto* starter method. Another, Musubi, is brewed with germinated brown rice.

On a tour of the beautiful eighty-year-old pine-and-cedar-constructed brewery, Terada shows us a cheesecloth-lined wooden barrel filled with soaking unpolished brown rice, pointing out the little horns that have begun to sprout after about five days soaking in water. "This helps the rice get a little softer, and it's easier to ferment," he explains,

The well-known Osaka woodworking shop that made this wooden rice steamer for Terada Honke came back from the brink of extinction thanks to renewed interest in traditional brewing techniques.

as we notice a slightly sour, cheesy, aroma wafting off the tank. After the five days of soaking in summer, or a week to ten days in the winter, it will be steamed and brewed into his Musubi line of sake. Since brown rice promotes very strong lactic acid activity, Terada explains, he can brew it during the hot summer with no danger of spoiling.

Next, he shows us the room where the kimoto starter is made in short wooden barrels. Brewing here begins in November when it is colder to allow low-temperature fermentation. Terada leads his crew in stirring the kimoto three to four times a day while singing a traditional brewing song from Hyogo Prefecture's Tanba Toji Guild. He adopted this ancient tradition a dozen years ago and says, "I do think it makes it easier, because it helps us keep time and stay in the same rhythm." A page on the brewery's website notes that singing songs also "transmits our joy to the sake."

We hop in Terada's van to make the ten-minute drive to see a few of his rice fields, which total a little more than 2,000 square yards (1,600 m²) and accounts for only about 5 percent of the total amount of rice he uses per year. He grows two heirloom strains, Shinriki and Kame no O and an old local table rice, called Chiba Nishiki. Heirloom varieties are much more difficult to grow, but worth it for what they bring to sake, Terada believes. Both Kame no O and Shinriki, he says, have a complexity that he likes, a slight sweetness and they produce an acidity that is a hallmark of his sakes. He'd like to increase the ratio of rice he grows himself, partly because even though he pays twice as much for organic rice as for non-organic, it's still hard to convince farmers to grow troublesome rice varieties like these.

In his pesticide-free rice fields he depends on the ability of beneficial insects to vanquish the type of insects that destroy crops. "There are a small number of predators, but there are also other bugs that eat those predators," he says. He will, though, plant a cover crop of Chinese milk vetch, which is well suited to wet paddies. A mainstay of agroecological farming, cover crops convert nitrogen in the

Above Masaru Terada breaks up the *koji* rice in his Chiba Prefecture brewery. **Below** Terada welcomes us to his brewery, which embraces all-natural fermentation in its sake and food products. Terada's wife, Satomi, runs a plant-based café, Ufufu, on the premises.

air into a natural fertilizer the plant can absorb in the soil, enriching the plant and improving its nutrient uptake.

Acquaintances passing by call out in greeting; in the distance we spot a white heron perched in the fields and hear a small frog croaking. It's easy to believe, surveying this peaceful tableau, that like the microbes in Terada's sake, all living beings, human and non-human are, as his father-in-law once said, "co-existing in diverse ways, supporting and making use of each other."

Aramasa Brewery: A Return to Edo-style Brewing

On the March day of our visit to Aramasa Brewery, we stroll from our hotel near the Akita City train station west to the Asahi River, grabbing a quick lunch of *tororoimo* (grated mountain yam) soba for Nancy and curry udon for Michael, and then walking south along the river until we spot signs in the Omachi neighborhood proclaiming it to be "Akita Beautiful Sake Kingdom." Akita Prefecture is justly proud of its rice and its sake and residents like to claim they have the highest per capita daily consumption of sake in the country.

Yet until the age of thirty, eighth-generation

Aramasa owner-toji Yusuke Sato was not among sake's fans. "For no good reason, I used to look down on it, claiming it didn't taste good," Sato recalls. He earned a degree in English literature at Tokyo University and did a stint in journalism. Covering left-wing politics and the counter-culture led to an interest in organic foods and in traditional Japanese culture. Then, on vacation in Shizuoka Prefecture, he tasted a bottle of Isojiman *honjozo* sake made for the local market. "I was shocked at how beautiful it was," he says. "It completely turned around the way I thought about sake."

Sato returned home and told his father he wanted to enter the brewery, which was founded in 1852. His father's reaction, he says, was, "Do it!" Sato spent a year studying brewing at the National Research Institute of Brewing in Hiroshima before joining the family brewery in 2007 at age thirty-two. Working alongside toji Takashi Suzuki, he systematically set about remaking the brewery into his dream craft brewery. His own interest in traditional Japanese culture led him to convert the brewery's production from regular to premium craft sake, turning the clock back from industrial to more hand-crafted practices.

As Sato explains, postwar industrialized sake relied on petroleum-based energy and brewing materials, production machinery, chemical lactic acid, commercial yeasts and often rice transported from afar, resulting in a low-cost, standardized brew. He considers this entire system unsustainable. His dream is instead to return to traditional Edo-era techniques of brewing with local ingredients made by harnessing the natural energy of the land and sun, with a diversity of local rice varieties.

Reverting to traditional methods, he explains, "is very difficult because you need a tremendous amount of technique—you have to proceed more by feeling. In that way," he adds, "we're really no match for the people of the Edo period. They didn't know the science, so they brewed by feeling. I want to return to that style of making sake." One of his favorite quotations is from his fifth-generation ancestor Uhee Sato (1865–1946), a brewing technology wizard who nevertheless still recognized the role of the mystical in sake. Uhee, Sato likes to point out, sat— along with the father of Japanese whisky and founder of the Nikka distillery Masataka Taketsuru—at the top of their class at Osaka High School of Engineering, later to become the faculty of engineering at Osaka University. The oft-quoted line of Uhee's, which is in line with Yusuke's desire to return to the intuitive, is, "Sake making is a matter of faith."

Aramasa is housed in a nineteenth-century riverside brewery to which a modern, wood-paneled front office has been appended. After our interview, Sato takes us on a tour of the brewery, explaining his progress as a brewer. In 2009, his first year at the brewery, he began brewing with Akita Prefecture rice and reviving old varieties. Then he decided to only use the brewery's famous Yeast No. 6, considered the forebear of all modern commercial yeasts in use. His ancestor Uhee is considered one of the originators of the yeast in the 1920s.

The *kioke* Edo-style wooden barrels at Aramasa are made with prized Yoshino cedar.

Are *Shizen-ha* Sakes the Natural Wines of Sake?

Though it's easy to equate *shizen-ha* ("natural clique") sakes to natural wine, some say this misrepresents sake. "There really isn't an equation," says Alex Bernardo, a wine merchant in San Francisco who carries artisanal wines and sakes. The natural wine movement was a reaction to an industry that had become industrialized, its wines adulterated to a degree not seen in today's conventional sake. Rice cultivation for premium sakes is done on such a small and careful scale, he notes, that even when pesticides are applied, amounts are moderate compared to the industrial scale seen in large wineries. Most brewers, he says, don't feel organic rice makes much of a difference in the quality of the final product.

He shifted to all-junmai sake and added the kimoto style of starter. In 2013, he purchased his first *kioke,* or Edo-style wooden barrels. Today, more than half of his tanks, forty-four in total (the largest number in use by a brewery in Japan), are kioke made with prized Yoshino cedar by a company called Fujii Woodwork in Sakai City, Osaka. It's the last cooperage of its kind, where the average age of its craftsmen is close to seventy, and just one of countless Japanese craft workshops that are threatened with extinction. Yet there is a bright spot. After witnessing a small renaissance in traditional brewing practices and corresponding kioke sales (Senkin and Terada Honke both use Fujii's barrels) an announced imminent closure has been postponed.

Sato extols the natural benefits of the wooden barrels, like the antioxidant-packed micronutrients that they contain, comparing their benefits to those of the natural lactic acid that flourishes in his kimoto sake. Because of these microorganisms, he explains, it has a much longer shelf-life than non-kimoto styles.

In 2017 the brewery began to manage its own rice fields, coaxing farmers to begin organic rice production. "To put it simply, technique is the barrier," says Sato, explaining why it's hard to get Japanese farmers to grow organic rice. Part of their hesitation might be due to the fact that when Sato says "organic," he means the most militant kind. While cutting out pesticides and fertilizers is expected with organics, he also does not believe in any type of organic fertilizer or natural amendments. At the suggestion of organic compost, a look of horror passes over his face and he says vehemently, "No, never! Compost brings disease and contains so much nitrogen. We hate nitrogen. The trees of the forest don't need fertilizer, do they?" he asks rhetorically. Sato also does not believe in crop rotation because he says that brings in weeds. Asked if his philosophy is synonymous with that of the famous advocate of "natural farming," Masanobu Fukuoka, he says immodestly, "It's close. But compared to his, my method reliably works."

Because converting rice fields to organic practices is a long process and one that's hard to convince farmers to take on, Aramasa's own organic sake rice accounts for only 20 percent of its total, the rest coming from local contract farmers. This, though, is a percentage that he plans to expand.

After our visit, we wend our way through the still-quiet entertainment district of Kawabata-dori, making our way to the small sake, shochu and wine shop Sugakyu, owned by the Sugawara family. Their sake section only stocks Akita sake. Fourth-generation family member Hidehisa Sugawara, whose father runs the shop, keeps a small handwritten list next to the cash register that displays the limited-edition Aramasa bottles he's stocked for the day and their prices. "In the past ten years, sales of premium, special designation sake have grown dramatically, he says. "Akita people are really proud of their sake and they like to give it as gifts to people in other parts of the country and to foreigners. Everyone who is on the receiving end is grateful to get such a gift."

In addition to the limited-edition Aramasa bottles, there are other hot items like issues from the Next Five collective (see page 182). We watch locals sidle up to the cash register, glance at the handwritten list as if shopping for contraband and request the addition of one or two of these rare bottles to their haul, then walk away, triumphant.

Senkin's "Nature" Sake

Senkin Brewery, which we described in chapter 12, is another member of the *shizen-ha* "natural clique" and a typical example of a brewery saved from extinction by forward-looking heirs. During our visit, toji Masato Usui let us taste the three lines of Senkin sake his brewery makes, Nature, Modern and Classic. Of the three, it's the organic Nature—brewed in the kimoto method with Kame no O rice, light-bodied, tart and clear-tasting despite its 90 percent polishing ratio—that Usui as well as taste-making bartenders like Marie Chiba (see page 196) are most passionate about. To Usui, "organics" is not a new trend to be chased, but a return to how sake was once made. The brewery's website evokes ancient times when there were no rice-milling machines, no such thing as premium sake rice and no commercial yeast. It extols the sake's "infinite life force" hidden in the heirloom grain, which they believe contains more than enough vital strength to

Masaru Terada inspects a barrel of rice that has begun to germinate. Fizzy and cider-like, it will be brewed into his organic, unpasteurized Musubi *junmai* sake.

summon wild yeasts and allow the fermentation of a totally additive-free sake.

When they found that the family brewery was going bankrupt, Masato's older brother Kazuki, the eleventh-generation heir, returned in 2003 to try to save it. Masato joined him in 2007. The brothers, influenced by Kazuki's work as a wine sommelier in Tokyo, adopted a low-intervention approach to sake making, to produce a brew with the body, crispness and astringent quality of a good white wine, putting themselves in league with a natural wine movement that had begun in France and was just making inroads in the US, Japan and beyond. It wasn't just a trend-chasing thing either, Kazuki explained. The way Japanese eat has changed, incorporating Western foods like ketchup and mayonnaise, boldly spiced ethnic foods and more fatty fried foods. These foods, Usui argued, demanded higher-acid, sweeter styles of sake, more like northern European white wines.

Their father was against the new, wine-like sakes, and at first, critics and the public panned them. But Masato says, "The company was about to be auctioned off. So it really couldn't fall any further at that point. There was nowhere to go but up." Within a decade, the brothers had turned around the brewery, led by their motto of *yokeina koto wo shinai*, or "do nothing unnecessary." This meant no charcoal filtration, no added water and no pasteurization. Usui laughs remembering the comments from other breweries. "They said, 'What's Senkin doing?' That high-acid, sour sake, that's stupid!'" To older brewers, high acid was something to be avoided at all costs, a sign of oxidation or spoilage. Consumers, especially young women, responded first to the crushably light and drinkable sakes, leading the brewery's turnaround. Reflecting the general trend in Japan among premium craft brewers, Senkin has dropped its production from 4,000 koku (a little under 200,000 gallons/900,000 liters) during the height of sake's popularity to about half that, but their bottles are now hand-crafted and more expensive than the *futsu* (regular) sake they were making before.

Some brewers want to go organic, but the supply is simply not there. At Saiya Brewery in Akita Prefecture, best known for its Yuki no Bosha label, toji Toichi Takahashi brews in the old all-natural manner, with a kimoto starter, native yeast and local rice. All the brewery need to be able to market its sake as organic was organic rice. But the brewery found that element too difficult to source. "It's difficult because it takes three years to convert to organic," explains Takahashi. "There were some farmers interested, but it's hard to convert if the surrounding farms use pesticides. So now, even though our brewing style is organic, we aren't making organic-labeled sake."

San Francisco wine merchant Alex Bernardo would argue that

Master brewer Nobuyuki Komai of Hachinohe Brewery, Aomori Prefecture.

Takahashi's sake, in its craftsmanship, is equal to any organic sake. What really matters is the brewer's artistry, and his or her manipulation of water, rice, koji and yeast. Yet a number of brewers we meet assert there is a palpable difference in the quality of sake brewed with organically grown rice, compared to conventional rice, in part because of its lower protein content resulting in better flavor. Yoshihiko Yamamoto, president and toji of Yucho Brewery, says he's noticed that the sake he brews with organic Akitsuho table rice has a taste that is "really pretty, very smooth and fine. A 65 percent polished rice sake tastes like a 50 percent polish."

We think of Senkin's Nature, and Terada Honke's Katori, both 90 percent polish and both far more refined tasting than the ratio would indicate. Perhaps the vibrancy we love in shizen-ha sakes is due to a combination of things—that "infinite life force" of Senkin Nature's heirloom Kame no O, the lack of chemicals andthe hewing to traditional techniques, from seed to bottle.

Niida Honke and Hachinohe Brewery: Sake Centered on Preserving the Natural Ecosystem

In Fukushima, eighteenth-generation Niida Honke Brewery president and master brewer Yasuhiko Niida's experience in the aftermath of Japan's 2011 earthquake, tsunami and nuclear meltdown strengthened his desire to expand the practice of "natural agriculture" his father pioneered in the late 1960s. Although his brewery is located forty-five miles (72 km) southwest of the nuclear-power-plant meltdown, it did sustain damage from the earthquake. His pregnant wife and toddler daughter had to evacuate to Tokyo while he spent a lonely six months assessing the damage and monitoring daily radiation levels. Sales fell, and it took the

wooden planks, the move makes his brewery both more self-sufficient and adds a complexity and depth to his sake, Niida believes. And he has also stopped using commercial yeasts, switching to all spontaneous yeast found within his own brewery.

Niida is an innovator in other ways, as well; along with Aramasa Brewery he was also one of the first breweries to swap the traditional yellow koji mold for the white koji mold typically used for shochu. Its high citric acid levels help give his sake a noticeably clean, sharp and sophisticated character that goes especially well with food.

When the Covid-19 pandemic hit in 2020, Niida's sales for April 2020 logged a 45 percent drop compared to the previous April. But that began to turn around the following month as sales shifted from in-house restaurant sales to more mail-order purchases. Niida foresees a future in which people will reassess their lives and move away from the urban concentrations of Tokyo and Osaka to a lifestyle more rooted away from the cities in the outlying regions. "It's a very Japanese way of life," he says, and one that he aims for himself—"self-sufficiency with the blessings of rural life."

Prefectural or even a more local-level pride, we begin to learn, is an effective way to cultivate and preserve the essential ecosystem that makes a distinctive regional craft sake possible. We see it in Aomori, where the organically minded Hachinohe Brewery has organized the three-hundred-member-strong Ganja Natural Sake Club.

The Ganja district is one of the few left in Aomori where the original landscape has been preserved. Through their dues and volunteer activities, club members help maintain the area's rich ecosystem, which includes the local spring water that gushes up from the limestone terrain. They participate in May *taue*, or rice planting, June weeding, September harvest and March bottling and labeling events. In a rural area where the population has been in decline,

brewery nine years to recover fully from the disaster, Niida estimates. Yet the disaster also resulted in a new cooperation between advocates of organic farming and mainstream producers and brewers that hadn't existed before.

Once he recovered from the initial shock and anger, Niida promised himself to "leave as many healthy rice fields as possible for our children." He began to brew with all-organic rice from fields enriched only by shell and straw fertilizer. To make his sake as low-intervention as possible, in 2014 he even stopped using the all-natural fermented persimmon extract that had acted as a sediment remover. In 2015, when two of his natural sakes won gold at the International Wine Challenge, it brought widespread attention to Niida and his organic efforts. Accolades like these don't make a sake good, Niida says, but it gives him a platform to "talk out loud" about his passion for all-natural sake. In 2020 he began using wooden tanks to mature his sake, constructed from the cedar trees his grandfather planted on the brewery grounds. Made in the traditional style using no glue or nails to join the

the brewery's sought-after sake has even managed to pull in outside members as well, from as far away as Tokyo to places such as Singapore, says brewery representative Yumi Takahashi. At the end of the brewing season, members receive exclusive organic sakes brewed with rice from the Kanizawa Ganja district as well as Aomori yeast, a taste of the land they have helped preserve.

A Tasting on Our Return to Tokyo

As we settle into our bus ride from Terada Honke Brewery back to Tokyo we crack open a bottle of Musubi, the brewery's 100 percent sprouted-brown-rice sake. It takes us more than two-and-a-half minutes to fully open it because there's so much still-living yeast inside of the bottle. Michael has to keep opening and then closing the reinforced anchor cap to keep the very active bubbles from overflowing. In our cups, we note that the Musubi is a pale orange color, with the cloudiness of an *usunigori*, or lightly pressed sake. We bury our noses in its initial sharp, cider-like aroma, catching the scent of apples, mushrooms and a bit of cheese. On the tongue, it carries the distinctly pleasing finish of roasted barley. It's the absolute embodiment of Keisuke Terada's utopian world of fermentation.

The sakes made by the natural and organic sake brewers we've met on our journey are each dramatically different from the other; Terada's barely tamed Musubi on one end of the spectrum and on the other, a soigné, crystalline, fruit-and-herb scented Aramasa No. 6 "X-type" sake. Yet their makers are each united in their shared vision of a more sustainable ecosystem. We raise our glasses to toast *kanpai* to their products, as harmonious and as vividly alive as the bright green rice fields unfurling outside our window.

Natural Flight

Sake name: Katori 90
Sake type: Kimoto junmai muroka nama genshu
Brewery: Terada Honke, Chiba Prefecture
Made with organic Koshi Hikari rice and designed to blow your palate away with full flavors and powerful umami.

Sake name: Tamura
Sake type: Junmai ginjo kimoto
Brewery: Niida Honke, Fukushima Prefecture
Niida Honke is a pioneer in organic sake. This sake is exclusively made from the brewery's own rice paddies, in cultivation since 1997.

Sake name: Sakura Cosmos
Sake type: Junmai kimoto
Brewery: Aramasa Co., Akita Prefecture
Fermented in wooden kioke barrels, made using local Kairyo Shinko rice and Aramasa's proprietary Yeast No. 6. A true taste of locality, with Aramasa's sublime trademark depth of flavor and roundness.

Chapter Fourteen

Bodaimoto: The Monk Starter

Our day begins at Kyoto Station, over steamed Chinese pork buns (the iconic Osaka comfort food Michael has an unholy obsession with and nose for) from 551 Horai, and bamboo-leaf-wrapped sticky-rice dumplings studded with dates for Nancy. Our trip to Yucho Brewery today is one we've been looking forward to for weeks, because of the way thirteenth-generation owner-*toji* Yoshihiko Yamamoto's products seem to touch on everything that the sake world is grappling with now. He's reviving long-forgotten sake-making techniques on the one hand, while on the other dreaming up cutting-edge brewing technology that will light the way to sake's future. And he's bringing back a lost sense of place to a drink commodified by war and the loss of the local *jizake* tradition.

On this sunlit March morning we sit at the station waiting for our train and discussing one of Yucho Brewery's signature sakes: *bodaimoto*, or monk starter. Developed by Nara temple monks in the fifteenth and sixteenth centuries, it is considered the first "modern" sake, a precursor to both the *kimoto* and *sokujo* methods in that it involves a starter, main mash, yeast and the koji-kin fungus. It was revived by Yucho and seven other Nara breweries in the early aughts, and has come into its own as consumer tastes have changed. Sour, creamy and slightly fizzy, with some pronounced cheddar cheese, lactic acid-like notes, it's like the Japanese cousin to a sour beer, but with an amped-up sweetness and hints of herbal spice on the finish.

From this bustling, modern station we're about to embark on a trip into the past, taking three local trains that wend their way due south, deep into the lush green Nara basin. We take in the Kongo mountain range to the west, which separates Nara from Osaka Prefecture and is the source of Yucho's pure, hard mountain water. To the south are the rugged Kii Mountains and to the east is Mt. Miwa, where the Yoshino cedar boughs were harvested for the first sake barrels and for *sugidama*, the perfectly

round, decorative orbs of tightly bound cedar branches seen in front of every brewery during the brewing season. They can take the *kurabito* hours to make; when they are hung in front of the brewery at the start of the October brewing season they are bright green, gradually turning brown as the season progresses.

Visit with Yoshihiko Yamamoto, Yucho Brewery
Alighting at tiny Gose Station, we hop in a cab and roll through a sleepy shopping arcade. We pass faded wooden homes—some shuffling through their third century of life—that seem to exhale the incense-scented breath of old Japan. Nara was Japan's first permanent capital during the eighth century and the seat of Buddhist spiritual teaching and political influence.

Inside the sliding wooden doors of his home (like many traditional breweries, the Yamamoto family's living quarters are attached to the brewery), Yamamoto greets us and ushers us into his cozy, bookshelf-lined study. Four hours and a short tour of the brewery later, we emerge, our brains lit up with images of warring feudal lords, brilliant monk-brewers and the mercantile glories of the Edo period. Perhaps most impressive to us, though, is Yamamoto's determination to follow in the footsteps of the Nara maker-monks of old with his ingenious technical innovations.

Wearing dark, horn-rimmed glasses and a navy lightweight down jacket, Yamamoto looks like a youthful, curious owl. Without much preamble, he pulls out an old map of Nara and the first of many historical sake-making books, and we plunge into the Nara of a thousand years ago.

At that time, the all-powerful Fujiwara clan, which had intermarried with and become synonymous with the imperial family, acted as a de facto government to the country. In 992 AD, the clan erected the Bodaisen Shoryaku temple complex in

Shoryaku Temple, where in 1999, Yoshihiko Yamamoto of Yucho Brewery and other Nara brewers came to collect native yeast and *koji* fungus in order to revive the *bodaimoto* "monk starter" method.

Nara. Shoryaku Temple, along with its eighty-six sub-temples, was a religious institution. It was also where the Fujiwara clan was educated, equivalent to today's national research universities and filled with scholars of every discipline.

The temple complex was erected during the peaceful, roughly four-hundred-year era of cultural splendor known as the Heian period (794–1185), when new forms of art and literature arose and Buddhist temples, the aristocracy and the imperial family were staunchly aligned. Rice cultivation, which had been imported from China, was well established, and most sake was produced at shrines and temples for religious and imperial celebrations.

The technical innovations that would become the foundational features of modern-day sake—the creation of a starter, (the *shubo*, or *moto*), the three-stage brewing method (*sandan shikomi*), pressing (*shibori*) and pasteurizing (*hi-ire*)—though, did not occur during this time of peace and

prosperity. Instead, they were inventions of necessity, made five hundred years later by Shoryaku Temple monks clinging to a fading power structure. As their wealthy patrons gradually lost control and were replaced by warring daimyo, or regional lords, the monks began to look for new sources of revenue.

The era known as the Warring States period (1467–1615) started with a battle over succession by the ruling clan and then devolved into a widespread, bloody turf war. "The Kyoto central government was unable to collect taxes," Yamamoto explains, "so in order to protect themselves, the monks had to make money." Shoryaku monks began manufacturing bamboo shakuhachi flutes, as well as sake, both of which bore the mark "Bodaisen," after the mountain enshrined at the temple. With society in turmoil, Shoryaku and other large temples also turned to producing sake from their rice fields to sell for profit, hiring private soldiers to aid in their efforts and help protect them and their property.

Sake's first *shubo*, or *moto* (starter), was the ingenious bodaimoto. To make it, raw rice and a small amount of steamed rice are soaked in water for two to three days until the water becomes microbe-rich and sour with naturally occurring lactic acid. The sour water is drained and saved, and the rice is steamed. It's then reunited with the sour water to begin the starter fermentation. During this ten-to-fourteen-day period, naturally occurring

yeast falls into the starter, protected from malign microbes by the high levels of lactic acid.

Reviving the Bodaimoto Starter Method

In 1999, Yamamoto's father and a group of Nara brewers banded together with local sake researchers to revive this all-but-lost way of making sake. They gathered both wild yeast and the *koji-kin* fungus native to Shoryaku Temple, where bodaimoto was first developed. Every year since, they've made a pilgrimage back to the temple to make the shubo for the season's present-day bodaimoto.

Nara Prefecture temples were responsible for other innovations in sake. Pulling down a volume of the *Tamon'in nikki* (Dairy of Tamon'in Temple), Yamamoto explains that the book originated in one of the temples of Nara's famed Kofukuji temple complex. There, monks kept the five-volume diary from 1478 to 1618, recording their daily doings. Yamamoto loves the diary for its detailed entries on sake-brewing. The book contains the first record of sake pasteurization, describing the "simmering" of sake before putting it in wooden casks, most likely made of Yoshino cedar. This technique, of course, pre-dates Louis Pasteur's discovery of pasteurization in the late nineteenth century.

A natural-born teacher, Yamamoto is partial to the Socratic method. He'll rhetorically pose questions before answering them himself. "Putting sake in casks, what does that mean?" he asks. He waits a beat then answers, "You can distribute and sell it." The diary describes famous figures of the day who drank the monks' sake. One story details a May 1582 party thrown by Oda Nobunaga—the all-powerful warlord who then ruled most of Japan—at his sprawling castle in Azuchi, Shiga Prefecture. Among the many presents the Tamon'in Temple monks sent—here Yamamoto consults the diary to confirm his memory—"were three casks of high-quality *morohaku* made at Bodaisen Shoryaku Temple." Morohaku, literally "white-white" is a sake in which

Kaze no Mori sake casks in front of the Yamamoto home in Nara. As with many old sake breweries, the owners' home is adjacent to the brewery.

white, or polished rice, was used for both mold-inoculated *kojimai* rice as well as for the *kakemai* steamed rice added to the main mash. A more common and less expensive alternative to morohaku was *katahaku,* which used brown rice for the *kojimai* and polished white rice for the *kakemai.*

"But why all the presents from the priests?" Yamamoto asks. "They were afraid of Nobunaga's power, of being overtaken by him," he answers. After more than five-hundred years of being protected by both the imperial family and the government, the priests were now out of favor. "Nobunaga wanted to cut the old feudal bonds of obligation," says Yamamoto. The priests had reason to be frightened of the warlord: in 1571 his men had attacked Enryaku Temple on Mt. Hiei in Kyoto, burning it to the ground and killing its monks.

By the Edo period (1603–1868), the center of sake-making expertise had shifted from Nara and Kyoto to Itami. The ruling Tokugawa clan had stripped the temples of their land, and Edo (today's Tokyo) was the commercial center of power. Sake making shifted to the merchant class, and new powerhouses of sake making sprang up along transport routes to Edo. Yamamoto shifts gears to another of his favorite books, a technical tome on sake making written by Konoike Brewery in Itami around 1670. Titled *Domo shuzoki* (Annals of the Domo Brewery), Yamamoto enthuses, "There are all kinds of interesting things in this book!" He reads to us passages that describe how sake brewers gauged whether sake had been heated enough to be safe to drink "by putting their hand in the pot and rotating it around the circumference three times." If it was too hot to keep your hand in any longer, the sake was deemed hot enough to kill harmful microbes.

"And another thing," adds Yamamoto, eyes still sparkling with enthusiasm, "Somewhere along the way, during the Sengoku period, sake had become

Monks at Shoryaku Temple, attending to the making of the starter for Nara Prefecture's revived bodaimoto-style sake.

clear." Sake had gone from *doburoku,* a kind of chewy drink that was essentially the main mash, to a more transparent elixir pressed from the lees, probably a commercially motivated invention. "Which one is better business?" Yamamoto asks. "Clear, you can keep it for three days. Cloudy, it's not stable, and doesn't last long." Ever the Nara booster, Yamamoto then asks, "Who did this? Who needed the money?" Before we can guess, he says, "It was the monks of Bodaisen Shoryaku Temple!"

The innovations kept coming. With a new product on their hands, Nara monks then came up with a value-added product to make with sake lees: *narazuke,* the alcohol-perfumed pickles of Nara, still famous today in the form of sake lees-pickled cucumber and *uri* (a kind of gourd).

For Yamamoto, learning about the development of sake technology isn't interesting unless one also understands the motivations behind these advancements. "They teach the terms today, *shubo, sandan jikomi,* but not the reasons behind why the methods developed. That's not interesting!" he says. "What I think is interesting are the reasons."

The discussion turns to the advent of the *jukkoku kioke* (giant ten-koku, or 1,800-liter/476,000 gallon) sake barrel. The wooden barrel had been in use for hundreds of years, but it was its super-sizing that led to another leap in brewing technology. As giant wooden barrels replaced smaller ceramic jars, the volume of sake produced by Edo brewers soared. The first mention of the use of the ten-koku barrel in the sake literature comes in about 1582, Yamamoto, says, reading from the *Domo shuzoki:* "Last night, in Takame [close to the present-day Nara train station] a seventeen-year-old young woman fell into a ten-koku-sized barrel of sake and died." A barrel a young woman could drown in would be roughly five times the size of the ceramic pots that had been previously used to store and ship sake.

Bigger barrels created the need for bigger-scale variations of the *sandan shikomi*, or three-step brewing process, which had been invented in the Nara temples. Yamamoto boggles our minds further by showing us detailed drawings of three different methods used to create the main mash.

Though today traditional craft sake making is thought of as a wintertime pursuit, back then sake was brewed year round, and each season had its own method. "For the Japanese," explains Yamamoto, "seasonal changes mean temperature changes, and therefore a change in microbes, too. In high temperatures there is one family of microbes working, and a different one in the winter." The different brewing methods were exquisitely tuned to both temperature and microbe differences.

Bodaimoto, the "monk starter" now made during the winter, was made only during July and August, when the water soured quickly and lactic acid dispatched any

harmful microorganisms. *Nimoto*, or boiled starter, was considered to be ideal for brewing during the months of August and September. The third method, *mizumoto*, was best, according to the *Domo shuzoki*, "when you can see people's white breath in the air," or the cold winter months.

Translated as "water main mash," the mizumoto method was developed around the mid-seventeenth century in Nada (to the southwest of Itami, on the water where the port city of Kobe is located). This method is considered the precursor to what we know as the kimoto method, popular again today among some breweries for its layered complexity, lactic richness and powerful umami punch.

Brewed in winter, mizumoto needed no boiling, since temperatures were much lower, keeping unwanted microbes at bay and allowing for a slow development of lactic acid and wild yeasts. "They figured out sake could be made year round, but along the way, why do you think we started to produce sake only in winter?" he asks again, going Socratic on us.

"Um, because of the need for off-season farmer help?" we venture.

Wrong. It had nothing to do with the availability of off-season farmers and fishermen, but everything to do with the Edo government's strict regulation—based on rice harvests—of when and how much

Yoshihiko Yamamoto displays a map of Shoryaku Temple, circa 1580, as he tells the story of how, in the tenth century, the powerful Fujiwara clan erected this temple complex the size of a small town.

brewers could produce. By mid-winter, if the government was assured there would be enough rice for the people to eat, it would give the go-ahead for winter-season brewing, Yamamoto says. "It was about stabilizing the price of rice."

The boiled, or nimoto starter was made in flat-bottomed half-barrels (*hangiri*) that resemble the wooden vessels used to mix sushi rice. Brewers kneaded the steamed rice and water starter by hand four times a day, a little like bread dough, until foam rose up the side of the barrel on about the tenth day. At this point, the mixture was boiled, killing all microbes. The water again became sour, and the kneading resumed until the water soured a second time, this time only with beneficial bacteria, thanks to the dominance of lactic acid. (The lower pH, the more acidic water kills potentially harmful bacteria). At this point, the starter is the ideal medium for ambient wild yeast to join the mixture and begin propagating. Brewers used multiple small half-barrels to make the starter. Yamamoto shows us a detailed drawing, where ten small hangiri are combined to make the starter, which is then added to the mash in stages: an old-fashioned sandan shikomi, or three-step brewing process.

"Edo-era brewers were amazing technicians, the cleverest sake-making people," concludes Yamamoto in admiration. His enthusiasm is catching; we're riveted by these tales he's brought back to life from the pages of his own library. But was all of this sake lore once lost and then somehow recovered?

The answer underscores an issue the brewer considers one of the biggest problems with today's sake world. "This information has always been here, but nobody looked," Yamamoto says. "There are so many teachers, but they're not heeded. Brewers today are too consumed with what type of rice to use, and how much to mill and which yeast to use." This view is not only limiting for sake making as a

Illustration from the 17th-century *Domo shuzoki* (Annals of the Domo Brewery) detailing the new *sandan shikomi* brewing method using *kioke* wooden barrels.

craft, he believes, it also limits the spreading of sake culture overseas. "We're Japanese, so naturally we make sake, but it's these stories are important. It's only through these that the depth and fascination of sake can really be explained."

As the talk shifts from what Yamamoto calls contemporary sake's "original text," to his own sake innovations, we're vaguely aware that we have been here for hours. We can hear the laughter of his young children playing outside, and the sound of women's voices. Switching gears from the past to the present, Yamamoto tells us that just as the ancient Nara brewers left a lasting mark on sake, "I really want to think of all kinds of new things and make my own style." Recreating old techniques like the bodaimoto starter method is interesting, he says "but what I really want to do from now on is create new technologies and innovations."

Better Fermentation Methods, New Ways of Evaluating Sake

Yamamoto's own innovations are arguably on track to one day rival his Sengoku- and Edo-era predecessors. In Yucho Brewery's Kaze no Mori line, Yamamoto is playing with the variables of sake—polishing ratio, fermentation length, maturing and pressing methods—like a virtuosic jazz musician bending notes, elongating the beat and reconfiguring our own sense of beauty. He's trying to conceive of a type that never existed before, or was once considered downright off-putting.

For example, with his Yamada Nishiki junmai, he's taking rice that has been polished only to a rustic 80 percent but giving it a long ferment at low temperatures, as one would brew the most ethereal junmai daiginjo. The familiar daiginjo melon and banana fruit elements are slightly more complex here. There's some jackfruit, Bartlett pear and a kiss of white peach. And in place of the delicate mouthfeel and slender elegance of most daiginjo sakes, this bottle has a complexity divorced from the old standard of excellence. It displays an unusual viscosity, richness and slightly bitter astringency that comes from fermenting the outer proteins and minerals of the rice grain—parts of the grain once shunned for their way of causing temperature and fermentation rates to spike which result in a host of unwanted flavors.

"We're able to control fermentation much better now," Yamamoto says (thanks to greater skill and the brewery's mineral-rich hard water, which promotes fermentation), "so it's much more interesting to think of sake from a lot of different directions."

For instance, who's to say that qualities once derided as *zatsumi* (off-flavors) are all bad? He suggests amending the pejorative term to *fukuza-tsumi*, a play on the word "complexity." And how about shifting consumer views so that when they see a polishing rate of 80 percent, they think, "oh, delicious sourness and complexity," and compare it favorably to the "clean and smooth" of a 45 percent polish? One is not inferior; they're just different.

Building a Better Nama, and the Alpha Line

Another aspect of sake that Yamamoto has thought a lot about is how to lengthen the shelf life of unpasteurized *namazake*. The entire Kaze no Mori line is unpasteurized because his father wanted customers to enjoy the full expression of fresh sake, without the flattening effect that can result from pasteurization. The downside is that nama typically needs to be stored carefully at low temperatures and consumed quickly. To achieve his goal of creating legions of new young converts, Yamamoto knew he needed a nama with a longer shelf life.

So he does no mixing, blending or filtering, and minimal pumping. Kaze no Mori tanks are designed to cut down on oxidation by limiting the surface area exposed to air. On the supply side, he brews his nama to demand, producing batches every three to four months year round so fresh stock is

always available, which also reduces storage costs.

While Kaze no Mori was his father's invention, Yamamoto's own contribution to the brewery's sake line-up is his Alpha line, brewed with a single rice, a humble local eating variety that he's revived called Akitsuho. He contracts directly with thirty local farmers and buys their entire stock, jokingly calling the rice the brewery's *shuzo kotekimai*—a term bestowed on rice varieties (never table rice) considered ideal for making premium sake.

To prevent oxidation, Yamamoto also invented an ingenious, patented tank and "pressing" process for the Alpha Type-4 sake label that is beautiful in its simplicity. It dispenses with any kind of cotton bag or accordion press. Instead, he puts the yeast to sleep with extreme cold temperatures, causing it to fall to the bottom of the tank. He then extracts the clear sake from the top of the tank through one hose, and with a second, replaces the oxygen in the tank with nitrogen.

Since most of Yucho's sake is unpasteurized, he has not until recently been able to offer a sake that can be served warm. So he came up with Alpha Type-5, his version of an aged sake that actually isn't aged at all. Instead, he creates a sour-water kimoto-like starter rich in lactic acid, and boils that. He adds his standard yeast No. 7, and then instead of aging the sake for a long time, he adds old sake that the brewery had in storage during fermentation. The result is a golden sake that drinks like a *koshu* (aged sake) and can be enjoyed at all temperatures. Red dots on the bottle's label act as a thermometer, changing color as the sake is warmed.

But the most subversive of the Alpha line is Yamamoto's Alpha Type-2 label. It's designed to showcase that humble table rice Akitsuho and again, to question the prevailing notions of what makes a "premium" rice or sake. He polishes the table rice down like a luxury Yamada Nishiki rice to an extreme ratio of 22 percent (meaning 78 percent of the outer husk has been removed) and calls it Alpha 2-2-2. Why? "To raise Akitsuho above Yamada Nishiki" he says. Most fans of this type of highly polished *daiginjo* will expect a clean, clear taste. But Alpha Type-2 is a different sake: its textural richness stays on the tongue longer, leaving a correspondingly strong impression of deliciousness in the brain, he explains.

"Everyone has heard of Yamada Nishiki and how it's expensive. When prices are high, farmers are happy. So brewers say Yamada Nishiki is the most expensive because it's the best quality rice for sake making," he says. But Yamamoto wants to challenge that received wisdom, and to value rice once considered less worthy, as well as the farmers who grow it. "In the near future, I want to buy Akitsuho at the same price as I buy Yamada Nishiki. That would be a very good thing for our local farmers." In a country where farmers are aging out and young people have all fled to the city, he knows that providing farmers with a sustainable, equitable livelihood is of vital importance to the community. Of course, this experiment will ultimately fail unless

the skills he brings to it as a brewer really do elevate the sake. His challenge is to make something delicious enough to change an entrenched way of thinking about sake, so that customers will willingly shell out daiginjo prices for a table-rice sake.

Outside, the sun has set. Yamamoto sends us off with two exquisite boxes of a Kansai seasonal delicacy: persimmon-leaf-wrapped pressed salmon sushi. It's a specialty that the writer Jun'ichiro Tanizaki penned an ode to for its evocation of traditional Japan. Like Yamamoto himself, the pressed sushi brings together the artisanal ways of past and present. The difference is that while the boxed sushi preserves the past in amber, perfect and unchanged, Yamamoto protects the old traditional ways, keeping that one tank of monk-starter bodaimoto, while sending forth his Alpha series like an arrow into sake's future.

Bodaimoto Flight

Sake name: Takacho
Sake type: Junmai bodaimoto
Brewery: Yucho Brewery, Nara Prefecture
Instrumental in reviving the bodaimoto method, Yucho and other Nara brewers worked with the monks of Nara's Shoryaku Temple to bring this one back.

Sake name: Hanatomoe
Sake type: Mizumoto muroka genshu
Brewery: Miyoshino Brewery, Nara Prefecture
Mizumoto is not much different than bodaimoto. In the seventeenth century it was used during the colder months while bodaimoto was a summer brewing method. Look for high acidity and body in this fantastic bodaimoto.

Sake name: Gozenshu
Sake type: Junmai usunigori bodaimoto
Brewery: Tsuji Honten, Okayama Prefecture
Fresh, fruity and not as funky as other bodaimoto-type sakes. The Omachi-rice-based sake's slight cloudiness adds body and sweetness, but remains in perfect balance with its acidity.

Part II
The Alchemists: Yeast, Mold, Makers and Cooks

For all that sake is a product of rice, water and earth, there are two more magical ingredients— microorganisms, actually—without which sake would not come alive. This section is devoted to these invisible microscopic workhorses and other agents of change that make sake a world and culture unto itself. Rice makes sake an agricultural product, but yeast and mold make it a fermented, living libation. We'll visit the yeast isolators, fungus cultivators and mold merchants who bring these agents to life, and other human intermediaries who lie between us and a carafe of sake: the brewery workers and master brewers, bartenders and home cooks (yes, we have recipes!) who bring nuance, beauty, craft and pleasure to the drink. We'll also tip our hat to the growing number of foreign breweries that are taking sake culture international. And we'll end our journey by enjoying the fruits of the Yokawa rice fields where we began.

Chapter Fifteen

The Father of Modern Kochi Yeast

The disorientation we feel this January afternoon as we step out of the Kochi Ryoma Airport on Shikoku island has nothing to do with sake; it's what happens when you leave a cool cloudy alpine town in the morning, and a few short hours later find yourself blinded by a southerly sun and feel a warm breeze that holds a faint promise of the ocean's tang. Such is travel in Japan, a long and narrow island country with a northeast to southwest orientation and excellent ground and air transport. Climate zones and terrain can change in the blink of an eye here.

Waiting at arrivals is Haruhiko Uehigashi, the father of the Kochi sake-yeast movement, who will be our guide for the next two days. His face is tanned, shingled with a jet-black head of hair. He wears a short, mint green–colored jacket that makes him look like a typical Japanese factory worker instead of the brewing and fermentation biochemist (zymurgist, if you want to know the technical term) that he is. He greets us with a big smile, perhaps anticipating the packed agenda he has in store for us.

Although Kochi is the largest prefecture on Shikoku island, it has the smallest population, in part due to its geography. In the north are mountains, and along the south, the Pacific Ocean. Most of the prefecture's population is strung along its narrow coastal plain, and this relative isolation and mild climate has created a unique dialect, cuisine and culture. Kochi's people are known for being big-hearted and fond of drinking and games.

Though they do not share a language, Uehigashi and Michael hit it off at the US National Sake Appraisal competition in Hawaii, where they communicated through the limited yet still-effective language of rice and yeast varieties. Our first car ride with Uehigashi proceeds along these lines.

"Kaze Naruko?

"Shinpaku too big."

"Gin no Yume?"

"Moving more toward Tosa Urara."

"Tosa Urara?"

"Parents are Kaze Naruko, Toji no Hana and Hitomebore."

"Which rice is best for Kochi yeasts?

"All of them"

Today there are many different kinds of yeast used in sake making. The majority are sourced from the Brewing Society of Japan, which now offers about twenty different kinds of numbered yeasts. Stabilized and preserved, they've been isolated over the years at various breweries and selected for their ability to make exceptional sake. Some breweries also keep their own private yeast stores.

Then there are the wild, ambient or *kuratsuki* yeasts, which spontaneously ferment in tanks, or those that are carefully selected from sake mash by observant brewers and scientists for their aroma and fermenting ability. Over time, some will become new *kyokai*, or commercial yeasts, distributed by the Brewing Society of Japan and available to all. Others will remain proprietary to the brewery. A fourth type of yeast, which is the kind Kochi is known for, is yeasts that have been developed, either at prefectural research centers, universities or at one of the industrial sake makers with large research departments. The development of these new yeasts, often adaptations of existing

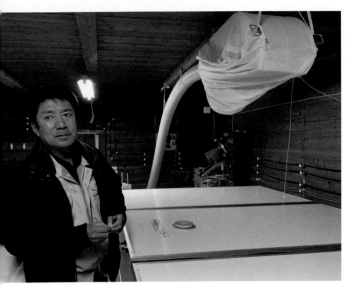

Kochi Prefecture zymurgist Haruhiko Uehigashi has developed a number of "modern yeasts."

yeasts, like their hybrid rice counterparts, are a way to set themselves apart from other regions of the country and instill a sense of place, or regionality, to their sake. Kochi has more than twenty of its own yeasts, the largest number in Japan.

These so-called "modern" yeasts are responsible for some of the crazy, amped-up aromas that have gained popularity in recent years.

In the Lab with Uehigashi-sensei

At his lab at the modern and nondescript Kochi Industrial Technology Center, Uehigashi's equipment includes a gas chromatographer, a machine for analyzing sake-mash aromas and a large freezer stuffed with vials of yeast kept at -112°F (-80°C). He hauls out a large cooler filled with sake left over from a tasting event and lecture that he gave the day before. This is our chance to work through eighteen of Tosa's best sakes. (Tosa is the ancient name for the prefecture, and is still heard everywhere, especially in reference to Kochi sakes. Not to be confused with the city of Tosa to the southwest of Kochi City.) We are also, in a sense, working our way through a catalog of Kochi yeasts as we taste the fruits of Uehigashi's life's work.

As we taste, the Kochi sake profile emerges in sharp relief: a light, refreshing dryness that makes

you want to drink more, and can sometimes push the envelope of aromatic intensity.

Of the nine yeasts that Uehigashi has developed at the center (with support from Kochi University and the prefectural research center), none has become more of a cult yeast than his Cel-24, which produces high levels of the ester ethyl caproate as well as malic acid. The sakes they shape are highly fragrant, green-apple tart and low alcohol as a result of the yeast's low fermentation ability. Yet ironically, Uehigashi absolutely detests Cel-24 yeast. As we taste Kameizumi Brewery's Cel-24 sake, which explodes with gewurztraminer-like aromas and sweet fruitiness, high acidity and an edge of effervescence, Uehigashi puckers up his face and says, "Crazy! I don't like it! Young women really like it. People who don't drink that much like it. It's for entry-level drinkers."

Over the past thirty years, Uehigashi has not only developed Kochi's suite of modern yeasts, he's also helped change the way sake is evaluated and judged in all-important national and international competitions. In 2015 he was invited to the US National Sake Appraisal for the first time, and noticed that all of the winning sakes were extremely sweet, the polar opposite of the Kochi style. In order to elevate the ginjo aromas of their sakes, brewers have introduced yeasts that will result in high ethyl-caproate levels. Then, to offset the increased bitterness that comes with these esters, they have had to increase glucose levels.

"These sweet sakes got really big because of the competitions," Uehigashi says. "People liked them for a while, but now, less so. They want sake they can drink with food." It's true. In our travels across Japan, the mantra we hear repeated everywhere is "I brew sake that you can drink with food." Kochi, says Uehigashi, is jumping on no bandwagon; it has always brewed food-friendly sake. He realized that

Kochi's light and dry sakes were severely handi-capped in a competition environment. He also knew that the order in which sakes are tasted affects judges' perceptions. After tasting several sweet, fruity junmai daiginjos, a dry sake would strike a discordant, even off-putting note on their palates.

Those running the US National Sake Appraisal, meanwhile, led by its executive committee director Shuji Abe, felt a growing concern as members noticed that the junmai category was overly dominated by highly aromatic junmais more typical of junmai ginjos or daiginjos. They considered omitting aroma entirely from the attributes on which junmai sakes are judged. At the same time, the effort to switch to glucose-based evaluations had been gaining steam for the past decade, but with no success. Uehigashi and his colleagues conducted an evaluation of the glucose levels of the Appraisal's award-winning sakes in 2016, which showed that sakes with higher glucose levels did indeed tend to do better in the junmai category. Kochi and Yamagata prefectures requested a change in the sake evaluation system at this same competi-tion: arranging the sakes on the judging tables from lowest to highest glucose levels. In 2017, after this change, Kochi sakes won four gold and eleven silver medals, ranking third in Japan, a clear vindication of Uehigashi's desire to even the playing field.

In addition to developing new yeasts and advocating for his prefecture in international competitions, Uegashi is the *koji* rice doctor on call to all eighteen of Kochi's breweries. Every Monday, he and his two-person team pick up 140 bags of koji and *moromi* mash from the breweries. Uehigashi analyzes them and provides feedback and advice to brewers on how to tweak these key components to make a better sake. Last year he analyzed 1,400 moromi samples, eight hundred koji-rice samples and three hundred sake-rice samples.

Birthday Party, with Space Yeast

Before we head to dinner, we stop briefly at our hotel, where Uegashi takes off his factory jacket and dons a sport coat in tasteful, muted brown colors, suddenly turning from professor-disguised-as-

Kochi sakes brewed with space-traveling yeasts, a plan hatched to bring attention to local sakes and test the effects of space travel on sake aromas.

brewery-worker to suave academic. At Akincha restaurant ("Aki's Place" in Tosa dialect), where we're dining with guests from the prefectural government export development office and trade association, Uehigashi has brought more Kochi sake to taste. Today is his sixtieth birthday, although no one would ever guess that; he looks twenty years younger. Although he was scheduled to retire in 2020 after logging thirty-five years at the technology center, he's agreed to postpone his retirement for a year. But he's getting itchy for more time to pursue his hobbies.

One of the unique and more endearing features of the Japanese is the passion and seriousness with which they pursue a galaxy of hobbies, from archery to tango dancing to curling. "I want to play with my radio-controlled helicopter and airplane," he tells us, proudly showing us photos of the five-foot (1.5 m) long aircraft he built himself. His other hobbies are making Japanese battleship models, surfing and snorkeling. "My wife likes snorkeling but not the radio control," he says. "She's angry—too expensive!"

As the dinner party gets going, Uehigashi opens a Suigei junmai ginjo made with a test batch of the local Yamada Nishiki hybrid rice Gin no Yume, and a super-dry banana-scented Kameizumi tokubetsu junmai, bottled earlier this month. Their fruity, bright acidity meshes seamlessly with a plate of fatty yellowtail sashimi served with Kochi's signature condiment, bright green garlic leaf *nuta*, a dressing made of young garlic leaves, miso, vinegar and yuzu juice (see recipe on page 213). Course after course emerges: tempura of fish cakes wrapped in nori seaweed, firefly squid with chili and grated daikon radish and the local *akaushi*, or red beef served with our choice of wasabi, soy sauce or salt. Then Uehigashi pulls out a trio of "space sake" from Matsuo, Akitora and Takagi breweries.

The "space yeast" idea is another Kochi scheme that Uehigashi seems to be at the center of. The idea was hatched as a way to raise flagging sake sales during the shochu boom of the early eighties. A four-year project, it involved sending six of Uehigashi's Kochi yeasts to the International Space Station and back on a Russian Soyuz rocket, then marketing the sake made with the outer space–tempered yeasts, branded as Tosa Uchu-shu (Tosa Space Sake). At this point, another stilted Japanese-English exchange takes place.

"Whose idea was it to start this?"

"The people of Kochi. Drinking idea." Uehigashi lets out a laugh.

"How many bottles of sake did you drink before getting this idea?"

"A lot."

The project, a collaboration between the Kochi Industrial Technology Center, the Russian government and the Japan Aerospace Exploration Agency (JAXA) yielded a space sake from each of Kochi's eighteen breweries, and touched off a rise in sales. Uehigashi says that the yeasts' ten-day voyage into space, traveling at speeds of 28,000 miles (45,000 km) an hour through the earth's magnetic fields quite possibly was responsible for their heightened aromatic powers. The Kochi yeasts also experienced the microgravity of outer space, and the crushing pressure of the re-entry into earth's gravity—they're yeast trailblazers. As if this weren't kooky enough, in 2019, the prefecture decided to see how its yeast would be altered by spending a year in icy waters at depths up to three-and-a-half miles (6 km) under the ocean's surface. At the time of this book going to print, the Tosa Deep Water sake series was approaching its release date.

By the end of the evening and after many more bottles of sake, Michael and Uehigashi are engaged in a slightly more drunken version of their usual sake diplomacy:

Michael: "Tomodachi!"

Uehigashi: "We are friends!"

Michael: "Tomodachi!"

Uehigashi: "We are friends!"

Brewery Crawl: The Maestro of Cel-24 Yeast

The next morning, Uehigashi is at our hotel bright and early, ready to take us on a brewery tour. Wincing slightly, he tells us he drank too much the night before. At Kameizumi Brewery in Tosa City, we meet *toji*, president and CEO Kazuhito Saibara, who is mixing a starter batch of Tosa Nishiki rice. Gravelly voiced and appearing perpetually amused in a low-key way, Saibara, we learn from Uehigashi later, is someone he considers a "self-taught brewer." Even though Saibara went to Tokyo University of Agriculture (Nodai), Uehigashi explains, "everyone knows he didn't study, he just played."

We lower our faces into a tank of moromi made with Cel-24 yeast. The powerful aromas and the sting of alcohol assault our noses, which feel like bees have buzzed their way in. Uehigashi paces around the brewery shaking off his hangover and muttering in mock despair before each labeled tank, "Cel-24! Cel-24! Cel-24! Cel-24!" while Saibara just smiles impishly. The brewer tells us that he loved the low-fermentation power of the Cel series from first whiff, and was the first in Kochi to brew with it. The yeast has been good to him, too; his Cel sakes are big sellers both in Tokyo and abroad. He still remembers when Uehigashi debuted 24's precursor, the full-flavored, flower- and tropical fruit-scented Cel-19 in 1993. "All eighteen sake makers in Kochi gathered. We were told that the apple aroma with this yeast was going to intensify three to four times the level typically found in ginjo sake at the time,

The maestro of Cel-24 yeast: *toji*, president and CEO Kazuhito Saibara of Kameizumi Shuzo, Kochi Prefecture.

and that we could use it for blending [with other yeasts] or to lower alcohol levels. I tasted it and knew I wanted to use it with a Yamada Nishiki 50 percent polish." The sake he envisioned panned out: the highly polished Yamada Nishiki rice gives the sharp sake a roundness and an elegance: a new level of class in a modern breed of sake that is often simply crushable and fun.

Tsukasabotan and the Drunken Whale

Tsukasabotan is the oldest brewery in Kochi, established at the dawn of the Edo period in 1603. Nestled in the Sakawa Valley along Sake Brewery Street, it used to be one of five breweries lining the road. It also enjoyed close ties to both the Edo government and—toward the end of its rule—the beloved Kochi folk hero Ryoma Sakamoto, a samurai who fought for the overthrow of the feudal government and the restoration of the imperial court. Today, in the slanting, late-afternoon sun, the street feels like a ghostly relic of the late Edo and early Meiji periods. The brewery's beautiful buildings seem little changed from what they must have looked like 150 years ago. Master brewer Toru Asano gives us a tour, walking us through a white walled 280-foot (85 m)-long brewery building once filled with wooden barrels and now used for sake storage. But inside the cedar-scented brewery, modern rice-washing machines, a conveyor-belt rice steamer and the clanking of machinery shows that this is now a modern, automated brewery.

While Tsukasabotan retains the charm and faded glamor of bygone days, Suigei Brewery's new ginjo facility in Tosa City—an hour's drive from the main brewery, and completed in 2018—is a glimpse into sake's future. Nestled against green hills where grapefruit and pomelos are grown, this state-of-the-art, temperature-controlled facility's goal is high-quality, small-batch brewing. It produces about six-hundred koku (about 29,000 gallons/130,000 liters) a year, toji Makoto Myojin tells us, less than a fourth of the volume of its main brewery. But through a combination of expediting the brewing process and adding more tanks, in the future the brewery will be able to easily more than triple that volume.

Suigei means "drunken whale," and is a name taken from the fifteenth-generation Tosa Domain clan head who called himself "Ocean Whale Drunk Lord." In the 1980s, the brewery's purchase by a large trading company that specializes in food enabled its expansion in size and also into the premium ginjo market. The sparkling new brewery we're visiting includes a sleek, modern gift shop and an outdoor tasting and dining area. Suigei's sakes are designed for the premium sake-hungry international market, where the growth in sake consumption now lies. While Tsukasabotan tries to uphold the "southern style" traditional dry, high-acid Kochi sake, Suigei is moving its premium Tosa sake to a fuller-bodied profile, using traditional Kumamoto yeasts (commercial Yeast No. 9 and its variants), and a few of Kochi's apple-scented varieties.

Suigei has set its sight on modernization and internationalization, while another brewery we visit, tiny Takagi Brewery, represents the small-town, old Tosa spirit of festivals, parties, games and stories. Takagi is located in what was once the smallest town in Japan, Akaoka, and is famous for its two festivals, one celebrating the small-fry fish known in Japan as *dorome*, the other to celebrate a hometown painter of macabre works for the Kabuki theater.

The main draw of the Dorome Festival, besides eating large quantities of raw goby fish, is a drinking contest to see who can drink the most Takagi sake in the shortest amount of time. The current record is 11.8 seconds to down 1.8 liters (a little less than a quart). Fifth-generation brewery owner Naoyuki Takagi shows us the oversized, red lacquerware bowl from which contestants chug their sake.

The fun-loving, storytelling side of the Kochi character is apparent in Takagi's prized Toyonoume junmai daiginjo Ryuso ("The Dragon God's Musical Performance"), an all-local bottle made with two Cel yeasts and Gin no Yume rice. Its name commemorates an event so otherworldly that it was attributed to the weather-controlling Dragon God. In 1994, a massive tornado whirled over the brewery, then miraculously disappeared. From that point on, the quality of the sake brewed at Takagi is said to have noticeably improved. Takagi shows us a laminated photo of his brewery over which towers a huge column of mysterious white light. "We think the sake-loving Dragon God descended from the tornado and is brewing here," the placard reads.

Something about this temperate prefecture, where people take fun and their drinking seriously but also make seriously good sake, reminds Nancy of her home state of California before wildfires became common, when Silicon Valley still seemed filled with the power to do good. It was a place where you could enjoy the sweet life, relax and dream about your next venture. It was, like Kochi feels today, a certain kind of paradise.

Kochi Flight

Sake name: Bunkajin Liseur
Sake type: Tokubetsu junmai
Brewery: Arisawa Brewery, Kochi Prefecture
Light, dry, exquisitely balanced and easy to drink.

Sake name: Kameizumi "Cel-24"
Sake type: Junmai ginjo nama
Brewery: Kameizumi Brewery, Kochi Prefecture
Much to the bewilderment of the man who developed this yeast, it has developed a huge following. Over-the-top tropical and strawberry aromatics.

Sake name: Tsukasabotan "Tosa Space"
Sake type: Junmai ginjo
Brewery: Tsukasabotan Brewery, Kochi Prefecture
This sake tends to sell out quickly but it's worth the hunt. Bone dry in the Kochi manner and out of this world.

Chapter Sixteen

The Yeast Hunters

During the earliest days of sake, whether it was shrine maidens or monks doing the brewing, makers were unaware of the existence of yeasts. Through trial and error, they figured out a way to brew sake, unwittingly enlisting these invisible microbes to help them do their jobs. The seventeenth-century invention, the kimoto starter, generated natural lactic acid with a taste for harmful microbes. By devouring those rogue agents, the lactic acid cleared the way for wild yeasts to propagate in the mash and set about the work of fermentation, creating a drink free of bacterial taint.

Eventually, scientists discovered the yeast *Saccharomyces cerevisiae,* which has been a part of baking and brewing since ancient times. It was first isolated by a Prussian scientist in Berlin in 1837; it took nearly another six decades for researchers at the University of Tokyo to discover that sake had its very own subspecies of this yeast. In 1895, they announced the isolation of Saccharomyces sake yeast, a name that has since fallen out of use.

Exciting advances in brewing microbiology were of great interest to the Meiji government since liquor taxes were an important way of fortifying its national treasury. Liquor taxes in some form had existed in Japan since the Kamakura period (1185–1333), but in the year that sake yeast was discovered, 1895, liquor taxes accounted for a full one-third of the national revenue. Having flung its doors open to the West after more than two hundred years of isolation under the Edo shogunate, tax bureaucrats saw in these advances a way of modernizing the sake industry, generating even higher sales and therefore tax revenues. So the government was happy to invest some of the spoils of victory from the first Sino-Japanese war into understanding the mechanisms of fermentation better.

So in 1904 the finance ministry launched the National Research Institute of Brewing, commonly referred to as NRIB, under the direction of Yabe Kikuji, a professor at Tokyo University. Two years later, Kikuji's subordinate Teizo Takahashi began working on a project to find and begin cultivating the best sake yeasts in Japan. NRIB research technicians lit out across the country to collect more than sixty strains of native yeasts from the sake mashes of the country's best breweries. Takahashi noticed that a yeast from Sakura Masamune Brewery in Hyogo (which we visited in chapter 9) made an especially flavorful, rich sake. It went on to become the first cultured *kyokai kobo,* or association yeast, Yeast No. 1 and was distributed by the newly formed Brewing Society of Japan (another government-affiliated body) which today still supplies cultured yeasts. Demand was bullish for large quantities of these stable yeasts because in 1911, Sawada Brewery in Aichi Prefecture, with the aid of an NRIB brewing engineer named Kenjiro Eda, had perfected the quick-fermenting *sokujo* starter method. It halved

Left A ceramic sake storage jar, over a half-century old, on display at Amabuki Brewery, Saga Prefecture.
Above Brewery workers at Amabuki Brewery cooling just-steamed rice before transferring it to the *koji* room.

the brewing time of the *kimoto* method and so became another revenue-boosting technology for the government. And a key component in the success of the sokujo method was stabilized yeast.

But it wasn't just speed that brewers were after. At the time, one of the biggest risks to their product was *hiochi-kin*, stink-producing types of bacteria that fall into the tank before the yeast has a chance to really get going. It could and often did ruin entire tanks. The sokujo method eliminated this costly risk by incorporating commercial lactic acid into the brewing process to clean out all unwanted microbes.

As beneficial as they were, the development and eventual dominance of commercial yeasts and lactic acid, and the widespread adoption of the sokujo method would—like so many other time- and labor-saving inventions—lead to a flattening and a loss of diversity in sake that many craft brewers today, as we've seen, are trying to recapture through their return to traditional methods.

We picked up the trail of Yeast No. 1 during our tour of Sakura Masamune Brewery, where master brewer Norihide Harada took the time to show us a vial of it. He described it as a robust yeast with strong powers of fermentation that thrived in high-temperature conditions.

After the isolation of Yeast No. 1 in 1906, four more yeasts from Kyoto and Hiroshima were isolated, including Yeast No. 2 from Gekkeikan Brewery and Yeast No. 5 from Kamotsuru Brewery. Harada explains that Yeast No. 1 was distributed by the Brewing Society of Japan from 1917 to 1935, but

The Newer, Better Yeast No. 6

In 1935 the Brewing Society of Japan started cultivating a new strain of yeast, Association Yeast No. 6. Tokyo University researchers Yoshikazu Ohya and Mao Kashima have described the close ties between academia, tax officials and brewers that have throughout modern sake history resulted in many technological advancements. They credit three highly accomplished yeast scientists who gave birth to Yeast No. 6. There was Masatsune Hanaoka, who worked first in the Sendai tax office and then the prefectural brewing institute, and who became known as the father of Akita sake brewing. The second man was fifth-generation Aramasa Brewery head Uhee Sato (see page 138) who made several prizewinning sakes that piqued the interest of the third man, Fujio Oana, a research technician at the National Research Institute of Brewing (NRIB), who went on to isolate Yeast No. 6 from an Aramasa tank in 1930.

Remember that 1934 Kodama Brewery junmai daiginjo sake we mentioned on page 50 that won first place in the national sake competition? To celebrate its 140th anniversary, Kodama brewed a replica of this sake, which paid homage to Oana for his role in the creation of the original prizewinning sake. In the deep cold of Akita's winter of 1934, Oana traveled from Tokyo to Akita to work closely with Kodama brewers and family members, using a recipe he had developed for the still-unnamed yeast he had isolated at Aramasa Brewery.

Until this point, all the association yeast had come from the warmer, western parts of Japan; no one thought it possible that snow country could produce a great yeast. Oana was convinced this new yeast could be a contender. The 1934 victory confirmed his belief, and caused a swelling of pride throughout Akita. The next year, Oana's application to have the yeast accepted by the NRIB was accepted.

As we noted earlier, since 2010, Aramasa has brewed only with Yeast No. 6. President Yusuke Sato loves it because "it's tough, and it has a long shelf-life," he says, comparing it to "us Tohoku people, who operate best in a very cold climate." Association yeasts 1 through to 5, he explains, are too dependent on the warm climate. "They can't work in the cold, but No. 6 can continue fermentation in temperatures of under 50° F (10° C) ," he adds. As the 1934 Kodama win showed the country, Akita Prefecture—and the Tohoku region in general—is an ideal place for ginjo-style, low-temperature brewing.

disappeared during the chaos of World War II. In 2001, Sakura Masamune Brewery learned that the yeast had somehow resurfaced at the Brewing Society, and once again began to brew with it; its Yomigaeri Hyakunen ("Revived after One Hundred Years") is brewed just as was it was a century ago, using 80 percent-polished Yamada Nishiki, Yeast No. 1, *miyamizu* water and the kimoto starter method. For a sake-yeast aficionado like Michael, learning about this throwback sake was like hearing that Paul and Ringo were bringing John and George back from the afterlife and staging a Beatles reunion tour. This was the very bottle he homed in on at the

brewery shop like a heat-seeking missile tracking vintage yeast vibes.

Lucky Yeast No. 7

Aramasa Brewery's Yeast No. 6 (see box above) had its run as top yeast for a little over a decade, until another prizewinning brewery caught the attention of brewing scientists. In 1946 Miyasaka Brewing Co., Ltd. in Nagano dominated the field at the regional and national sake appraisals. This time it was NRIB scientist Shoichi Yamada who isolated Masumi's Kyokai No. 7 yeast, a mutation of the Kyokai No. 6 that the brewery had been using. Its ability to ferment very reliably at lower temperatures and lend an enhanced set of aromatics and flavor to sake made it a game changer. Today it is the most widely used sake yeast in the world. As for Yamada, the discovery was only one among a career studded with achievements. He went on to become director of the NRIB, "the best one they ever had," says sake importer Chris Pearce, "a prodigious publisher, research innovator and renaissance man."

At Miyasaka Brewery, the Miyasaka family has had to work out what it means today to be the caretaker of a yeast legacy. Heir apparent Katsuhiko Miyasaka pushed for focusing only on the family's iconic yeast, the way Aramasa has decided to do with Kyokai No. 6. At first, his father, Miyasaka Brewery president Naotaka Miyasaka, was resistant—couldn't they keep it a strong part of their story while still innovating with other yeasts and sake styles? In the end, Naotaka was convinced that brewing exclusively with No. 7 was the direction to take, and the brewery began focusing its research on teasing out new, more modern variants of the yeast that will speak to contemporary sake tastes.

We got a glimpse of this (not exactly action-packed) process during our visit to Miyasaka Brewery. When we enter the large lab at the brewery's Fushimi site, our first encounter with the brewery's microbiologist and yeast researcher Hirosato Asaki is startling because he's wearing a large exoskeleton-like frame on his back that lends him a futuristic cyborgian look. It turns out it's a piece of equipment designed to help carry heavy loads of sake on his back without injury. One of his current projects is to take the oldest stable form of Yeast No. 7 that exists, from 1967 (samples before this have mutated too much) and find a winning modern variant. The process is painstaking. Asaki creates a yeast culture, isolates its most promising mutations, grows them out and then brews miniature test batches in mason jars (complete with the standard *sandan shikomi* addition of three batches of steamed rice, koji and water).

It's not just one version of No. 7 that Asaki is working on, either, but three different versions. Each requires culturing forty-five different lines, each line housed in its own petri dish. The project is appealing, says our guide Keith Norum, International Sales Director of the brewery, because "this isn't something that's already been done, and it's something that keeps us close to our roots." If Miyasaka can come up with a sake with a modern balance of acidity, sweetness and alcohol it will have it all: taste, story and brand integrity. Yet it could take as long as a year to come up with concrete results, Norum says. "Whether or not they will be good results, we don't know. It's a matter of luck and fate."

The Yeast Individualists

As our time at Miyasaka has shown us, in the highly competitive world of premium craft sake, the push to stand out, to show individuality and originality, whether through rice, water or yeast, is fierce. Another way to attract consumers is by

Amabuki Brewery Chairman Takefumi Kinoshita and his son, eleventh-generation president Sotaro Kinoshita.

developing your own proprietary yeast. Terada Honke
Brewery relies on native yeast,
as do a growing number of
brewcries. But Saiya Brewery, in
the southern Akita town of
Yurihonjo near the Japan Sea,
has been doing this for more
than thirty-five years now.

On a sunny March morning,
our bullet train wends its way
through Tochigi en route from
Tokyo to Akita. We're obsessed
enough with sake regionality to
get excited when we see
mountains from Michael's
textbook appear in real life: Mt.
Takahara, and in the background, Mt. Nanatsugatake.

Toichi Takahashi has spent thirty years
perfecting his ability to nurture Saiya
Brewery's proprietary yeast.

proprietary yeast began in the
late 1980s when fourth-generation president Senshiro Saito
told him, "I want to make a sake
that no other sake brewery is
making. Others are making
ginjo, so how are we going to
differentiate ourselves?" At the
time, isolating one's own yeast
was considered fraught with risk
because you never knew what
kind of sake was going to emerge
from your tank, or if you would
be able to replicate it. Takahashi,
who had spent his first several

Michael's day will be complete if we catch a glimpse
some of the other mountains in the Ou range that
bisects the length of Tohoku.

We arrive at the small town of Yurihonjo with just
enough time for a quick lunch. At the closest place
to the train station that we can find, Restaurant
Miya, a picture of a Roman chariot hangs on the
wall, and the friendly proprietor, Naoki Abe, regales
us with tales of the TV crew who came to his place
to film a documentary on local foods. *Tara nabe*—
cod hot pot made with *hakusai* cabbage, Japanese
parsley, leeks, mushrooms and tofu in a miso broth
was one example. Abe ends up giving us a ride to
the brewery so we won't be late.

Well known in the Western market for its Yuki no
Bosha line of sake, Saiya brewery launched in 1902
when fifth-generation president Kotaro Saito's
ancestors broke off from the *honke*, or head house,
to set up its sake-brewing business. Like many other
breweries during the postwar boom it took up ginjo
sake brewing, tasking master brewer Toichi
Takahashi with figuring out how to get it done.
Along the way, Saiya also gained renown for its
brewery-cultivated yeasts.

Takahashi, who is difficult to understand because
of his thick Akita accent, tells us that Saiya's use of

years at Saiya brewing with Association Yeast No. 9,
spent two weeks at the prefectural research center to
learn the science of isolating and cultivating yeast.

Saiya became the first brewery of the postwar era
to do this on its own. This isn't what's known as
kuratsuki kobo, or wild yeast that falls from the
rafters into the fermenting mash, but a careful
process of monitoring the season's production for
the tank with the best flavor and most beautiful
aroma, then using yeast from that tank in the next
year's production. Every year, Takahashi searches
for just such an outlier. Every one of Saiya's sakes is
made with self-isolated yeast cells; the brewery does
not use any Brewing Society yeasts.

Asked how long it took to perfect the technique,
Takahashi answers, "Thirty years. It takes a lot of
time and patience." First, he explains, it requires
scrutinizing every tank of fermenting mash daily.
"The microflora are not always the same," Takahashi
says. "You look, taste carefully and say, 'Is this the
taste of the future? Is it going to be necessary,
essential for the future?' Once in a while, that taste
emerges." When that happens, he isolates the
bacteria, cultivates it and then preserves it. A long
period of experimentation follows, and if he's lucky, a
new proprietary yeast is born. There are years that

yield no new yeasts; in an exceptionally great year, it might happen two or three times. To date, Takahashi has isolated eleven different yeasts—an impressive accomplishment that other breweries now emulate.

Takahashi seems to relish the fact that sake-brewing styles have caught up with Saiya Brewery. "Finally," he says, "people are making all kinds of sake with all kinds of yeast. The age of just association yeasts is no longer viable."

Visit with the Flower-yeast Professor

We travel today from Tokyo's Shibuya Station to the leafy Tokyo district of Setagaya to pay a call at Japan's premier agricultural school, Tokyo University of Agriculture (Nodai for short). Here, for the past sixteen years, brewing and fermentation professor Takayuki Kazuoka has made it his mission to help widen the flavor bandwidth of sake by discovering new sake yeasts extracted from the native flowers of Japan.

Founded in 1891, Nodai is a junior college, four-year university and a graduate research center

all rolled into one. It's also a finishing school of sorts for the *atotori*, or the brewery heirs who are destined to take over their family breweries. The school is the UC Davis of the sake world.

We extract Kazuoka from his impressively disheveled third-floor lab office—books, papers, coffee cups and somewhere in there among drifts of paper, a computer. His office opens onto an equally messy mad-scientist lab, strewn with rows of flasks, petri dishes and test tubes. Dressed in a white lab coat, its breast pocket well-supplied with pens, his head is covered in a thatch of black hair and his voice is soft-spoken. He leads us to a quiet, spotless meeting room where we can talk.

Since his lab started in the late 1960s it has isolated more than one hundred viable flower yeasts, about thirty of which are now being used to brew sake in Japan. Saga Prefecture brewery Amabuki's Abelia sake and its Oshiroibana ("Marvel of Peru") sake, are two that are direct results of Kazuoka's research.

The process is simple enough, but laborious and time-consuming. What makes it possible is Kazuoka's secret weapon: the "yeastcidin," or enrichment culture, that was developed by his mentor, the late Hisayasu Nakata. The culture contains an

Takayuki Kazuoka's goal is to expand the regional expression of Japanese craft sake by isolating sake flower yeasts from different parts of the country.

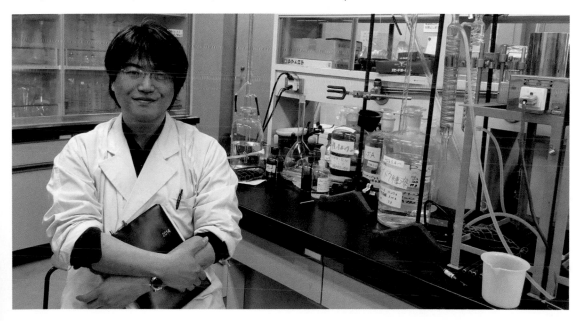

who must be highly attuned to the moods, images and sense memories that different aromas will evoke in consumers. "With flower yeasts, there are strong likes and dislikes. Those who love them really love them, and those who don't tend to detest them," he explains. To isolate a cherry-blossom yeast, Kazuoka spent nine years working with blossoms sourced from across the country, from Okinawa to Hokkaido. "There were a lot that could make good sake," he recalls, "but we wanted a sake that would best match the Japanese image of sake."

For the Japanese, *sakura*, or cherry blossom, evokes a bittersweet mixture of joy at the ineffable, euphoria-inducing beauty of cherries in full bloom, and sadness, even spiritual pain, over its fleeting nature, echoing Buddhist notions of the transience

antibacterial substance isolated from *Aspergillus oryzae* (or koji mold) that conveniently suppresses the growth of most yeasts except for sake yeast. Using it significantly speeds up the flower-yeast isolation process. No one outside his lab has access to this technology.

Breweries, local governments, botanical gardens and students collect fresh flower samples from across Japan, delivering them to the gunmetal gray Nodai lab. A small, ten-gram sample of the fresh flower is placed in a jar in the yeastcidin culture made of sugar, water, koji and mold isolate. The mixture rests for three weeks at 77°F (25°C). When it enters its enrichment culture bath, the flower is teeming with microorganisms. But Kazuoka is after only that very specific sake yeast. The enrichment culture calms down the unruly mixture, suppressing all organisms other than sake yeasts, which are allowed to happily gorge on the sugars. Beer yeasts, wine yeasts, all but sake yeasts will fall by the wayside.

Kazuoka's lab extracts yeast from a thousand or so flowers around the country every year, isolating from two thousand to three thousand yeasts. Out of those they will isolate an average of ten yeasts that are suitable for sake making. If his lab can release one good new flower yeast a year, he is happy, says Kazuoka.

His job is pure science, but there is also an aspect of it that comes close to the art of the perfumer,

Non-foaming Yeasts

The world of sake yeasts, of course, extends way beyond Kazuoka's burgeoning garden of flower yeasts. One major milestone in sake yeasts, for example, was the development of *awanashi kobo*, or non-foaming yeast. First reported in the early twentieth century, these yeasts do the job of fermenting without creating the thick cap of foam that normally develops on the surface of the fermentation tank. In the early 1960s, it was successfully used for the first time by previously mentioned master brewer Takao Nihei of the Honolulu Sake Brewery. Some brewers still like to use foaming yeasts because the foam itself can offer valuable clues about the state and quality of the mash below. But for the industry as a whole, the advent of non-foaming yeast was a game-changer; it allowed brewers to produce 30 percent more sake per tank.

of life itself. *Hanami*, or flower-viewing gatherings, are an ancient rite celebrated in the novels of Tanizaki, popular song, poetry and manga. The season has turned into a marketing bonanza, too. On our first, late March visit, sake-shop refrigerators were bursting with a riot of special-issue pink labels, glowing with foil lettering, laser-cut flower images and festive gift wrapping: bottles brewed just for seasonal parties, featuring delicate, light, springlike aromas and textures. We spy pink-blossomed-themed merchandise in every shop and department store as well, from sakura-themed rice cakes, Pocky and Asahi beer. There's even a pricey, special-edition sakura Moleskine notebook set.

Kazuoka isolated ten different cherry-blossom yeasts that would yield good sake, but, he says, only one was deemed to best match the "image of sakura." To get the typically rich, aromatic profile of a classic ginjo, brewers look for yeasts that produce high levels of the esters ethyl caproate, which yield apple-like aromas and isoamyl acetate (responsible for banana-like aromas). Although Kazuoka and his team did isolate sakura yeasts with these specific qualities, they found that the sake those yeasts produced didn't have the "calm" and "gentle" qualities they were looking to express in their sakura blossom sake. They ended up selecting an outlier, a robust number known as SA-2, which is low in ethyl caproate, but with enough isoamyl acetate to deliver the specific sakura qualities they sought.

Five breweries, starting with Sekigen in Nagano, Sansha in Gifu

and Amabuki in Saga make this seasonal sake. Like all of the breweries using flower yeasts in Japan today, they are headed by former students of Kazuoka, who is like a one-man yeast association to his spreading network. "I want a *nakama* (circle of comrades)," he says simply. That nakama may one day help realize his own personal dream: a time when every region of Japan can claim a sake that expresses the aroma and character of its representative native flower.

Before ending our visit with Kazuoka, we are curious what he thinks of the current boom in "modern" yeasts, including the "mutant cerulenin-resistant" yeasts that—in their ability to survive the aroma-quenching fatty acid cerulenin—are able to produce the billowing aromas that are taking sake into wildly expressive new territory. (The Cel series that Uehigashi developed in Kochi is an example of this type, and its name is a coded reference to its defining characteristic.)

The new Association Yeast No. 1801 is another. It creates a high level of aroma-inducing ethyl caproate, but with weak flavor. To balance the effect of No. 1801, brewers have begun mixing other yeasts into the starter, often the classic Yeast No. 9, which adds balanced flavor and acidity. Brewing is getting more complicated, Kazuoka says, ushering in an era of exciting new aroma and flavor profiles.

The Miyasaka Brewery shop, Cella Masumi, opened in 1996. Housed in a late-Edo period building, the structure was gutted and rebuilt after a 2010 incident in which a truck rammed into the shop.

Amabuki Brewery's lineup of flower yeast sakes: begonia, dianthus, sunflower, strawberry and rhododendron.

whose yeasts provide their aromas.

We've come to this small town to taste the work of Amabuki president Sotaro and his younger brother Daisuke, former sake manufacturing team manager. Both are Nodai graduates who were deeply influenced by Nodai's flower yeast lab—Daisuke in fact now chairs it—and have popularized a new breed of sake.

Miyaki also happens to be the hometown of Nancy's paternal grandparents. But she's not expecting to walk into the tatami-matted sitting room where our interview is to be conducted and find her father's first cousin, Takao Ohkubo sitting at the table with a Cheshire cat smile on his face. Dinner is planned later with the family, but Takao—along with his local Lion's Club buddy and Amabuki chairman, tenth-generation Takefumi Kinoshita—were responsible for this surprise meeting.

A former land-owning family in the domain of the Nabeshima clan, the Kinoshitas began brewing sake to add value to their rice fields. Until about two decades ago, Amabuki brewed regular sake with Association Yeast No. 9 for the local market. Then the two brothers returned from Nodai, where they had fallen under the sway of Professor Hisayasu Nakata (Takayuki Kazuoka's predecessor, page 165), and had their first taste of flower yeast sake.

"I drank the trial sake they had brewed at Nodai and thought, 'This is wonderful,'" Sotaro Kinoshita recalls. He and his brother had discovered a world of limitless possibility, and, even better, something that might attract new young fans to sake. Nakata provided the flower yeasts, and the brothers began experimenting with different rice and yeast combinations. The *nadeshiko* (pink dianthus) yeast, they decided, worked best with Omachi rice because the pretty, sweet softness of the flower

Yet Kazuoka cautions against over reliance on new yeasts, or novel yeast combinations alone. Brewers are using modern yeasts to get the aromatic highs of ginjo-style sake, he explains, but without the traditional ginjo-making technique of carefully calibrated low-temperature fermentation. The latter is where the craftsmanship, the art of the brewer, shines. Without this component, a sake may achieve a kind of inexpensive blowsy aromatic high, yet without the structure of a truly well-crafted ginjo, causing it to shift and change after bottling because it lacks a certain balance. As importer Chris Pearce puts it, only truly great craftsmanship can yield sakes that "are so well-structured you have the sense that every molecule is exactly where it is supposed to be."

The Flower Yeasts of Amabuki Brewery

The handsome wooden doors that welcome visitors inside Amabuki Brewery in Miyaki, Saga Prefecture are fitted with a beautiful, round stained glass window in pink, orange and gold colors that bring to mind a blazing sunset. It's unusual to see so much color at a traditional brewery, especially one that is more than 330 years old as Amabuki is. But as eleventh-generation president Sotaro Kinoshita explains, this is no accident. "We are colorful," he says—a lot like the labels on his bottles and the array of flowers from across Japan

yeast tempered the rich umami of the rice. Young women, especially, took to this sake. Sotaru tells us that many of these women say the nadeshiko Omachi was their gateway into sake.

While the commercial yeasts from the Brewing Society of Japan have been used for more than seventy years now and a large body of technical expertise has accumulated around them, flower yeasts are relatively new. The fact that in practice they are only available to Nodai graduates limits the chance for brewers to experiment with them. Whereas association yeasts have been cultivated to express very specific traits, says Kinoshita, brewing with flower yeasts is more like trying coax good behavior from a rambunctious child. "They have a lot of idiosyncratic quirks, so what we try to do is foster an environment where the unique qualities of that yeast are best expressed, while also

protecting the yeast's individual traits," he explains.

In order to support local farmers, Amabuki Brewery tries to use as much Saga rice as possible, prioritizing locally grown Yamada Nishiki over Hyogo-grown crops and also focusing on the locally grown hybrid Saga no Hana. A flower yeast from Saga, which would help strengthen the brewery's all-local nature and help fulfill Kazuoka's dream, has not yet been developed. "We've put in our request," Kinoshita says, "but they have not succeeded yet."

Sake yeasts are a labyrinthine world unto themselves, all the more tantalizing for being both invisible and yet so important to the final brewed sake product. But they are only half of the invisible microbial universe that makes our favorite drink possible. For the other half, we head back north, to Akita Prefecture, to investigate.

Sake Yeast Flight

Sake name: Kohro Institute
Sake type: Junmai ginjo
Brewery: Kumamoto Prefecture Sake Institute
The institute is home of the famous Yeast No. 9—one of the world's earliest ginjo yeasts— and also brews the Kohro-brand sake that showcases it. Moderate ginjo aromas that suggest apple and melon, with a good dose of flavor to back it up.

Sake name (Japan): Amanoto "Land of Water"
Sake name (US): Heaven's Door
Sake type: Junmai ginjo
Brewery: Asamai Brewery, Akita Prefecture
Made with local Miyama Nishiki rice and AK-1 (Association Yeast No. 1501). Delightfully aromatic without being pretentious, allowing rice-driven flavors to come through on the palate.

Sake name: Amabuki "Strawberry Yeast"
Sake type: Junmai daiginjo nama
Brewery: Amabuki Brewery, Saga Prefecture
From the brewery that specializes in flower yeasts. Juicy yet creamy flavors and a long finish.

Chapter Seventeen

The Merchants of Mold

Dampness hangs in the air this morning as our train makes its way southwest from Akita City through the rural rice-producing Senboku district. In a typical February, this Akita landscape would be buried in snow. Yet in this warmer-than-usual winter, it's filled with browns, beiges and muted greens, which seem to reflect the slight weariness that has accumulated at the end of our sixteen-day research trip. Taiheizan Brewery is the last of our fourteen brewery visits, eased by the warmth of the Kodama family. Today Eiko Kodama is taking us to meet with her husband's old classmate from the National Research Institute of Brewing (NRIB), Hiroshi Konno, PhD. He's a microbiologist and head of his family business, Akita Konno, Tohoku's largest producer and seller of *koji-kin*—the fungus, or mold without which sake would not exist.

The super mold koji-kin (*Aspergillus oryzae)* is what enables the breakdown of the starch in rice into fermentable sugars, converting them from an inedible to an edible food for hungry yeasts to feast upon. While other countries adopt flowers, plants, or animals as national symbols, so central is koji-kin to Japanese culture and cuisine that the Japanese government in 2006 named it the "national fungus of Japan." And it truly is: *Aspergillus oryzae* plays a role in almost all of Japan's basic seasoning agents, from miso to soy sauce to mirin. Fermented foods have been at the center of the Japanese diet for millennia, and are often credited for its population's longevity. As one Japanese microbiologist bluntly put it, "No koji mold, no Japanese taste."

Koji-kin has been embraced by the top kitchens of the world, too. It plays a central role at chef René Redzepi's Noma in Denmark. In the book *The Noma Guide to Fermentation*, he and co-author David Zilber wrote, "We find koji indistinguishable from magic—the best kind of magic, in fact, because anybody can wield it." (In English, "koji" is often used to refer to koji-kin mold, but in Japanese "koji" or "kojimai" refers to koji mold-inoculated rice, and koji-kin refers to the mold itself.)

While koji mold can be harvested in the fields on the heads of rice stalks, or from partially germinated rice, these are labor-intensive processes that yield a koji-kin that is less stable than the commercial variety. So most breweries today rely on professionally cultivated *Aspergillus oryzae*, choosing different strains for their effects on sweetness, acidity, umami level and even the final flavor of the sake.

Out of the 97,000 known species of fungus—some experts estimate there are as many as 1.5 million—there are precious few that have been proven safe for human consumption, and only one that is used in Japanese sake. A thousand years ago koji-kin merchants selected for and carefully cultivated this very specific, invisible and difficult-to-control fungus, selling it to sake breweries in feudal Japan. And they did this all without the aid of modern scientific knowledge or equipment to control moisture, oxygen and nitrogen concentrations as is done today. In a way, commercial koji mold is Japan's oldest biotech product.

How Koji-kin is Used in Sake Making

The essential brewer's mantra goes, *Ichi koji, ni moto, san tsukuri,* or "first koji-making, second yeast starter and third, main mash." Step one involves seeding the initial small batch of steamed and cooled rice with the koji-kin mold spores in order to produce *kojimai* (koji rice). If you've seen Erik Shirai's popular film *The Birth of Sake*, you'll know this seeding process is also the most photogenic part of the sake-making ritual, often rendered in poetic, sensuous slo-mo—the sake world's equivalent of NBA slam-dunk highlight reels.

In the hot and humid *koji muro*, or koji room, the *toji* shakes out delicate, greenish-brown wisps of koji-kin from what looks like a fine-holed salt shaker over a bed of freshly steamed rice. The Italian priest and biologist who first catalogued the fungus *Aspergillus oryzae* in the late eighteenth century thought that under the microscope it resembled an aspergillum, the liturgical ornament at the end of a rod that Catholic priests use to sprinkle holy water on supplicants. The name is

The incubation room at Akita Konno. The mold is incubated on a substrate of minimally polished rice and placed in wooden trays to complete the two-week process.

oddly apt: the toji is indeed sake's high priest, and the koji room the church where his or her flock of rice grains waits to be anointed.

The process looks ephemeral yet those wisps aren't even the mold spores, which are invisible; they're the medium (usually potato starch) with which the mold spores are mixed and weighted to keep from flying away into space, enabling them to make contact with their target, the pearly rice. The mold invaders will multiply and blanket the softened rice-grain exteriors, penetrating the *shinpaku* (heart) of each grain with their probing hyphae, beginning the conversion of starch to sugar.

The rice is then bundled up and swaddled like a baby. As the hyphae burrow into the steamed rice, they digest its starches and release an array of enzymes that—in combination with the yeasts they will later encounter in the fermenting tank—will create a unique range of intoxicating aromas.

Three enzymes in particular are key to sake making. Alpha-amylase breaks down the rice grain's starchy bonds to create gummy dextrins and other by-products. These are ideal feed for the second

enzyme, glucoamylase, which turns them into sugar. The delicate job of the master brewer is to coax out the right balance of these two enzymes through careful tending of the koji as it develops, regulating temperature and humidity and turning and mixing it on trays to keep it oxygenated. A third enzyme, protease, breaks down proteins into amino acids, which will lend umami to the final brew. The brewer aims for a minimally appropriate level of protease to do the job; too many amino acids will result in off-flavors. Countless other compounds emerge as well, turning the koji rice into a nutrient-dense mix of sugars, vitamins, minerals, amino acids, peptides and acids that can affect both the flavor and texture of the final product.

To allow electron-microscope viewing, *koji-kin* must be free of moisture and its surface covered with a thin layer of gold or platinum.

About forty to forty-five hours after bundling the mold-innoculated rice, it is spread out to dissipate some of the heat it has generated. The koji mold, given the optimal heat and humidity it needs to flourish, has thoroughly colonized the rice.

This process ramps up exponentially when the koji rice is combined with freshly steamed rice, water and yeast to make the *shubo* or *moto* (yeast starter). This is where that elementary principle of every sake education course begins: multiple parallel fermentation. The rapidly growing koji mold continues to colonize the newly added rice, breaking it down into sugars, while in a parallel universe, the just-introduced yeast gets to work fermenting those sugars into alcohol. Mold and yeast share a tank amicably, and are an indispensable team. That's why Yamagata brewer Tomonobu Mitobe had a band record an ode to the duo called "Yeast and Mold" (Check out Mitobe Sake Brewery's Vimeo page to watch one of the best sake music videos ever made, and shot, in a brewery.)

Bespoke Molds and Bacteria: Akita Konno

Our host, Eiko Kodama, tells us that when her husband, Shin'ichiro, was classmates with Hiroshi Konno in the early 1980s at the National Research Institute of Brewing (NRIB), Konno's nickname was ParaKon, short for Paradise Konno. It was a reference to his habit of returning to the dorm after a long night of drinking, falling into bed and exclaiming, "Paradise!" Decades later, we're curious to see what has become of that happy, hard-partying brewing student.

As we approach our stop, Kariwano Station, Eiko points out a long wood-and-glass display case. In it, what looks like a long brown snake turns out to be the rope used in the village's annual *tsunahiki* tug-of-war contest, part of a five-hundred-year-old festival, one of several held in Akita, all of which are tied to the rice harvest. The village is divided into two teams, red and yellow. The winning team is believed to determine the nature of the rice harvest: a red-team victory presages an abundant rice harvest, while a yellow-team victory predicts the price of rice will be high.

In a small meeting room lined with framed koji-kin posters, Konno, dressed in a sharp dark suit with a pocket square and a striped tie, welcomes us. Later, he'll tell us that many people think he's a dead ringer for the actor Tom Selleck. With the same mustache, bushy eyebrows, dark hair (now gone salt-and-pepper gray) and familiar broad, confident smile, he does, in fact. And in his eyes, which twinkle with a kind of merriment, we can see the carefree student he once was.

Until the early twentieth century, he tells us, the Konno family made sake and soy sauce here in Kariwano. The direction of the family business changed when first-generation founder Seiji Konno graduated from Osaka Imperial University [where another Akita-born sake pioneer, Aramasa Brewery's revered patriarch Uhee Sato, studied]. Staffed by faculty members from England and Germany, the school stood as a shining symbol of the Meiji-era government's adoption of Western science. In 1910 Seiji and two of his brothers opened a Kyoto business selling brewing materials to the large breweries of Fushimi and Nada. In 1915 they moved the business to Osaka and began cultivating koji-kin the next year. Their imported Western microscope made possible single spore isolation and germination. Along with state-of-the art glass flasks for culturing, these tools and techniques ushered in a modern age of koji-starter cultivation. The resulting high quality koji-kin allowed the Konnos to quickly build their business and even expand into China and Korea.

Rice shortages and the destruction of its factory in Osaka during World War II led the brothers to return to Akita, where their close ties to southern Akita's Dewatsuru Brewery gave them access to the brewery's warehouse—shuttered during the war—for koji mold cultivation.

Today's visit gives us a new understanding of the large, if largely unheralded role, that koji-mold merchants play in so many of the sakes that we admire. For example, much as yeast researcher Haruhiko Uehigashi is sake-mash doctor to all eighteen brewers in Kochi Prefecture, Konno is his sake-mold equivalent. He receives daily samples of his customers' *kojimai*—the mold-inoculated rice that will go into the yeast starter to convert its starch to sugars—for analysis.

"We check how it's working, all day we're checking enzyme activity," he says. The checking includes whether the enzyme activity is strong enough to dissolve the rice, and levels of glucoamylase, the enzyme that converts starch to glucose. Ginjo sakes, he explains, need a very high level of glucoamylase in order to give the yeast sufficient food to produce the high aromas that are a hallmark of this class of sake.

Laboratory Tour

On a tour of his lab, Konno shows us clear cones filled with different strains of dried *Aspergillus oryzae*, for soy sauce, shochu, *katsuobushi* (smoked, dried and fermented bonito), camembert and

Earliest Records and the Koji Wars

Written records of koji-mold use in Japan go back to at least 714, when it was mentioned in a set of public documents known as the *Harima Fudoki*, an almanac that recorded the flora, fauna, crop production and folklore of a portion of present-day Hyogo Prefecture. Earliest records of commercial koji-kin pop up about eight hundred years ago.

At the end of the Heian period (794–1185) the government established the *koji-za,* or seed koji–making guild, bestowing on members the exclusive right to cultivate seed koji. For the government, this was a way of controlling and maximizing tax revenues from alcohol sales. The guild's best-known production site was at Kyoto's Kitano Tenmangu Shrine. However, as sake transitioned from being a costly product made by brewer-priests for the imperial family and cultivated aristocrats to a beverage also enjoyed by the masses, the system grew shaky. The rapidly growing ranks of Kyoto's sake breweries chafed at this lock the guild had on koji-kin cultivation. Many breweries began making their own seed koji. At first, the government backed the guild, destroying the sake makers' koji-kin cultivation rooms and putting down their attempt to break its monopoly. But an escalating series of events turned the tide, culminating in the mid-1400s when a large horde of angry sake makers faced off against the guild at Tenmangu Shrine. Soldiers stormed the shrine to unseat the koji guild, a fracas that ended in a conflagration and the death of dozens of people.

Roquefort cheeses. He keeps a few plastic bags in his pocket at all times to hold any new fungus he might come across on plants, flowers, or fermented foods. Near an electron microscope, there's a framed poster of a rogue's gallery of cute cartoon characters, each depicting a different type of koji mold. The contrast illustrates one of the dualities of the Japanese character: hard-science co-exists alongside *kawaii* (cute) anime culture. In another room, Konno shows us his culture bank, a −112°F (−80°C) freezer that holds one thousand cultures. The entire lab houses over ten thousand different cultures Konno says. About eighteen are sake koji molds, and another thirty are used for shochu. In addition to supplying sake brewers with koji-kin, the company works with cosmetics companies, chemical and medical research companies; makes various koji-mold-based health food extracts; and a line of microbial, chemical-free pesticides.

A few minutes later he shows us an impressively indecipherable print-out, a chemical analysis of a sake. Another service he provides clients, he explains, is to help them come up with the right koji-kin to brew an award-winning sake. To do this, he analyzes the chemical fingerprint of various prizewinning sakes the way a sports coach might analyze tape of an opposing team's play in preparation for playoff season. With this detailed intelligence at his fingertips, he advises his customers on different ways they might brew a prizewinning sake.

"We have ready-made and order-made" koji-kin, he explains. Most of his client breweries use bespoke order-made formulas. Lactic acid formulas are another of the many different products

Hiroshi Konno, PhD, president of Akita Konno, manufacturer and seller of *Aspergillus* molds.

that Akita Konno sells. "If a company wants to make a new version of their sake, they'll change their starter—this is a way to expand their business," he says. And this can mean playing with lactic acid, which, in addition to killing unwanted microorganisms, produces various organic acids that can lend different tastes to sake. Konno offers four or five different strains of lactic acid to breweries. And, as with his koji mold, he offers select customers made-to-order strains.

How Koji-kin is Cultivated

Although our schedule does not allow us a visit to the koji-kin cultivation factory, Konno describes how it's done. While sake brewers make their koji rice to produce enzymes that will convert the rice's starch to sugar and jump-start fermentation in the mash, the purpose of making seed koji is to produce *Aspergillus oryzae* spores in bulk to make koji rice. Propagation takes about two weeks.

To breed high-quality seed koji, the fungi are cultured on steamed rice that has been polished to a ratio of only 96 percent, meaning only 4 percent of the bran is taken off, just enough to allow the desired amount of water to infiltrate while soaking and steaming. After steaming and cooling, the rice is mixed with trace amounts of mineral-nutrient-rich camellia ash, a technique that ancient koji-kin cultivators discovered increases the rate of spore harvest. Most microorganisms, if subjected to the high alkalinity of wood ash, simply die, Konno explains. "Conversely, if *Aspergillus*, or koji-kin, is mixed with wood ash, it's able to use the potassium in the ash to grow a large number of spores." Wood ash was the perfect medium to cultivate koji-kin: it eliminated harmful microorganisms and promoted the growth of *Aspergillus* spores, allowing

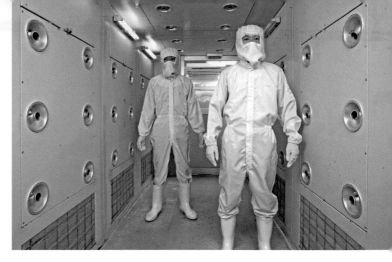

Akita Konno's bacteria-cleansing "air shower" creates a sterile environment for mold cultivation.

breeders to obtain an exceedingly pure koji-kin.

"Not only that," adds Konno admiringly, "wood ash plays an active role in the preservation of the original seed koji-kin used for propagation, which is the lifeblood of the mold dealer. Koji-kin made with wood ash is more durable than koji-kin made without it, and it is able to retain its high germination rate even when stored in poor conditions. More than four hundred years ago, no one even knew of the existence of microorganisms, but brewers were using wood ash for the separation, culturing and long-term storage of koji-kin," he says. "I admire the wisdom of the Japanese people who did this before any other people of the world."

New koji-mold strains are created through a lengthy process of induced mold transformations that involve irradiating microflora or subjecting them to ultraviolet light to speed the rate of random, naturally occurring mutations. These microflora then grow new mold spores that are examined for sake-making potential. Konno does not use any genetic-engineering techniques.

As Terada Honke's Keisuke Terada intuited through his fermented foods explorations, the potential to harness the strength and intelligence of microbes and molds—whether through the human microbiome, non-chemical pesticides or new medicines— is only now beginning to be understood. "As the technology advances," Konno predicts, "we'll find new species that will be applied to other fields and industries."

Visit to Koji-kin Purveyor Higuchi Moyashi

On a sweltering July day, our taxi driver, seemingly lost, circles around our target before finally zeroing in on the narrow residential street we're looking for in the Abeno Ward of southern Osaka. Our destination, Higuchi Matsunosuke Shoten, is a study in nondescript gray: gray wall, gray siding, grayish silver aluminum window frames.

Appearances are deceptive. Higuchi Moyashi, as the company is informally known, is Japan's largest purveyor of koji-kin. *Moyashi* means bean sprout, a reference to the fact that when magnified, koji mold, with its long hyphae, looks a lot like bean sprouts.

In a spare, second-floor wood-paneled office furnished with a desk, three chairs and a rack full of test tubes, company director Koichi Higuchi, who's in line to become the seventh-generation head of the company, greets us. He grew up across the street from these headquarters; out the window, we can see his mother's spacious rose garden and her smaller traditional Japanese garden. Like other Japanese kids, he was raised on a diet of miso soup and soy- and mirin seasoned foods. But very few had his understanding of the invisible alchemy in these foods that his family's company makes possible.

Higuchi studied biology in college and worked as a visiting researcher in the US before facing the fact that as the only child, he was destined to one day step into his father's shoes as president of the family company. The company was founded in 1855, yet is not nearly the oldest koji-kin company in Japan; that would be the more-than-350-year-old Kyoto-based company Hishiroku. The two companies, along with Akita Konno are among the seven active licensed sellers of purified, shelf-stable koji-kin.

Higuchi Moyashi sells koji-kin to makers of soy sauce, miso, mirin, sake, *amazake* (a creamy, sweet lightly fermented rice drink) and shochu liquor— the gamut of Japanese fermented products. But not every product takes the same type of mold. In the family of the *Aspergillus* mold, there are three different types. Sake is made with the rice-friendly *Aspergillus oryzae* mold, which is also used to make miso, soy sauce, mirin and amazake. Typically, the koji-kin used for sake is yellow koji. The second is known as *Aspergillus sojae*, and is used exclusively for certain kinds of soy-sauce production. The soy sauce giant Kikkoman, says Higuchi, is so big it has its own in-house mold-breeding operation. We picture an Amazon-style giant warehouse for mold, though it is probably relatively compact, so microscopic are these hard-working spores.

The third type is *Aspergillus luchuensis*, known in the US and

Left Different forms of the *Aspergillus* mold are used for different fermented products. **Below** Koichi Higuchi, director of *koji-kin* producer Higuchi Matsunosuke Shoten.

Europe as *Aspergillus awamori* because it's used for the distilling of Okinawan specialty *awamori*, an indigenous beverage distilled using a base of long-grain rice, and believed to be the predecessor of shochu liquor. This mold is ideal for shochu because of the rich citric acid, and hence a sourness that it produces. Some adventurous brewers, have started to use *Aspergillus awamori* in sake in place of lactic acids to create a slightly sour flavor profile.

Higuchi then pulls a tightly stoppered test tube to show us some brown koji used for rice and barley shochu. Another is for miso, and another for soy sauce. All look a uniform, green-tinged brown tone except for the black koji which is espresso colored, and the brown, the color of light brown sugar. The very light-colored one is a white mutation of *Aspergillus oryzae* and has become popular for amazake and white miso production. The color white exerts a powerful pull on the Japanese psyche; to cater to consumer's preference for light-colored

drinks and condiments, makers will use white koji-kin even though it results in lower enzymatic activity.

Despite the profusion of new yeast varieties and hybrid rice strains, Higuchi describes the world of koji-kin as changing a little more slowly. Ginjo makers, for example, will usually start with one of four varieties of koji mold, likely the Hikami variety, which is relatively easy to control and grows quickly. About fifteen years ago, to cater to the trend for sakes that are both sweeter and higher in acidity, Higuchi created a new strain called High G, now a bestseller. This mold creates higher levels of glucoamylase, the enzyme that facilitates the production of fermentable sugars. Several years ago the company launched the next-level version, Super High G and Milk High G to meet demand, especially from Tohoku makers whose brews tend to be richer in glucose amylase.

For an up-close look at how koji-kin is cultivated, we take a tour of the factory. Although it was built in 1995, this phase of koji-mold-starter cultivation, at least, is as old-school as it gets. In many ways the cultivation process closely mirrors that of the koji-rice-making process. The cultivation room has to be spotlessly clean to prevent the growth of stray bacteria. As with the traditional brewery koji room, this one is lined with cedar, which, in addition to possessing antimicrobial powers, absorbs excess water yet keeps the koji room moist. Similarly, the room's thick walls are insulated with rice and barley husks to regulate temperature and humidity. We see some old-fashioned wooden trays, similar to those used in sake-brewery koji rooms, as well as their modern replacement, sterile metal trays. Nearby is a cylindrical container for soaking and steaming the rice that will be used as the substrate, or base material, on which the koji spores will flourish A brand-new facility is under construction now, in which, Higuchi promises, "we'll change everything."

There are certain aspects of koji cultivation that are off-limits to outsiders. There have been efforts to steal the company's koji strains, sometimes by foreign countries. "We sell to all buyers," Higuchi explains. "But I make sure of their purpose. If someone is trying to steal our strains to make a koji starter, I worry, because it can be very dangerous if done incorrectly on an industrial level."

The Koji Universe Keeps Expanding

Although Higuchi has told us the pace of new koji-kin development is not rapid, koji producers

are nevertheless continually engaged in research to bring forth new strains. One of the more recent strains, from Akita Konno, reflects both the changing taste and aroma profile of sake and the way the development of new yeast and molds are connected. Made in collaboration with the prefectural research center, this Akita Konno strain is called N54G, and was released in 2008 largely to counteract the bitterness that can be a by-product of the super-aromatic modern yeasts that have become popular in recent years.

Yet no matter how high-tech and advanced his profession becomes, Hiroshi Konno never wants to lose track of the ancient knowledge on which the roots of the mold merchant's business stand. He points to the wooden plaque in his office, bearing the company motto in an archaic form of Japanese script. It reads "Learn a lesson from the past in order to create something new."

Koji Flight

Sake name: Yoshidagura "U"
Sake type: Yamahai junmai
Brewery: Ishikawa
From the brewery featured in Erik Shirai's Birth of Sake *documentary, a solidly built sake with fresh-cut grass aromas and a savory yet sharp, precise palate.*

Sake name: Mutsu Hassen
Sake type: No grade
Brewery: Hachinohe Brewery, Aomori Prefecture
The brewery uses the novel method of combining white koji to make a starter bursting with acidity, then transitioning to yellow koji to build the main mash. The result is a sake that is ultra clean, pure tasting and finely balanced.

Sake name: Kuro Kabuto
Sake type: Junmai ginjo
Brewery: Ikekame Shuzo, Fukuoka Prefecture
Juicy, round, with strawberry flavors. Made with Yamada Nishiki koji rice and Yume Ikkon rice for the main mash.

Chapter Eighteen

Master Brewers and the New Collectives

Along with the rapid development of Akita Prefecture's sake industry in the late-nineteenth and early twentieth centuries, the demand for seasonal brewery workers expanded. The village of Sannai (today part of Yokote City), with its large population of farmers who were free during the winter months, became a hub for *kurabito* (brewery worker) recruitment. Every fall, the farmers of Sannai set out from their home village for their winter brewery workplaces. One subset of this group of farmers was known in Akita dialect as *sakaya wakazei*, or "sake breweries' young energy"; workers with the youth and vigor needed to make it through the brewing season's bitterly cold winters, early mornings and late nights.

The grueling work was well paid, and was considered good training for the enlistment exam to enter Japan's armed forces. As they became more skilled, workers emerged from the ranks who were not only highly competent brewers, but also possessed executive leadership skills. They formed their own *kurabito* teams, often made up of blood relatives, which traveled with them each brewing season. The Sannai Toji Guild was officially formed in 1922 and reached a peak membership of roughly six-hundred members. Demand for members' skills was so high that some were called to staff breweries as far away as China, Korea and the Sakhalin islands.

Widely admired master brewer Toichi Takahashi was born in Sannai and is a third-generation member of the Sannai Toji Guild. For the past thirty-seven years, he's worked at Saiya Brewery in Yurihonjo, Akita, maker of the Yuki no Bosha brand of sake. On our visit to the brewery, we find him dressed in a uniform of white lab coat and baseball hat. At the age of seventy-six, he still exudes a boyish passion for his craft. Takahashi's family history spans the rise and fall of the toji-guild era in Akita Prefecture, beginning with his grandfather Yokichi, who was born in 1878 before the advent of

sanbai zoshu, the triple-volume, adulterated sake born of wartime rice shortages. Toichi's father Kokichi only knew and brewed this diluted *futsushu* or "regular" sake.

Takahashi says, "From the time I was a very small boy, I was raised by my grandfather because my father was always working. My grandfather taught me about junmai, because that's all he had ever brewed. I was raised on tales of his natural-starter

Toichi Takahashi, master brewer at Saiya Brewery, makers of the Yuki no Bosha line of sake.

sake. I was very close to the sake-making process because everyone talked about sake making, and I read a lot about it, too. My grandfather would criticize my father and say, 'That's not sake you're making.' He refused to drink my father's sake." Not surprisingly, father and grandfather did not get along. But decades later, this early inculcation made Toichi the ideal toji to help revive junmai brewing, which he began to do in 1987, three years after his 1984 arrival at Saiya Brewery.

The Roots of the Sake Guild System

The earliest sake guilds go back to sixteenth-century pre-Edo times. During the Warring States period (1467–1615), the powerful feudal lord Oda Nobunaga swept through Japan's main island of Honshu, consolidating power in an effort to unify the country. He and his successor, Tokugawa Ieyasu, viewed the Buddhist temple complexes of Nara—seats of power as well as sake-brewing expertise—as existential threats. Their destruction of the temples resulted in the demise of the brewing culture that had been nurtured there. But remnants of that knowledge, including written diaries, migrated to Itami in the northeast, centered on a village called Konoike. There, Nara techniques were preserved by makers who gathered rice from farms and villages along the Ina and Muko rivers and brewed sake. The Konoike and Nara toji guilds are considered the country's earliest, collecting, advancing and disseminating the accumulated wisdom of the monk master brewers from a previous age.

During our visit with Yoshihiko Yamamoto, president and toji at Yucho Brewery in Nara, the topic of the guilds comes up. Referring to one of his favorite books, the *Domo shuzoki* (Annals of the Domo Brewery), issued in the 1600s by Konoike Brewery, he says it's full of information on Konoike Guild sake-making techniques and mentions other sake guilds as well. The book also includes the Nara Guild and the importance of Nara to brewing history, which feeds Yoshimoto's sense of local pride and makes him happy, especially one passage that describes the Nara "monk starter" technique as "the beginning of sake making."

Yoshihiko Yamamoto, owner and master brewer of the Yucho Brewery, makers of the Kaze no Mori brand.

Heyday of the Guild System

At its peak, the toji-for-hire system and the guild system were powerful forms of knowledge sharing, creating distinctive regional styles of brewing, like those of the venerable Tanba and Tajima toji guilds of Hyogo Prefecture, the soft-water brewing expertise of the Hiroshima Toji Guild that grew up around ginjo sake pioneer Senzaburo Miura, and the signature *tanrei karakuchi* (crisp and dry) style of Niigata's Echigo Toji Guild. Guilds came in all different sizes and complexions, too. While most toji were farmers in the off season, the Echizen Nuka Toji Guild of Fukui Prefecture developed as a subgroup of the local fishing industry. And while some guilds' influence was limited to their home prefectures, others influenced sake brewing on a national or even international level as skilled members traveled to less technically advanced

Left to right Naohiko Noguchi from the Naohiko Noguchi Research Center; Yasuhiko Niida from Niida Honke Brewery; and Yusuke Sato of Aramasa Brewery.

regions and passed on techniques and styles. Among the latter, are the Echigo Guild of Niigata and the Nanbu Guild of Iwate, currently the largest guild in Japan. As well as the Sannai Guild, the Noto Guild of Ishikawa and the Bichu Guild of Okayama have had success exporting their expertise to other Asian countries.

The Toji as God

In any brewery, the toji is treated with the utmost respect. While rank-and-file *kurabito* brewery workers are housed in communal dormitories, the toji will often get his own room. Philip Harper, the renowned British toji of Kinoshita Brewery in Kyoto, has described working at breweries where during staff meals, no one picks up their chopsticks before the toji does. When the toji puts his chopsticks down, the meal is over for everyone. Baths, too, are taken in order of seniority.

During the pre- and postwar years, the guild system produced a number of toji who achieved widespread, even legendary, status in the sake world. Third-generation Noto Toji Guild member Naohiko Noguchi is one of these people and his reputation encompasses not just himself, but his employer, Kikuhime Brewery in Ishikawa Prefecture, where he spent thirty-six years and along the way revived the old-school *yamahai* method of brewing. He retired at age sixty-five, did a second stint as toji at another brewery for another twelve

years and at age eighty-four came out of retirement a second time to launch his eponymous Naohiko Noguchi Research Center. Sake expert John Gauntner visited him there when he was eighty-six, finding him spry and working as hard as anyone on the team. But Noguchi's reputation for being a fearsome taskmaster was such that he earned the nickname, *Oni*, or Demon, meaning that he was both feared and respected for his fanatic work ethic. One former kurabito told Gauntner that in twenty years of working with the master, he never once spoke directly to him.

The guild system could also be competitive and contentious. Toichi Takahashi of Saiya Brewery explains how the Sannai Toji divided into five or six different factions, each with different philosophies. His group was made up of younger brewers with progressive ideas. One group picked up and went to work for Gekkeikan in Fushimi. When it came to guild elections, there could be friction: in the early 1980s, Takahashi was in line to receive a promotion, but it was derailed by factional politics. In the end, he says, it was the best thing that could have happened, leading to his move to Saiya Brewery.

Perhaps in reaction to the cult of the toji that formed around Noguchi during his tenure at

Kikuhime, brewery patriarch Tatsushi Yanagi devised his "meister" system of brewery workers based on the German apprenticeship system. He began employing students with a background in science, who could gradually rise to the level of toji or *kashira* (the toji's right-hand person), or other positions. Each worker holds the highest level of the two-level government certification system, Yanagi notes, so could become a toji at any other brewery.

Yanagi believes the toji has become overly exalted, and that because today there are so many other kinds of manufacturing jobs that farmers—or any young people—can do, the part-time kurabito worker is going the way of the dinosaur. Kurabito are hard to find, and so more and more breweries are moving to full-time staff brewers and toji.

At Niida Honke Brewery in Fukushima, eighteenth-generation president Yasuhiko Niida, as part of his holistic vision of taking care of land and people, provides his staff year-round employment. Each of his employees masters all aspects of the sake-brewing process, spending the winters brewing together and the summers cultivating the brewery's organic rice fields.

The Rise of the Owner-Toji

As the guild system has faded, other institutions have come to the fore to fill the void. Nodai, the Tokyo University of Agriculture, where Niida himself graduated, is often a stop for brewery heirs preparing to take over the family business, and has helped usher in the rise of president-toji like himself. Yasutaka Daimon, the sixth-generation heir to Daimon Brewery in Osaka, believes the rise of the brewer-toji has been good for sake. "Sake brewing is very risky, so people were afraid of experimentation—no challenge, no creation," he says. But with the rise of the *kuramoto-toji*, or owner-master brewer, that's changed. "When owners, as well as their sons and daughters, take on the master brewer role, they have more leeway: they can afford to make mistakes," he adds. "That's why we're seeing so many different kinds of sake now."

Wearing both toji and owner hats can be complicated, and selling sake today is also far more difficult than it was when everything being made was "regular" sake that practically sold itself. Kamoizumi Brewery owner-toji Kazuhiro Maegaki says that with breweries making a number of different styles and often labels of sake, the owner-toji "has to think about issues like brand image, and how to make a sake with consumer tastes in mind." The upside is that when it's the owner-toji overseeing both production and marketing, one person can realize his or her concept for a sake faster than under the old toji system.

In Niigata Prefecture, the realization that the old toji-guild method of passing on sake-brewing knowledge was fading, coupled with a desire for technological advances, led a group of sake brewers to team up with their prefectural research center to launch the Niigata Sake School in 1984. In 2018, an academic/industrial/government collaboration resulted in the opening of Niigata University's Sakeology Center, which educates students on production, history, culture and sake's connections to agriculture, finance and medicine.

Some toji, like Harper, who learned at the feet of seasoned elders with a lifetime of brewing experience at their fingertips, feel nostalgia for a fading way of life in sake. Yet most of the toji and brewery presidents we spoke to feel that the system, like the times, must change, and say there has been no loss of expertise. Kosuke Kuji, a trained toji and president of Nanbu Bijin Brewery, who learned both from his brewer grandfather and at Nodai, says although the old ways may be changing, his dedication to the Nanbu Guild style of brewing will never waver, and that the guild itself is strong.

"Every summer we meet for four days, lodge together and have a training camp. Through those types of meetings, things such as social media techniques are passed on," he explains, "The speed of transmission is totally different from the old days." Turf and timelines are carefully drawn too; a week after the Nanbu meeting, the Sannai Toji Guild holds its week-long training retreat.

But what is the Nanbu style, or the Sannai style these days? More often than not, when we ask, "What is the fill-in-the-blank toji guild style of

Fukumitsuya master brewer Kazuhiko Itaya has worked with four different *toji* guilds and is guided by all of them.

brewing?" or "What is the regional style of fill-in-the-blank region?" we get the same answer: "It's hard to say." It's clear that one thing that has been lost with the passing of the traditional seasonal toji and the guild system is a strong sense of regional brewing styles. Yet interrogating the notion of whether regionality as such exists is still a valuable organizing principle, a lens through which to learn about sake.

Kazuhiko Itaya, the toji at Fukumitsuya Brewery in Ishikawa Prefecture, agrees that "while each toji guild has its various technical strengths and types of sake, the distinctiveness of each guild is being lost as sake styles diversify, and also because there's such a rapid spread of knowledge in our society." Itaya himself has learned from and worked with the Tango, Echizen Nuka and Noto guilds. He considers the lessons he learned at each to embody "the core of his brewing." But he adds that at Fukumitsuya Brewery, the kurabito combine skills they've learned from other guilds to help the brewery make its own kind of elegant, rich and often aged sake.

Beyond simply sharing brewing techniques and a regional style of brewing, the guilds were a labor union, a hiring center for brewers, protecting their rights to fair wages. "The original purpose of the guild was not to share knowledge, but to ensure no one was earning more than others," says Kazuhiro Maegaki, of Kamoizumi Brewery. Keichirou Katsuki, formerly special advisor to the Matsumoto Brewery's production department, says "Now there's no need for a union because kurabito are too expensive to hire." Brewing has gone in-house, and so in effect, each brewery is a guild, he explains.

Where the guilds were once secretive societies that rarely divulged their techniques, Katsuki believes that today, all brewing knowledge should be open-source , and says it is already happening: brewers frequently visit each other and hold study meetings. Each brewery, he says, is a small thread in a rope, and "all have to work together" to keep sake viable. "I want as many different brewers as possible to survive," he says. There's no danger in losing individuality by doing this, he believes, because water is the biggest single differentiator in sake. "Even if all information is shared, the finished expression of each sake brewer will be different."

The New Brewing Collectives

Katsuki's vision of an "open-source" knowledge sharing both harks back to the past—Senzaburo Miura's open-source approach to publishing and sharing all the secrets of Hiroshima-style brewing— and to the forward-looking collectives that have popped up around the country.

In Akita Prefecture, five brewers began collaborating in 2010, mainly, says Aramasa Brewery owner-toji Yusuke Sato, because they were young and inexperienced and wanted to help and learn from each other. The members, who called themselves the Next Five, were from Akita, Aramasa, Fukurokuju, Kuribayashi and Yamamoto breweries. They met regularly to discuss brewing techniques and management challenges, and began producing one joint sake project a year, a practice unheard of in the sake world. Each year a different member took the lead, and a batch of two tanks, or about four thousand bottles, was brewed. The project was a hit, each issue with a sold-out waiting list. At the end of five years they thought the project was over. "Everyone's sake had gotten better, and our management, too," says Sato. But the demand for more sake was there, so they began collaborating with artists in various fields: the painter Takashi Murakami (who designed a label splashed with his colorful, smiling flowers), the deejay and sake fan Ritchie Hawtin, and star architect Tane Tsuyoshi (who designed a clear bottle covered in textured spikes, like the back of an armadillo). In 2018 they collaborated with a manga artist who created the label design; each bottle in this series came packaged

with a ceramic sake cup from one of forty-nine different pottery artists. Through these efforts the group has not only raised its collective brewing and management skills, it has succeeded in building excitement and cachet around each new release.

Other collectives have emerged, too, including DATE7 in Miyagi and Yamakawa Mitsuo in Yamagata. Think of them as smaller, contemporary and way hipper versions of toji guilds, with an appeal closer to that of a popular (albeit aging) boy band than to the farmer-toji guilds of old. As one Japanese journalist described the Next Five concept: "It was an explosive hit and became the driving force behind the popularity of Akita Sake."

By now you may be wondering, where are the women? In the next chapter we'll introduce some female toji who are making their mark on sake.

Toji Flight

Sake name (Japan): Yuki no Bosha
Sake name (US): Cabin in the Snow
Sake type: Yamahai junmai
Brewery: Saiya Brewery, Akita
Master brewer Toichi Takahashi has inspired brewers throughout Akita, using only proprietary yeast for sake that is light and fragrant. Unlike Yamahai's umami- and earth-driven backbone, this is fruity and elegant.

Sake name: Naohiko Noguchi Sake Institute
Sake type: Yamahai Gohyaku-mangoku
Brewery: Naohiko Noguchi Sake Institute, Ishikawa Prefecture
Exhibits elegance, precision and mastery of temperature control, all marks of Noguchi's deft touch.

Sake name: Koshi no Kanbai "Bessen"
Sake type: Ginjo
Brewery: Ishimoto Brewery, Niigata Prefecture
This esteemed brewery, headed by brewer Shinichi Takeuchi, offers up classic tanrei karakuchi sakes with both Gohyakuman-goku and Yamada Nishiki rice.

Chapter Nineteen

Reclaiming Their Place: Women Master Brewers

In 1991, Rumiko Moriki and her husband Hideki were struggling to run Rumiko's small family brewery in Iga, Mie Prefecture. Three years earlier, when her father suffered a stroke, Moriki quit her job at a nearby pharmaceutical company to try to keep the family business alive. Newly married, her husband, who did fermentation research at a large food company, reluctantly joined in the effort. She was twenty-eight and he was twenty-nine. Times had been hard for the brewery for some years already; unable to afford a full staff, her parents had been producing the sake themselves with the help of a seasonal *toji* and one brewery worker. Her father wanted to shut down the business, but Moriki had always loved sake, and loved what it stood for: she wanted to take over.

The work, however, was more than she and her husband could handle. "We were like dancing mice, running around in circles every day, and we were at the limits of our physical endurance," she recalls. "Financially we weren't doing well either, but we didn't want to grumble about our situation."

Then late one night in 1991, Moriki finished reading the twelfth and final volume of a recently published manga series called *Natsuko no sake* (Natsuko's Sake) by Akira Oze. In Japan, manga are not just a storytelling vehicle for kids; the more sophisticated titles are comparable in their breadth and complexity to the serialized newspaper sagas that nineteenth-century Western authors wrote. This series was about a young woman, Natsuko, a gifted sake taster who works at a Tokyo ad agency. When her brother suddenly dies, she quits her job and returns to her family's brewery in the countryside to continue her brother's quest to revive a mythical heirloom rice and with it, brew the best sake in Japan.

The series, which is a highly realistic reflection of the sake-brewing industry and the hard times it was

Left Rumiko Moriki, one of the first women master brewers in Japan. **Above** Rie Toyomoto, center, and Moriki, immediate right, transferring rice from steamer to cooler.

going through in the late eighties and early nineties, struck a chord with Rumiko. Like the struggling brewery depicted in the manga, many of those around her were trying to stay afloat by cutting costs, which inevitably sacrificed quality. Most were making *futsu*, or regular, sake, but Moriki and her husband had been increasingly attracted to the junmai sakes that were just starting to be revived. Philosophically and even physically, they felt their bodies were telling them to return to making pure rice sake. The manga's exploration of agricultural practices in Japan, the return to more traditional forms of sake making and Natsuko's desire to make truly great sake lit a fire under Moriki and made her commit to following in Natsuko's footsteps.

There were also striking, uncanny similarities between Rumiko Moriki and the fictional Natsuko.

Like Natsuko, Moriki had grown up in a sake brewery. "The brewery building is right next to our kitchen, so it was like I was living in the *kura* (brewery), it was so familiar," she says. She remembers the yearly arrival of five *kurabito* from the Noto Peninsula at the start of brewing season, when she was a child. But when she and her husband took over the brewery they struggled to get the work done. She remembers once waking up at four in the morning and carrying a 66-pound (30-kg) batch of steamed rice up a ramp to add to the fermentation tank; she was also carrying her unborn baby.

In one key scene of the manga, Natsuko presses her first batch of the heirloom "phantom sake." (The story's fictional Saeki Brewery is based on Niigata's Kusumi Brewery, makers of the Kiyoizumi brand, and its owner Norimichi Kusumi's quest to revive the Kame no O heirloom rice strain.) The reader also learns that the day is doubly special: It is February 7, Natsuko's birthday. "The date of my birthday, too, is February 7," Moriki says.

For all these reasons, she explains, the series "was like a declaration. It really gave us strength. We had been thinking of quitting the business, but this made us want to continue for the next generation." She closed the manga and immediately penned a letter to Oze.

"It is one in the morning on June 22, 1991," she wrote. "I have just finished reading *Natsuko's Sake.*" After briefly explaining how she came back to work at the family brewery, she added, "Like Natsuko, I grew up next to the fermenting tanks with the scent of koji and sake, learning the taste of sake before I knew anything else about the world.

"When I was in elementary school, I already understood the deliciousness of the *arabashiri* that drips from the tank mouth. When I got home from school I would secretly steal some from the tank. I'm not an expert taster of brand-name sake like Natsuko, but I think I understand delicious sake."

Before Moriki sent off the letter, she made a copy of her driver's license, which showed that her birthday was identical to Natsuko's, and sent off the letter. Among the bags of letters that Oze received, he later said that Moriki's stood out. He shared it with close friends of his, a brewer and sake shop owner, in Saitama Prefecture where they all lived. These friends of Oze were so moved by Moriki's heartfelt letter and her story that they visited her in Mie to help with the brewing and offer professional advice. Oze also invited Moriki to a sake study group meeting in Tokyo with a group of illustrious brewers, all of whom were experimenting with making junmai sake. She traveled there with her one-and-a-half year-old son on her back, while pregnant with her third child. She was in awe of the forty or so famous brewers assembled to talk about junmai sake. Among them was Yoshimasa Ogawa-hara of Shinkame Sake Brewery in Saitama, who would become an important mentor to her.

She and husband Hideki—now fully committed to their mission—began brewing their first junmai sake that same year, 1991. For its label, Oze drew a beautiful likeness of her, gentle and dignified, in the style of his manga. Naturally, it was called Rumiko no Sake, or "Rumiko's Sake."

The Natsuko character was based on a male brewer, Norimichi Kusumi, but to make a point about sexism in the brewing world, and, as Rumiko says, "to stick up for the disadvantaged," Oze had made her a woman who faced objections from male brewers. Rumiko was the real-life version of Natsuko, and it was through this surreal blend of fiction and reality that Oze's vision was in a way realized. Moriki became one of the first women toji in Japan, and as far as she knows, the first woman owner-toji in the country, splitting the job with her husband. She is in charge of koji making, while Hideki, who studied fermentation science at Hiroshima University, handles the making of the starter and the main mash.

The Role of Women in Early Sake Making

In early Shintoism, shrine maidens called *miko* were the brewers of sake, beginning their ritual by chewing and spitting out rice and letting their body's own enzymes start the process of fermentation. During the Edo period (1603–1868), the belief evolved that menstrual blood made women "un-clean," and so they were barred from sake breweries. Yet the word *toji* (杜氏) itself is believed to hark back to ancient times when the woman of the household brewed the sake; the word is thought to be a corruption of another rendering of the word using the characters 刀自, meaning "madam" or "lady."

The start of her toji career was "at the very end of the period when women were prohibited from entering breweries," Moriki explains. Though the prejudice against women in sake breweries was fading, she notes, "there were still subtle shades of that. It was so rare to have women on the brewing site that it was considered strange; it would become the source of talk." When she first entered the brewery, it was also pre-Internet, pre-social media, when breweries were relatively closed and one really did not know what was going on in other breweries.

Yet during those first early years of being a master brewer, Moriki says she did not suffer any discrimi-nation, or at least did not stop to notice anything of the sort. "I was doing the work as a desperate effort to keep the company alive, so I didn't care about any

Mariko Chino, master brewer at Nagano Prefecture's oldest brewery, Shusen Kurano. The prefecture is especially rich in women master brewers.

group and fifty or so are women owners or master brewers. Members are scattered throughout the country, but one prefecture that stands out for its wealth of female brewing talent is Nagano, home to seven women toji.

Leading the way is Mariko Chino of Shusen Kurano Brewery, the oldest brewery in Nagano (founded in 1540), maker of the Kawanakajima line of sakes. Born in 1967, she became toji at her family's brewery in 2000. The youngest of the group is Mami Wakabayashi, who was born in 1987. "Nagano has the second largest number of breweries in Japan after Niigata," Chino explains, "and many more small breweries, so there are many more successors." There also happens to be an abundance of daughters. Midori Okazaki, the toji at Okazaki Brewery, for example, is the youngest of three daughters.

"If you have a small sake brewery, rather than bringing in a toji from elsewhere, you can make the sake by yourself," Chino explains. "You reduce labor costs, you don't waste money and you can also make a sake that's close to your ideal." It is also true that all of the women we spoke to are owner-toji whose rise coincided with both the owner-toji movement and the same hard economic times for the brewing industry that led Rumiko Moriki to return to her family brewery. It was economic necessity as much as women's empowerment that placed them in the master-brewer position.

The only child of the family, Chino left her hometown of Kawanakajima to attend Nodai. Although she met her husband Kenichi while they were students at Nodai, it was she, not him, who went on to become toji; he fills the position of brewery manager. "I was the heir to the brewery and was the toji before I got married," Chino explains. "So I asked him to be the brewery manager."

In 2007, as the number of farmers in Nagano decreased and more fields fell fallow, Chino began collaborating with local farmers. She uses the

of that." By 1999, though, she did feel the need for some type of forum for women to support each other and exchange information, so she launched the first Women in Sake-Brewing Summit.

Moriki Brewery, which now employs between five and six kurabito, has made a reputation for itself as a maker of organic, minimally manipulated sakes, old-school kimotos and yamahais that are exactly the kind that Natsuko wanted to make. Moriki is now in her sixties, and says she hopes to continue brewing until she's seventy. Her successor, Rie Toyomoto, a graduate of Tokyo University of Agriculture (Nodai) who has worked alongside Rumiko and Hideki for twenty years now, took over toji duties in 2016. Rumiko's younger son, Yu, will one day take over as president and her daughter Nozomi, a Nodai graduate with an interest in natural wine, may one day become master brewer.

The Women Brewers of Nagano Prefecture

In 2018, there were twenty-four women master brewers in Japan; today there are about sixty registered members of the Women in Sake-Brewing

prefectural rice that they grow, Hitogokochi, to brew her own creation, the elegant Kawanakajima Genbu sake.

For Mie Oguchi, assuming the position of toji at her family's Koten Brewery in Suwa, which she did in 2016, was not an easy thing to do. Obsessed with softball in her younger years, she didn't think about entering the family brewery until she was in high school. At that point her family showed her around the brewery for the first time, and she got a glimpse into what life inside might be like. As a child, she explains, she had not entered the brewery because it was considered a dangerous place, not suitable for girls and women.

"I saw the tank bubbling with fermentation and thought, 'This is really interesting. You can't see the workings of microorganisms with the eye, and there's that nice aroma,'" she recalls. She attended Nodai for four years, then stayed on for two more years of graduate work. During her graduate studies she participated in joint research projects with the National Research Institute of Brewing (NRIB), then went on to become a researcher there.

When she finally returned to the brewery, her parents suggested she shadow the toji, Satoshi Ito. Even with the support of her brother and sister in the sales and management side of the business, it would be

another ten years before she was deemed ready to take on the toji role. Ito was an old-school *dekasegi* (itinerant) brewer who, from age fifteen, made sake during the winter and farmed during the summers. He gruffly told his new charge, "If you're going to get married and then quit, I'm not going to teach you." Then he added as an afterthought, "but then, you're over thirty and not married yet," as if that were insurance enough for him.

Oguchi learned the technical aspects of brewing from Ito, but says, "running the brewery is more than just technique." What she found most challenging was hiring and managing the brewery staff

The Wakabayashis, left to right: Yoko Wakabayashi; her son-in-law Makoto Wakabayashi; Makoto's wife, master brewer Mami Wakabayashi; Mami's father, Fumio Wakabayashi; Mami's older sister, Misa Wakabayashi.

each year. When she began doing this, most of the seasoned old kurabito were retiring or had retired and it was hard to find workers who would return each year. "Ascertaining aptitudes, finding good technicians and stabilizing the team, all of that was very difficult," she says.

The team members that she inherited didn't immediately welcome her with open arms, either. "If Ito-san said something, they would listen, but not to me," she recalls. "At first I wondered if I could do it, because there was the issue of strength. And then knowing I went to university, they may have thought I was just book smart and self-important. So the first year was hard." But Ito let her rotate through every job in the brewery, and when the other kurabito saw how hard she worked, they softened. "After a year or so, they began to acknowledge that I could do the job," Oguchi says. For support outside the brewery, she found the network of women brewers extremely valuable, as was her classmate network both at Nodai and at the NRIB. Her former professors, too, became a source of support, "to the point where they kind of became friends," she adds.

From her first year as toji, she's seen her brewing mission as twofold. On the one hand, she wants to protect the dry, traditional sake that Ito pioneered, geared toward the loyal local market. This is sake that's designed "to take people's fatigue away, and not surprise them," Oguchi says, "the type that's presented as a gift outside of Nagano to give outsiders a taste of the region's produce." Her other objective is to nurture her own brand, Mie Special. This is a sake that she changes every year to keep challenging herself, one that she hopes will attract more women and newcomers to sake. "Making it is really fun, but selling it is really hard," she says. "From now on, I want to work more on that."

Despite what her mentor Ito said, Oguchi did get married, in 2017, but continued her work. She and her husband Kojiro, who works in an accounting

Mami Wakabayashi, holding her Tsukiyoshino sake.

firm, named their son Junpei (純平), an homage to sake and harmony. Its two kanji characters are the "jun" from "junmai," meaning "pure," and "pei," meaning "peace," or "pure peace."

The name is not far in meaning from a common saying heard in breweries, *wajo ryoshu*, which can be interpreted as, "harmony creates good sake, and good sake, in turn, creates harmony." Both Mariko Chino and Midori Okazaki invoke this motto to describe the atmosphere that they try to create in their kura. Okazaki is the twelfth-generation owner of the family's Okazaki Brewery which was established in 1665. "However much technique you possess, teamwork is the most important thing in a brewery," she says. "When it's there, it is expressed in the sake." Like Rumiko Moriki, Okazaki has childhood memories of the seasonal toji and his team arriving in the fall, the bustle of activity that followed, and the steam that would rise all day from the brewery's chimney.

During her studies at Nodai she thought that she would, like her parents and the generations before them, manage the brewery but not brew the sake herself. But when the family couldn't find a new toji, she stepped in. "I had no idea how hard the job was going to be, which in retrospect was a good thing," she adds. But the confidence she felt when she stepped into the job turned into a daily sense of anxiety as she juggled brewing and management duties. When her children were born, she was supported by her husband, Kenichi, a former Tokyo metropolitan government employee and now president of the brewery, and by her parents.

One characteristic that both Okazaki and Mami Wakabayashi feel that women toji bring to the job is an innate talent for nurturing life. "Making sake," Wakabayashi says, "is the same as raising children." Okazaki points out that each tank of sake, like each of her children, has its own individuality, which she

Master brewer Midori Okazaki, twelfth-generation owner of her family's brewery, in the *koji* room with her husband, Kenichi, brewery president.

nurtures with an eye toward developing its innate personality to the fullest. In fact, over a decade ago, she made three types of sake that she named after her three children, Mei, Futaba and Taki. The first two were brewed from sprouted brown-rice sakes, and the last was a plum liqueur that was made with premium sake. She eventually discontinued those lines in order to focus on strengthening the company's flagship premium-sake production. Yet she still takes valuable lessons from being a parent and applies them to sake. She believes that, as with child-rearing, you can't coddle sake by, for example, overheating it; you have to know the optimal conditions under which it will thrive.

Okazaki's commitment to small-batch hands-on sake making led her in 2017 to begin contracting with local farmers to grow and hand-harvest the brewery's own rice; it now accounts for more than half of the yearly volume the brewery uses. Around 2015, she began looking to expand from local sales into the Tokyo market. "The local people look on us kindly and support us, but going into the Tokyo area, they didn't really care about our history. It was hard, and every year was a learning experience," Okazaki says. "But when people are judging you with a cold, impartial eye, it kind of lights a fire under you, and drives you to do better."

When her Shinshu Kirei daiginjo won the grand prize at the prestigious Kanto Shinetsu sake competition in 2015, she was not only the first woman toji to win the award, but her mother was also president of the brewery. "So it was a double female presence at the awards ceremony," Okazaki says. The media called her prizewinning bottle "the toji-mom's sake" and her small-batch sake became a much coveted item in the metropolitan market.

Not far away from Okazaki Brewery, in the same Nagano town of Ueda, Mami Wakabayashi, the youngest of Nagano's seven women toji heads her family's Wakabayashi Brewery. She embodies the outward-looking perspective of today's young brewers. The brewery was founded in 1896 but by the 1970s it was selling its sake to wholesalers for bottling and distribution. She didn't intend to enter the business, instead taking a job in the apparel industry in Tokyo. But in 2013, when it became apparent that there was no one to take over the family business, she decided to return home, apprenticing first at other breweries and then with a revered Nagano master brewer from whom she learned the ropes. When he died suddenly less than a year into her apprenticeship, she studied for three years at a different brewery before taking on the position of master brewer at her family's brewery. She admits that stepping into the toji job was hard. "It's not just making the sake, but selling it, public relations—there was a lot more to think about after I became toji," she says. As Midori Okazaki puts it, being an owner-toji means "carrying a year's worth of the family's fortune on your shoulders."

Yet for Wakabayashi, the benefits of running her own brewery outweigh the challenges. With the help of her husband Makoto, she focuses on brewing exactly what she herself wants to drink— small-batch, *fune* or old-fashioned vat-pressed sake, in which cloth bags of mash are stacked in a wooden vessel and then pressed. Wakabayashi collects the pressed sake in 18-liter (5 gallon) *tobin*

jars and then sells it under the Tsukiyoshino label.

While these Nagano women toji are making exemplary sake, it is not all available abroad. This is where Wakabayashi, fluent in English, has broken through, and where for many sake brewers, success must come in the future. Wakabayashi, who exports to Singapore and Italy and began exporting her Tsukiyoshino brand to America in 2020, says the keys to success are "the quality of the sake we make and the partners we work with."

But it is also the stories these women brewers have to tell, the cultural shift they reflect, and the diversity of talents, tastes and opinions they bring to the craft that help make the business so exciting today. In the rapidly internationalizing world of craft sake, it is stories of determination just like theirs that can connect them to a global audience and add immeasurably to our enjoyment of sake.

Women Power Flight

Sake name: Rumiko no Sake
Sake type: Junmai ginjo muroka nama genshu
Brewery: Moriki Brewery, Mie Prefecture
A rich and balanced sake, made with as little intervention as possible, with no pasteurization, charcoal filtering or the addition of water after pressing.

Sake name: Shinshu Kirei
Sake type: Junmai ginjo
Brewery: Okazaki Brewery, Nagano Prefecture
Toji Midori Okazaki crafts a tiny amount of sake (250 koku, or 12,000 gallons/45,000 liters per brewing year). The unassuming power on the palate is worth the journey to northern Nagano to discover it.

Sake name: Tsukiyoshino
Sake type: Tokubetsu junmai genshu
Brewery: Wakabayashi Brewery, Nagano Prefecture
Fruity, floral, with notes of bubblegum, honeydew, apple and an intriguing saline undertone.

Chapter Twenty

Sake Bar Nights

Our days on the road chasing down the country's great sake brewers and their stories have by now settled down to a routine filled with familiar actions, sights and sounds: the flashing of our Japan Rail pass at every station entrance and exit; the rolling rice-paddy vistas, vivid green or fallow brown, depending on the season. The polite, recorded voice asking us to watch our step when leaving the train and to please be careful not to forget anything has become white noise to us. There's a timelessness to these scenes, too. If someone from the 1950s were to be teleported into these rickety rural trains, the experience—other than all the electronic devices in passengers' hands—would not feel so different to them.

Breakfasts and lunches are grabbed and quickly consumed on the road. In the evenings, on our way back to the hotel, we see the dozing salarymen, the uniformed schoolkids glued to their smartphones. We do a quick online search for the best sake bars in the area. We should be better prepared, but lining up and making our brewery visits and the logistics of travel leave little time for R&R (even though these outings are research, too).

Next is a quick stop at the hotel to drop off bags and freshen up, then a rendezvous in the lobby before heading out for dinner and sake. Wardrobe changes are carefully calibrated: we're now masters of minimalist packing in order to leave enough room for the sake we're buying along the way. Each of us has an extra suitcase for our *nihonshu* stash.

The routine makes our packed days bleed into each other. But in memory, what can make them stand out in bright relief are those nights that showcase the best of Japanese bar culture—convivial, unfettered drinking sessions with fellow sake fans, where social hierarchy and honorifics are thrown out the window and we take part in the vast, nightly national ritual of sipping alcohol, airing our innermost feelings and letting off steam. Fukuoka City, the prefectural capital located on Kyushu's northern shore, brings us such a night.

The humidity feels around 120 percent, and just walking through the thick July evening air is a resistance workout, leaving us drenched in sweat. After fifteen minutes we arrive at our destination, Kumorebi, a tiny nine-seat bar across the Naka

Left At Kochi City's boisterous Hirome Ichiba food market, draft beer is the drink of choice to accompany bonito, gyoza and more. **Below** Server Aiko at the Fukuoka sake bar Kumorebi, which serves craft sakes from across Japan and as far away as New Zealand.

River from our hotel, in Fukuoka's Haruyoshi district. We slide open the door to catch a glimpse of wall-to-wall blond wood, warm lighting and the inimitable cozy comfort of a well-run Japanese bar.

Then comes the bad news. "No reservation? Sorry, we're full." The server, a young woman in a striped blouse, seeing our crestfallen faces, gestures for us to take a seat on a piece of wood in front of the bar, just a few notches above a concrete parking lot wheel stop. So we sit, peruse the menu and ask for her advice on local sakes. There are always good local sakes, many that never make it out of the prefecture. Our server arrives with a tray holding three *isshobin* (1.8 liter/2 quart bottles), one a sweet, umami-laden brew from Morinokura Brewery in Fukuoka, another a tokubetsu junmai from Kiyama Shoten in Saga Prefecture (a month ago it took home a grand prix award at the US National Sake Appraisal) and the third, a collaboration between Zenkuro in New Zealand, Kanhokuto in Fukuoka and Kumazawa Brewery (maker of the Tensei brand) in Kanagawa, to celebrate the Rugby World Cup that is about to take place in Tokyo.

We sip, gazing out at the banal scene before us: a small parking lot, a modern apartment building across the street and one of Japan's ubiquitous hot-and-cold beverage vending machines glowing like a small spaceship in front of it. The sake is delicious. Grudgingly satisfied, we're about to head out in search of someplace else when our server arrives to tell us that two seats have opened up.

Inside the bar, which feels as snug and welcoming as it looked from outside, we befriend an intellectual property lawyer and sci-fi movie fan named Yoshinori, and the sake keeps flowing. For food, we start with *iburigakko*, the delicious smoked pickles from Akita, and *gomadofu*, silky and rich sesame tofu sprinkled with toasted white sesame seeds. Food is often only the sideshow to these evenings.

The chit-chat starts out tentatively. Yoshinori explains that Kumorebi, the name of this bar, is a clever play on words, referring to the comfort one feels on a cloudy day, when rays of sunlight pierce through cracks in the clouds. Among the thousands of sake bars in Japan, he embellishes, the sunlight glints off this blessed little bar, where guests feel the warming comfort of those rays.

Soon, though, the talk turns to sake, and a scene that's grown familiar to Nancy unfolds. Michael, who is quiet at first, pulls out his phone and begins scrolling through his sake textbook infographics, which read like a road map through the contents of his sake-infused brain. The periodic table of rice. The sake yeast galaxy. The maps of each prefecture and their most important breweries. On cue, eyes pop out, exclamations are uttered, Michael's phone is passed around for all to gawk at. Our server, Aiko, almost starts crying, she's so amazed. Japanese love few things more than gasping over foreigners who know more about their culture than they do.

Then a funny character straight out of a manga cartoon enters the bar, mopping his brow furiously, huffing from the heat and humidity. On his shoulder is a bag made from the kind of indigo-and-orange sake brewery aprons that are seen in breweries across the country. Nancy eyes it covetously, but

he tells her it's handmade by someone he knows. He sits down and immediately begins a disquisition on his many sake fridges at home, and how many bottles he's got now. He reminds us of a kinder, gentler Comic Book Guy from *The Simpsons*. Then he begins enthusing about his new sake find, "an amazing brewery called Shigemasu" in Fukuoka. Their high-end brew is now served in first class All Nippon Airways, he tells us, but he recommends a more affordable bottle. He tells us we can find it at the Hakata train station. Alas, we tell him, we might not have a chance to pick it up because of our early departure the next morning.

"I'll send you a bottle," he says. "I don't care if it's to America," he adds. "I've got plenty of money from playing pachinko [a Japanese gambling game]."

"Her family lives in Saga," Yoshinori tips him off, referring to Nancy.

"I'll send it to your grandmother!" he exclaims.

In the hubbub of this exchange, Yoshinori has quietly asked Aiko to put our food on his tab. By the time the evening ends we are all slightly drunk and best friends.

The Izakaya Tradition

Sake drinking and food-service establishments began to appear in the Kyoto area in about the eleventh century, taking firm hold by the early fourteenth century. The Fushimi roadside rest stop dating from the Muromachi era (1336–1573) that the Masuda family ran before starting the Masuda Tokubee Brewery would have been one of these *nakayado* rest stops, explains sake writer and educator Ayuko Yamaguchi. When Edo began taking shape in the early seventeenth century, the male-dominated population of merchants, laborers and craftspeople grabbed quick meals and sake at humble shops known as *niuriya*, where sake and warm comfort foods were sold: each had a specialty: soba, *unagi* (eel), or tempura.

Unlike Edo pleasure-quarter establishments with courtesans and musicians, the humble soba shop was considered *iro ga nai* ("without color") says sake importer Chris Pearce. The only things on the menu, says Pearce, were soba and sake, a dab of miso for your appetizer and the fellowship of your friends."

Records of the earliest taverns go back further. In the 797 book *Shoku nihongi* (Chronicles of Japan Volume 2) is the story of mean-tempered King Ashihara. In 761, while gambling and getting drunk at a tavern, he flew into a rage and stabbed a man to death. Then, using the dead man's chest as a cutting board, he chopped up the man's genitals and ate them. Thankfully, gambling is not allowed in any restaurant or bar today, and violence is rare, though there is one chain, Zauo, where customers fish for their own dinner.

In today's Japan, izakaya range from garishly lit *gado shita* (under the girders) drinking holes tucked beneath the tracks of Tokyo's Yurakucho train line,

Above Kokushu no Shiwaza chef Katsumi Shimoju shows off a bag of Omachi rice. Shimoju serves it steamed, with boiled, soy sauce–laced wasabi greens. **Left** Bartender Marie Chiba's rich *katsu sando* ham sandwich is offset by a creamy *doburoku* sake pairing at Gem by Moto in Tokyo's Ebisu district.

to soigné bars where food pairings are considered and sake warming and serving rise to the level of high craft. There's Maishin in Tokyo's Shibuya district, where you can enjoy simmered gourd and sausage with unpasteurized junmai daiginjo from cult brewer Takagi, makers of the Juyondai label. Or Komejirushi, an eight-seat, pay-by-the-hour bar in Asakusa's underground shopping arcade and its neon-lit neighbor, Ninja Bar. The latter features an array of cup sakes, servers dressed as ninja and cosplay outfits for customers. Getting there is half the fun, as you wind past cheap noodle joints, fortune tellers and barbershops that take you back to Japan of the 1950s.

A Night on the Town with Shigeki Tonoike

Outside of Tokyo, we can hazily recall countless bibulous evenings, like the one spent at Utsunomiya's Kokushu no Shiwaza, the favorite izakaya of Tonoike Brewery president Shigeki Tonoike. We sample the local specialty of rubbery *konnyaku* (konjac, or devil's tongue) with hot mustard, yuzu-accented blowfish milt and bowls of sinus-clearing house-pickled wasabi greens served with steamed Omachi rice. Meanwhile, the Tochigi sake—including bottles from Sawahime and Watanabe Sahei breweries, and a cave-aged brew from Shimazaki Brewery—does not stop flowing.

Tonoike, descended from a long line of Omi merchants (see page 44) and so perhaps not surprisingly, possessed of an incessantly churning marketing mind, makes the acquaintance of every person in the small restaurant one by one. Soon, he's presiding over the room like its mayor. There's the two young women who buy sake for a big traditional Japanese inn in Nikko, the engineer for Honda and the former Watanabe Brewery *kurabito* who returned to his family's pearl business. Tonoike regales us with stories of the Kiss rock-and-roll sake label he once dreamed up, the ten export companies he works with ("I must think about the future") and why sake classifications don't matter anymore.

Nancy is introduced as "the Atsuko Sando of Canada," high praise indeed since Sando is among the best known sake writers in Japan, and soon the evening has arrived at that point where Michael starts pulling up photos on his smartphone. He shows the two young women a photo of himself posing with matinee idol Kenchi Tachibana, a fellow Sake Samurai, leading them to gasp, cover their mouths and swoon audibly. Off to one side of the bar, a grizzled veteran server whisks hot *kanzake* sake in a little pitcher over a flame, casting a jaded eye on the scene while carefully monitoring the sake's temperature.

Like all good bar evenings, this one keeps morphing with each new guest. Yasuhiro Watanabe, seventh-generation president of Watanabe Sahei Brewery, shows up late, and asks for a plate of yakisoba. And Tonoike is off, on another round of introductions and *kanpai* toasts.

The Bartender: Marie Chiba

If you could peek inside the mind of Marie Chiba you'd see a fantasia of floating sake aromas and flavors in a multitude of shapes and colors. Chiba's got synesthesia—a perceptual superpower that allows her to see tastes as shapes and sounds as colors—an ability that brings new dimensions to her food and sake pairings. When she leans into Michael for a selfie, she raises an eyebrow and whispers, "coconut," nailing the fading scent of his body lotion, which in her mind's eye appears as a marbled mix of flesh, cream and pink colors.

In 2010, before she found out about this hidden talent, Chiba (whose first name, Marie, is pronounced *ma-ri-eh*, with the accent on the first syllable) just knew she liked sake a lot. She became the manager of *tachinomi* standing bar Nihonshu Stand Moto in Shinjuku as a part-time side hustle while working full-time as a systems engineer. Nihonshu Stand Moto quickly gained a following for showcasing sakes by a strong list of small producers, many of whom became her friends. She's gained celebrity status as a sake bartender, sake pairing expert and sake producer, collaborating with her favorite breweries to conceptualize new sakes. She's even started her own collaborative sake line, the Dot Sake Project, designed to bring new sake fans into the fold. In 2015, she took charge of a second bar, Gem by Moto, in the much sleeker and more international Ebisu neighborhood.

Outside the building, a sign for Gem etched in brass is placed inside a *futa koji,* the wooden tray used during the *koji*-making stage of daiginjo sake brewing. This obscure symbol of premium-sake making is a secret handshake extended to sake initiates. The name of the restaurant is also a sake reference: the word *moto* refers to the yeast starter, or mother, in sake brewing. "Gem" is what Chiba would like the sake she serves to become, buffed to perfection by the ambience, serving style and food pairings of her bar.

Inside, surrounded by a twelve-seat wooden counter on three sides, a micro kitchen to their backs and the hum of alt-rock, Chiba and her staff of five use a worn, brass-fitted trunk as their counter and staging area. Small plates of her specialty— breaded, deep-fried ham *katsu* (cutlets) stuffed with creamy, blue cheese—arrive, paired with glasses of thick, milky *doburoku,* the traditional unfiltered sake brewed by farmers in her native Iwate Prefecture. A perfect pairing like this gives her the synesthete's satisfaction of fitting the missing wedge of pie chart into the whole with a satisfying click.

A little later, our server pours a small pitcher of junmai daiginjo that has been aged for three years in sherry casks and puts it through a warm water bath. She whips it with a whisk in a small silver *chirori* or metal pitcher, puts her nose to it, and decides it needs more heat. After a short re-immersion, she hands the chirori to her boss to taste. Chiba nods, and the drink is poured for us to be savored with rose-colored-slices of grilled duck breast resting on a pool of a silky egg-white and miso sauce, the whole concoction topped with a tangle of bitter *nanohana* (rape blossom) greens.

In the book *Saisentan no nihonshu pearingu* (State-of-the-art sake pairings), which she co-wrote with Hitoshi Utsunomiya, director of the Japan Sake and Shochu Makers Association and one of Japan's pre-eminent sake experts, Chiba defined nine different—sometimes mind-bending—rules for pairing sake with food. These include "match according to complexity and depth of flavor—capture sake on its time axis," and "dismantle existing dishes and reconstruct flavors stored in memory." An example of the latter would be a deconstructed apple pie she serves, made of caramelized apple, aged rice, potato and cinnamon, which she pairs with an aged sake with apple-like acidity. In the customer's mind, the combination is supposed to reassemble itself into the best apple-pie memory ever banked.

The duck-and-aged-sake combo, meanwhile, is an example of the rule of "layering flavors," where the duck is considered to be the base and the sake as a second sauce that will amplify the complexity and harmony of the dish.

Gem's white walls are covered with scrawled messages from brewer friends, a number of them Chiba's collaborators. She has partnered with hip, highly esteemed breweries like Aramasa, Senkin and Kidoizumi breweries, and for her Dot Sake Project, with Nagayama Honke, Akebono and Hachinohe breweries. Geographically diverse, what they all have in common are their forward-thinking outlook, organic-skewing rice and a combination of old and new brewing techniques that yield more wine-like, higher-acidity sake.

The point of the Dot Sake Project, says Chiba, is to disrupt sake and "make it more accessible and fun." The line's pixelated labels are designed in homage to 1980s-era video games, and since customers at her bar are always staring at their phones, Chiba put a QR code on the bottle that links to a short video about each bottle. The label on her Cream Soda junmai, a collaboration with Aomori's Hachinohe Brewery, suggests that people do exactly the things they've been taught not to with sake: add ice, or lemon, or pepper. That aged sake we tried earlier? That was another collaboration of hers, with the Jokigen label of Sakata Brewery in Yamagata.

"There are some sake that are perfect in and of themselves," Chiba explains, though many more are flawed. "Our job," she says, "is to make those palatable." For a too-strong sake, for example, add a bit of cheese, or fruit or ice, and what was a negative becomes a positive. "I realized that through pairing, a sake can become complete," she adds: the hidden gem that she, through her out-there mash-ups and her bar's many tender mercies, has chiseled to perfection.

Okayama Bar Hopping

At the weathered, old-school sake bar Sakabayashi, near Okayama City train station, we're seated on red-leatherette-covered stools facing a wall of fridges filled with large *isshobin* sake bottles. Our server, Takeshi Kawai, looks like a kindly retiree called up for bar service duty for the night, and in fact we learn that he sort of has. "I'm a *nombe* [heavy drinker]," he tells us. "I've been here about a month and before that I was visiting friends at sake breweries." Over bites of corn-kernel tempura and rolled sushi filled with tuna and glass noodles and striped with mayonnaise, he pours from bottle after bottle of fantastic Okayama sake. The first is a treat: the unpasteurized Blue Bottle version of Nine sake from local brewery Tsuji Honten, which boasts the first female master brewer in the prefecture, Maiko Tsuji. It's an unpasteurized bodaimoto, creamy, lactic and mellow.

Seated next to us, a man in a business suit who looks like a traveling salesman says he is in town for business, and that he makes it a priority to taste as many sakes as he can while he's on the road. "I've tasted 2,500 sakes," he tells us modestly. His favorite: Shinkame from Saitama Prefecture. If you recall the story of pioneering woman master brewer Rumiko Moriki (page 186), this is her mentor's brewery.

One of the best things about immersing ourselves in the world of craft sake is seeing how the dots connect, each leading to a new sake for our bucket list, a new story to unearth. Another great thing about drinking local is that it often means drinking *nama*, super-fresh, unpasteurized sake. The first one Kawai-san places in front of us is an all-natural nama junmai ginjo made by Kurashiki City's Kikuchi Brewery with local Asahi rice. The label says it's been grown agroecologically according to the "Kimura method" pioneered by an apple farmer in Akita who works along organic principles.

Kawai-san is looking increasingly harried and put-upon, and for some reason, his phone keeps going off with his selected ringtone, Scott Joplin's "The Entertainer." Andy Russell, the Scottish kurabito at Fukucho in Hiroshima will later tell us that Kawai is well-known in Okayama—"a lovely man who is crazy about sake," and even known by some as the city's "godfather of sake."

We don't mind the lulls in service; there's plenty in front of us to drink, including another nama, called Hare, part of an attempt to revive a dying Okayama farming village called Takebe through a collaboration of farmers, industry and the local university. The village's own Omachi rice was brewed by Kumaya Brewery in Kurashiki, and the colorful striped label is the creation of university design students. They came up with an imaginary character, a twenty-year-old student named Takeo, who is taking part in a joyful *hare* coming-of-age party, at which he will have his first legal drink of sake. The campaign seems to reflect the wishes of all sake makers, who worry over the fact that the younger generation is less interested in drinking alcohol than their parents and grandparents were.

The next sake is another fresh taste of the region and an ingenious concept: Triple A, from Okayama's Shiragiku Brewery, unpasteurized, banana-scented and slightly effervescent, with a lively acidity. This limited-edition sake is made with three varieties of local Okayama table rice, Akebono, Akihikari and Asahi, hence the name and royal blue logo of three interlocking "A"s. Okayama may be synonymous with Omachi rice, but it's the experimentation that's going on with less exalted local varieties that truly gives the visitor a sense of the breadth and depth of the sake culture here.

Partly to give Kawai-san a break, we take our leave, heading to the standing bar Okayama Eki-Mae Meishu Center, where we down some satisfying *oden* (a soy-flavored hot pot filled with daikon, konnyaku and boiled eggs), *onigiri* rice balls and more great sakes.

In Tokyo's oldest underground shopping arcade, in the Asakusa district, Ninja Bar carries hundreds of brands of one-cup sakes, served by costumed ninjas. Cosplay is optional!

Sapporo: Dropping in on a Sake Thoroughbred

The izakaya Minoriya is located on the fifth floor of a modern building in the Susukino entertainment district of Sapporo. Our friend and guide Carlin Kumada has brought us here on this late-January evening because the food is good and the restaurant is a loyal customer of his family's sake shop, Meishu no Yutaka. Since there are fewer local breweries in Hokkaido than in places like Okayama or Fukuoka, we drink sake from across Japan—Niwa no Uguisu from Kyushu, Kaze no Mori from Nara, and Denshu from Aomori. We eat glistening slices of sashimi and chicken thigh *tataki*. The latter is charcoal seared, still raw in the center, drizzled with sweet soy sauce and showered with minced garlic and thin slices of *myoga*, a woodland flower bud that tastes like an exotic, slightly bitter ginger. Broth from the bones of the chicken are used to add a subtle note of umami to the accompanying *dashi-tamago* omelet. Cigarette smoke hangs in the air, something we haven't experienced in a bar in years, and the movie *Transformers* is on the TV screen.

This is only the prelude to the main sake drinking attraction though, which happens about a five-minute walk away, at Bar Kamada. The eighth-floor bar is dimly lit and feels a little like a classy pool hall, with violet-hued ceiling lights, *Tom and Jerry* cartoons on the monitor and jazz on the stereo. Owner and sake- and wine somme-lier Takeshi Kamada comes out to greet us. By way of introducing himself he tells us, "My father worked in the Sapporo beer factory and my mother was at Kita no Homare brewery. A sake woman and a beer man married and raised me—a sake thoroughbred. When I was five they told me you can drink anything but please don't drink in front of other people." He pauses a beat and then adds, "I've always appreciated my parents."

Kamada starts us off with a flight of local Niseko sake. The brewery uses almost all Hokkaido rice, so this flight includes sake brewed with Ginpu, Suisei and Kita Shizuku varieties. The fourth rice we're not familiar with, an offspring of Hokkaido's first prefectural rice, Hatsu Shizuku, called Kita Mizuho. Michael is beside himself with joy to make a new sake rice discovery.

"Shut up!" is all he can manage in response to Carlin's introduction of the rice.

When Kamada learns that we're expecting Carlin's wife Rie and local celebrity Shinji Kawabata, master brewer at Kamikawa Taisetsu Brewery, Kamada is almost as excited as Michael was about the rice. When Kawabata arrives, looking seriously natty in a crew-neck sweater and a tweed jacket, he tells us about his meeting with people who run the largest sake competition in France, Kura Master, and how they compared sake to champagne. "Fifteen years ago champagne was just used for toasting and now it's enjoyed throughout an entire meal," he reports, the idea being that sake, too, could enjoy a similar widening of popularity internationally.

On the subject of sake competitions, Kawabata tells us that his thinking has changed. "First," he says, "making contest winners and making good-tasting sake are two different things." When he was asked to be a judge at a contest last year, he did not

At the tiny, pay-by-the hour sake bar Komejirushi in Asakusa, owner Haru Egawa offers a well-curated selection of sakes and bar snacks.

think much of the sake competition concept. But after the event, his thinking changed. "These contests do affect the direction of sake," he realized; it was necessary to play the game.

Then a man who looks like your average salary-man separates from a group that is breaking up nearby, comes over and stops at our table. "Do you eat sticky rice?" he asks in English. "Yes? Good, because sales are going down. Please eat more." Then he simply walks away. Seeing our baffled faces, Kamada stops by to explain. "They are all guys who are selling Kita Mizuho, the new sake rice." Still baffled (Why "sticky" rice? Why tell us to eat more sake rice?), we chalk this encounter up to the Alice-in-Wonderland–like aspect of certain long sake nights.

From beginning to end, we realize, starting with snowbound Kamikawa Taisetsu and Otokoyama breweries and ending at this local hangout for rice merchants trying to earn a living, our day has been all about sake. Tonight's last exchange is a fitting finish.

Kochi City Bonito and Bar Crawl

Sake yeast scientist Haruhiko Uehigashi is a happy man. He's got a glassful of Bijofu junmai on the rocks in front of him, just how he likes it. Next to that is a heaping plateful of sliced garlic to pile on to the blood-red slices of *katsuo* (bonito) *tataki* that is the local specialty. *Tataki* means that the fish is seared, in this case over an open fire fueled by rice straw. It's cheap, easy and imparts a pleasing aroma. But the main purpose of searing the fish is to kill off the parasites. It's then served Tosa style, which means it comes with garlic, *yuzu kosho* (fermented chili paste made with the citrus fruit yuzu) and salt.

"It's really important to have food with sake," Uehigashi says, and we couldn't agree more. We're sitting in the restaurant Myojin Maru, named after a highly successful bonito fishing boat, framed photos of which are hanging up on the wall. There are three different locations of the popular chain, including one at the sprawling and raucous Hirome Market food

Co-author of this book Michael Tremblay with Haruhiko Uehigashi at Tosa Sake bar, which showcases Kochi Prefecture's eighteen breweries.

hall, where we started out the evening. But Uehigashi insists on dining at this one down the street, where the garlic is fresh and plentiful. Garlic does not tend to figure that prominently in most Japanese cuisine, but here in southwestern Japan, it's one sign of the influence of the Korean peninsula. As we start off with a round of unpasteurized Akitora junmai, Uehigashi explains that while Chinese fishermen use large nets to fish for bonito, Tosa fishermen's single-rod fishing practice is much more sustainable. Of the mass net killing of fish, he says "This makes Japan angry, very angry!"

Kochi residents know how to eat bonito as well as catch it, showing their love for the fish by consuming an average of nine pounds (4 kg) per person a year. Uehigashi shows us how to eat the fish, first with just salt, then salt and yuzu kosho, then with garlic. "More! More!" he eggs us on as he watches us timidly place a few slices of garlic on our fish. Then he adds happily, "Kochi people always smell like garlic." He's not too far into his cups and garlic to know exactly what's going on in his glass though. When the next glass arrives, he takes a sip and a disgusted expression crosses his face. "Hine!" he says, almost spitting the sake out. *Hineka* refers to the unpleasant aroma of Japanese pickles gone south. In sake, it's a serious flaw, the result of decomposing amino acids and their metabolites.

At our next stop, the chic Tosa Sake Bar, the specialty is sake from all eighteen of Kochi's sake breweries. A mobile of plexiglass squares printed with names of all of those breweries hangs from the ceiling, and a map on the wall pinpoints their locations in the prefecture; this is a true *jizake* (local sake) bar. We taste an unpasteurized Minami Brewery junmai daiginjo that was bottled this very month, a Bunkajin Liseur tokubetsu junmai, and a Tosa Yamada Nishiki junmai ginjo, downing them to the recorded sounds of Japanese bands performing Beatles' covers, and endless toasts of "*Tomodachi!*" ("Friends!") For our last stop, we reunite with Uehigashi's wife Yoshiko, who left us earlier to have dinner with friends. Satisfying bowls of steaming-hot Susaki-style *nabeyaki* ramen appear before us. A local specialty prepared in an earthenware pot, our server dramatically uncovers it at the table to reveal the soup, bubbling and fragrant.

When the time comes to finally say goodbye after our marathon crawl, we feel like little kids parting after an intense summer camp experience—sad-happy, with a mental filing cabinet filled with endless memories and snapshots to pore over once we've returned home to our daily lives. We realize that alcohol is a social lubricant in any culture, but there's something special about getting to know friends better over their own national drink, and especially their own jizake. After all, the drink that draws you closer together is a product of this place, this land and these people. It's the closest thing modern life has to becoming blood brothers and sisters.

Sake Bar Recommendations

Our recommendation for your own trip to Japan: Walk into a bar with no expectations and place your blind trust in the sake expert. Then wait to have your mind blown.

Chapter Twenty-One

Recipes and Stories

For sake-brewing families, life unfolds according to the rhythms of the brewing season. The foods they prepare and serve change with the seasons, and have evolved to match the family's livelihood and brewing style. We asked the brewing families we visited for a cherished family recipe and their recommended pairing. Perhaps because sake making is traditionally winter work we received many recipes for warming soups and hot pots. And naturally, many recipes made use of *sake kasu*, or pressed sake lees, the plentiful and fragrant by-product of the sake-making process. A related ingredient is the flavor enhancer and tenderizer *shio koji*, made with dried koji mold-inoculated rice. Where necessary, we have adapted the recipes to work with the ingredients that can be found easily in the West at grocery stores or Asian specialty stores.

APPETIZERS, SOUPS AND STOCKS

Stewed Chinese Cabbage with Fried Tofu

Masuda Tokubee Shoten, Kyoto Prefecture

This is a typical lightly seasoned Kyoto-style dish. If you prefer more heavily seasoned soups, add more soy sauce, and a bit of mirin and sake. The dish is made with dashi stock (see facing page), the foundation for many Japanese dishes. You can also find instant dashi at most Japanese markets.

Recommended pairing: Brewery president Tokubee Masuda recommends something without a very high ginjo aroma, like an 80 percent polish Iwai junmai sake, maybe warmed. It also goes well with a Tsuki no Katsura Yanagi junmai ginjo.

Serves 2
7 oz (200 g) napa cabbage
2 sheets abura-age (ready-made fried thin tofu)
1¼ cups (300 ml) dashi stock (see page 203)
1 Tbsp light-colored *(usukuchi)* soy sauce
Powered sansho pepper, to taste

Stewed Chinese Cabbage with Fried Tofu

1. Finely slice the cabbage on the diagonal into bite-sized strips.
2. Cut the sheets of abura-age into rectangles, roughly ¾ x 2 in (2 x 5 cm) each.
3. In a large pot, mix the dashi and soy sauce, then add the cabbage and abura-age.
4. Bring to a boil, then reduce the heat. Simmer until the cabbage is tender. (Making this ahead and then reheating later in the day or after refrigerating overnight will allow the flavors to deepen.)
5. Ladle the stew into bowls, and sprinkle with the sansho pepper to serve.

Dashi Stock

Yields 2 quarts (1.9 liters)
2 pieces dried kelp *(kombu),* **each 4 x 4 in (10 x 10 cm) 2 quarts (1.9 liters) water**
1 cup (10 g) lightly packed dried bonito flakes *(katsuobushi)*

1. Wipe the kelp with a damp cloth or paper towel.
2. In a large pot, bring the water and kelp almost to a boil over medium heat. Let cook for about 10 minutes, removing the kelp once the water reaches a full boil. Reduce the heat.
3. Immediately add the bonito flakes all at once, and return the heat to medium.
4. Let the broth simmer for 10 seconds. Turn off the heat, skim off any foam, and let it stand for 2 minutes.
5. Strain the stock through a sieve lined with a tightly woven cotton cloth.
6. Discard the bonito flakes, or save along with the kelp for use in other stock.
7. Let cool, then pour the stock into a tightly covered container. Refrigerate for up to 4 days, or try freezing the stock in an ice tray to create ready-to-use cubes.

Root Vegetable Soup

Hakkaisan Brewery, Niigata Prefecture

This recipe is excerpted from the book *Okasama no jinsei ryori* (Mother's Life Cooking), by Hiroshi Morita. It tells the turbulent story of Ai Nagumo, who came to the then-poor Hakkaisan brewery as a young bride, and spent more than sixty years as the wife of brewery president Kazuo Nagumo. Around the brewery, she's affectionately known as *Okasama,* or "honorable mother." This is her recipe for *kenchin-jiru,* a hearty, vegetable-studded, fish-based soup.

Recommended pairing: Hakkaisan Tokubetsu Junmai

Serves 3–4
½ burdock root
1 piece of daikon, about 5 in (12 cm) long
1 large taro potato
Canola or grapeseed oil, for sautéeing
2 cups (480 ml) Niboshi Dashi stock (page 204)
Dash soy sauce
Pinch of salt
Canola or other neutral oil, for seasoning
1 scallion, for garnish

1. Remove some of the outer layer of the burdock by scrubbing with a brush under running water, or scraping the washed burdock root with the back (dull side) of a kitchen knife. Cut into 1½ in (3.5 cm) matchsticks.
2. Peel, slice and quarter the daikon into bite-sized pieces, ⅜ in (1 cm) thick. Repeat with the taro potato.
3. Coat the bottom of a small saucepan with the oil, and place over medium-high heat. Add the burdock, daikon and taro and sauté for 2–3 minutes. Add the Niboshi Dashi stock, bring to a simmer and allow to simmer until the vegetables are cooked through, about 8 minutes. Skim off and discard any foam that rises to the top.
4. Adjust the seasoning, adding a few drops of soy sauce, a pinch of salt and a few drops of neutral oil. Garnish with thinly sliced scallion.

Rice Cracker Soup

Niboshi Dashi Stock

Yields 2 cups (480 ml)
1 Tbsp dried sardines
1 piece dried kelp (*kombu*), 1½ in (3 cm) square
2 cups (480 ml) water

1. Place the sardines, kelp and water in a pan and let soak for at least 30 minutes and up to several hours.
2. Place the pan over low heat and bring the broth to a slow simmer. When bubbles begin to form around the kelp, remove it and save for use in other dashi stock.
3. Simmer the dashi with sardines for a further 5 minutes.

Rice Cracker Soup

Nanbu Bijin Brewery, Iwate Prefecture

In this hearty soup, rice crackers in the bottom of the bowl add a soothing and feather-light texture to the dish. Minimally seasoned, hard, baked rice crackers are preferable, but even large round soy-sauce-flavored crackers will do.

Recommended pairing: Nanbu Bijin tokubetsu junmai

Serves 2 as a main; 4 as a side
1 Tbsp neutral oil
4 oz (115 g) chicken thigh or pork meat, sliced into bite-sized pieces
½ carrot, sliced on the diagonal ¼ in(6 mm) thick
2½ oz (75 g) daikon, sliced in quarters ¼ in (6 mm) thick

2½ oz (75 g) julienne-cut burdock
2½ oz (75 g) enoki mushrooms, trimmed
4 green onions, cut into 2 in (5 cm) lengths
1 bag shirataki noodles, about 7 oz (200 g), boiled
    briefly in water, then cut in half
2 rice crackers per bowl

For the stock
1 cup (240 ml) rich chicken stock
2 cups (480 ml) dashi stock (see page 203)
1 Tbsp soy sauce
1 Tbsp sake

1. Combine the stock ingredients.
2. Coat the bottom of a separate saucepan with the oil, fry the chicken or pork until browned, then add all the vegetables except the green onions. Stir the vegetables to coat with the oil, add the dashi and bring to a simmer. Cook for 12–15 minutes until the vegetables are soft.
3. Add the green onion and the noodles. Simmer for 3 minutes or until the onions are softened.
4. Place two rice crackers in the bottom of each bowl, and ladle the soup over.

Eggplant and Green Peppers with Miso (page 206)

Sake Lees Crackers
Terada Honke Brewery, Chiba Prefecture

Taken from the book *Koji, amazake, sake kasu no hakko gohan* (Koji, Amazake and Sake- lees Fermented Foods) by Masaru and Satomi Terada, these are a great snack with sake, eaten plain, with a dip, or topped with cheese. The goal is to mix the ingredients into a crumbly dough. They scorch easily, so keep an eye on them while baking.

Recommended pairing: Terada Honke Daigo no Shizuku bodaimoto.

Makes 80–100 crackers
1¾ cups (200 g) all-purpose flour
1½ oz (40 g) sake lees
4 Tbsps canola oil
1 tsp salt
4 Tbsps water

1. Place all ingredients except for the water into a bowl. With the palm of your hands and fingers, mix to the consistency of crumbly dough.
2. Add the water, and without kneading, press the dough together until it coheres. If it is too dry and does not hold together, add extra water a small amount at a time until it does.
3. Place the dough on a cutting board. Use your judgment as to whether or not the board needs flouring. For a dry dough it will not be necessary. Roll out to ¹⁄₁₆ in (2 mm) thick, and cut into oblong shapes about 2½ x ½ in (6.5 x 1.5 cm).
4. Prick the dough with a fork. Bake at 300°F (150°C) for 25–30 minutes, until crisp.

SIDES AND MAINS

Eggplant and Green Peppers with Miso
Sohomare Brewery, Tochigi Prefecture

This dish is a specialty of Junko Kono, a trained architect and wife of Sohomare president Jun Kono. Their son, brewery managing director Michihiro Kono, recommends Sohomare's kimoto tokubetsu junmai as a pairing, explaining that kimoto-style sake generally goes well with oily or strongly flavored dishes. The more highly polished kimoto junmai ginjo is better suited to seafood.

Recommended pairing: Sohomare kimoto tokubetsu junmai

Serves 3–4
4 medium-sized slender Asian eggplants, about 1 lb 6 oz (625 g) total
3 green peppers, about 15 oz (425 g) total
2 Tbsps miso paste
2 Tbsps sugar
4 Tbsps sake
3 Tbsps sesame oil

1. Cut the eggplant roughly into bite-sized pieces. Slice the green peppers into ¾ in (2 cm)-wide strips.
2. In a small bowl, combine the miso, sugar and sake until smooth.
3. Heat the oil in a frying pan on high heat, then fry the eggplant until charred along the edges and soft.
4. Add the miso, sugar and sake mixture and stir to coat the eggplant. Add the green peppers and continue to stir-fry, taking care not to overcook the peppers. Their color should stay bright.

Nozawana Tempura
Okazaki Brewery, Nagano Prefecture

Owner-*toji* Midori Okazaki and her family pick and pickle local *nozawa* greens in December and eat them as a condiment throughout the cold brewing season. In early spring, the last of the pickles are battered and deep-fried, tempura-style. Any type of pickled greens may be substituted; we found pickled *takana* mustard greens at our local Japanese market.

Recommended pairing: Okazaki Shinshu Kirei Hitogokochi junmai

Serves 3–4
3½ oz (100 g) tempura flour
¾ cup (200 ml) ice-cold water
10 oz (300 g) pickled nozawa greens, or other pickled greens
Grapeseed, sunflower or other high smoke point oil, for deep-frying

1. Mix the tempura flour and ice-cold water lightly, being careful not to over mix. It's okay if the batter is lumpy; occasionally give it a stir while you're using it.
2. Squeeze out the liquid from the pickles well. Cut into about 1-inch (2.5 cm) lengths.
3. Put about about 2 in (5 cm) of the oil into a small saucepan and heat to 340–350°F (170–180°C).
4. Gather a small clump (about 1 Tbsp) of greens, and dip into the batter. To prevent the clump from separating in the oil, first place it on the lip of a ladle or large spoon. Slowly lower it into the cooking oil. When the batter has set slightly, loosen it from the ladle and let it float free. Turn once, until lightly colored and crisp. Drain on paper towels. Since the pickles are salty, serve as is, without additional salt or dipping sauce.

Nozawana Tempura

Okra with Taro in Ponzu Sauce

Tenzan Brewery, Saga Prefecture

"We are the Shichida family so we eat traditional sake brewery food," fifth-generation president Toshihide Shichida says. His wife Yoko cooks a lot of vegetable dishes that pair well with the family's rich, umami-filled sakes and two of them are included here. She serves this refreshing cold Okra with Taro several times a week, and touts it for its health benefits as well as taste. Both okra and taro potato have the *neba-neba*, or sticky quality prized in Japan, which is offset by the tart acidity of the ponzu sauce. For the sauce, Yoko keeps the yuzu citrus fruit well-wrapped in her freezer; you can substitute bottled yuzu juice.

Recommended pairing: Tenzan junmai ginjo, chilled.

Serves 3–4
12 oz (340 g) okra
3 taro potatoes, about 8 oz (220 g)
For the sauce
1 Tbsp soy sauce
1 Tbsp mirin
1 Tbsp yuzu juice (or ½ tsp zested yuzu peel)

1. Wash and parboil the okra for two minutes. Pat dry, and slice on the diagonal into ½ in (1.5 cm) pieces. Chill in the refrigerator.
2. Peel and slice the taro into 2 x ½ in (5 x 1.5 cm) batons.
3. Combine the soy sauce, mirin and yuzu and use it to dress the vegetables to taste. Reserve any leftover dressing for use with another dish.

American Eggplant, Tomato and Cheese

American Eggplant, Tomato and Cheese

Tenzan Brewery, Saga Prefecture

Recommended pairing: Tenzan junmai genshu jizake

Serves 3–4

1 medium "American" eggplant (not the long, thin
   Asian type)
Salt, for salting
2 small ripe tomatoes
¾ cup (200 ml) grapeseed, sunflower or other
   high-smoke-point oil
½ cup (110 g) grated mozzarella cheese

1. Wash the eggplant and cut in half lengthwise.
Score the cut surface of the eggplant with a knife
in a crosshatch pattern two-thirds of the way deep
into the eggplant, to allow for even cooking.
2. Salt the eggplant, let rest for 30 minutes then
wipe off the salt with a paper towel.

3. Remove the seeds from the tomatoes and finely
dice.
4. In a fryer or deep saucepan, heat the oil to 350°F
(180°C).
5. Fry the eggplant halves until soft.
6. Drain the eggplant on paper towels, then top
with the finely diced tomato and grated cheese
7. Heat in a 350°F (180°C) oven or toaster oven for
about 7 minutes or until the cheese is melted and
the tomatoes are warmed. Eat with a spoon.

Shio-koji–seasoned Vegetable Rice
Terada Honke Brewery, Chiba Prefecture

This is excerpted from the book *Koji, amazake, sake kasu no hakko gohan* (Koji, Amazake and Sake-lees Fermented Foods) by Masaru and Satomi Terada. The *shio koji* (mold-inoculated dried rice) gives this dish a slight fermented scent, plumps the rice and softens the vegetables. Shio koji can be found ready-made in bottles in Japanese stores, or is available dried online for you to ferment at home. The recipe is just as delicious with russet or any other widely available potato as with taro potato, and you can substitute any type of mushroom for the shimeji.

Recommended pairing: Terada Honke Gonin-Musume (Five Daughters) junmai

Serves 3–4
1⅛ cups (225 g) Japanese rice plus ¼ cup (45 g) glutinous millet (or glutinous rice)
½ pack of shimeji or other mushrooms, about 2½ oz (75 g)
4½ oz (130 g) taro or other potato
1½ Tbsps shio koji

1. Combine the rices, rinse in cold water and drain.
2. Remove the clumped bottoms of the shimeji mushrooms. For other mushrooms, slice into bite-sized pieces. Peel the potato and cut into bite-sized pieces.
3. Place the washed, drained rice into a rice cooker, and add the specified amount of water for this quantity of rice. (See below for stove-top cooking method)
4. Add the shio koji to the rice and mix well. Place the vegetables on top, and turn on the rice cooker.

To cook without a rice cooker
1. Follow steps 1 and 2 above.
2. Place the washed and drained rice in a medium-sized, heavy-bottomed pot with a tight-fitting lid. Add 1¼ cups (300 ml) of water. Let soak for 20–30 minutes.
3. Add the shio koji to the rice and mix well. Place the vegetables on top.
4. Put the lid on the pot and place over medium heat. When the water comes to a boil, turn the heat to low. Continue to cook, covered, for 12–13 minutes until the water is completely absorbed and the vegetables are cooked through.
5. Remove the pot from the heat and allow it to steam, covered, for 10 more minutes before serving.

Shio-koji–seasoned Vegetable Rice

Hamburg Steak

Kamoizumi Brewery, Hiroshima Prefecture

Japanese cooks have made this German dish their own. Kazuhiro Maegaki, president of Kamoizumi Brewery, says, "I loved my mother's hamburg steak. The one I love now is made by my wife, Miyoko. There was a Western-style restaurant in Hiroshima, called Port Rouge. Their hamburg steak really embodied the Maegaki family's taste. After they closed down, we invited the owner over, and we all learned the recipe."

Recommended pairing: Kamoizumi Shusen junmai ginjo

Serves 4

For the patties
14 oz (400 g) 75% lean ground beef
3½ oz (100 g) ground pork
1 small onion, about 3½ oz (100 g), finely diced
1 large egg
⅓ cup (20 g) panko breadcrumbs
¼ tsp salt
1 pinch white pepper, or to taste
1 Tbsp canola oil
¼ cup (60 ml) water (half wine or sake, if desired)
3 Tbsps ketchup
3 Tbsps Japanese Worcestershire sauce
1 Tbsp butter

1. Mix the meats, onion, egg, panko, salt and pepper untill just combined. Handle as little as possible. Divide into four elliptical patties. Lightly toss each patty between your hands to remove air pockets. Make an indent with your thumb on one side of each patty.
2. Put the oil in a 9-inch (23-cm) pan on medium-high heat. Place the four patties indentation side up and sear for 2 minutes on each side.
3. Add the water, cover with a lid and let the patties steam cook for 3–5 minutes. The patties are done when fat bubbles up to the surface.
4. Turn off the heat, whisk in the ketchup and Worcestershire sauce and let rest for five minutes.
5. Remove the patties from the pan, add the butter and whisk the sauce thoroughly to combine.

Hamburg Steak

Hokkaido-style Salmon Hot Pot

Otokoyama Brewery, Hokkaido

Goro Yamazaki, president of Otokoyama Brewery says, "Back in the day, this was a dish you would eat at home, but it's now something I eat when my family and I go out. It's a dish that visitors from Honshu or from abroad like to order at an izakaya because the balance of flavors of the salmon, butter and miso is really delicious. And depending on the restaurant (or the home), the taste will be different." In 2007, Japan's Ministry of Forestry and Fisheries named this Hokkaido dish among the 100 best regional cuisines of Japan.

Recommended pairing: Otokoyama kimoto junmai, either extremely chilled, or at room temperature.

Serves 4
4 salmon fillets, skin on, total about 14 oz (400 g)
Salt and pepper, for seasoning
½ head of cabbage
1 onion
⅓ carrot
2 potatoes
1 pack shimeji mushrooms
2 Tbsps butter

For the sauce
6½ Tbsps miso paste
4 Tbsps sake
2 Tbsps mirin
2 Tbsps sugar

1. Season the salmon with the salt and pepper.
2. Cut the cabbage, onions carrot, potatoes and shimeji mushrooms into bite-sized pieces.
3. Set a medium-sized frying pan over medium heat. Melt the butter in the pan, then add the salmon and cook, turning, until brown on both sides.
4. Surround the salmon with the vegetables. Mix the sauce ingredients, pour into the pan, then cover to steam.
5. Cut the salmon into pieces and serve with the vegetables and sauce. Or, you can shred the salmon, mix it with the vegetables and serve.

Akita Kiritanpo Hot Pot
Kodama Brewery, Akita Prefecture

After the autumn rice harvest, the people of Akita Prefecture like to eat *kiritanpo nabe*, a one-pot soup dish made with local Hinai chicken, maitake mushrooms, aromatic fresh *seri* (dropwort or Japanese parsley), burdock root, *naganegi* (Japanese long onion) and *kiritanpo*—steamed rice that is pounded, shaped around a stick and roasted. The dish originated in northern Akita, where bear hunters carried kiritanpo rice sticks into the mountains for lunch, adding them to a soup of freshly picked mushrooms and vegetables. Today kiritanpo nabe is a popular seasonal family hot-pot dish. You can shape the rice kiritanpo-style around

Hokkaido-style Salmon Hot Pot

211

a bamboo chopstick (see step 2), or you can form into balls (see step 3).

Recommended pairing: Tenko junmai daiginjo or Chogetsu junmai ginjo. If you prefer warm sake, try Taiheizan kimoto junmai or Shingetsu kimoto (brewed with soft mountain spring water).

Serves 4–6
2¼ cups (450 g) rice
Salted water, to moisten hands
Neutral oil, for grilling
1 large or 2 small burdock roots, shredded
Vinegar, for soaking
1 pack (7 oz/200 g) shirataki noodles, optional
3 cups (720 ml) Unsalted Chicken Stock (see recipe below)
2–3 cups (425–640 g) boneless chicken thigh, sliced into bite-sized pieces.
½ cup (120 ml) sake
½ cup (120 ml) soy sauce, or dashi soy sauce
1 tsp salt, or to taste
2 cups (170 g) maitake mushrooms, torn by hand into pieces
3 scallions, sliced diagonally about ¾-inch (2-cm) wide, using white part and a little of the green part
2 cups (100 g) seri (Japanese parsley), or watercress

For the rice
1. Steam the rice and transfer to a bowl. Pound and grind the hot rice with a pestle until it is about 70% pulverized.
2. To shape the rice kiritanpo-style on sticks, wet hands with the salted water, take a 3½ oz (100 g) clump of rice and shape into a ball. Insert the bamboo chopstick, then shape the rice into a cylindrical shape about 5½ in (14 cm) long. Squeeze lightly to compress the rice around the chopstick.
3. To shape the rice in balls, wet hands with the salted water, and form the rice into golf-ball-sized balls. Lightly coat a grill or cast iron skillet with neutral oil (omit if using non-stick pan), and grill the rice sticks or balls until golden brown.

For the hot pot
1. Scrub the burdock with a brush under running water, until it whitens a little. As if sharpening a pencil, shave off 1½-inch (3.5 cm) lengths of burdock. Soak the burdock pieces in a bowl of cold water mixed with a few drops of vinegar. When the water turns dark brown, drain and refill. Repeat 1–2 times to remove bitterness, then drain.
2. If using shirataki noodles, cut them in half, place in a small saucepan and cover with water. Turn the heat to high. When the water has nearly come to a boil, drain the noodles, and rinse in cold water. Drain well.
3. If you have shaped your rice kiritanpo-style on sticks, remove the stick and break each piece of rice in half.
4. Heat the chicken stock to a boil, then reduce to a simmer.
5. Add the chicken thigh and burdock to the chicken stock, and simmer for a further 2 minutes, discarding any foam that rises to the top.
6. Add the sake, soy sauce and salt to the soup. Add the mushrooms and simmer for 2 minutes.
7. Add the shirataki noodles (if using), the scallions, the halved pieces of kiritanpo rice or the rice balls, and simmer for 1 minute.
8. Add the seri or other greens just before serving so the green color remains fresh.
9. Adjust the taste with salt, sake and soy sauce.
10. Divide into small bowls to serve, or allow each person to serve themselves if the hot pot is prepared at the table.

Unsalted Chicken Stock

Yields 2 quarts (1.9 liters)
3 lbs (1.4 kg) chicken carcass/bones/wings
4 quarts (3.8 liters) water

Place the chicken in a large pot and add the water. Slowly bring to a boil then immediately reduce the heat to a simmer, skimming and discarding any impurities that rise to the top. Simmer for 2–3 hours, until the liquid is reduced by half.

Yellowtail Sashimi with Garlic Leaf Nuta Pesto

Yellowtail Sashimi with Garlic Leaf Nuta Pesto

Akincha Restaurant, Kochi Prefecture

Garlic leaf *nuta* is a condiment seen all over Kochi Prefecture and which we enjoyed at Akincha, the Kochi-style restaurant in Kochi City, headed by chef Akihiro Tani and his wife Saori. Its delicious mix of miso umami, garlic spiciness and acid tang from the vinegar is a perfect foil for fatty yellowtail or even grilled and sliced well-marbled skirt, flank or sirloin steak. This recipe is our own, thicker, more pesto-like version of the sauce we had at Akincha.

Recommended pairing: Tsukasabotan Senchu Hassaku junmai, served lukewarm

Serves 4
Half a bunch of garlic leaves or ramp leaves,
    about 2 oz (60 g)
Small clove of garlic, optional
5 oz (150 g) white miso paste
½ –¾ tsp sugar
2½ –4 tsps rice vinegar
1–3 tsps yuzu juice
A few drops of soy sauce
1 lb (450 g) yellowtail sashimi

1. Roughly chop the garlic leaves or ramp leaves. If you like your sauce on the spicy side, add some of the white bulbs of the garlic or ramp leaves, or a small clove of garlic. Place in a food processor with the white miso and process until smooth.
2. Place the garlic-miso mixture in a mortar, add the sugar, vinegar, yuzu juice and a few drops of soy sauce, and mash together until you have the consistency and taste you desire. The beautiful bright green color of the nuta deteriorates after the addition of vinegar, so it's best to make this dish on the day you plan to eat it.
3. Serve as an accompaniment to sliced yellowtail sashimi.

Sake Lees Hot Pot

Miyasaka Brewery, Nagano Prefecture

Kumi Miyasaka, the matriarch of the Miyasaka Brewery family, prepared this delicious and warming dish for us at the family's home in the mountain town of Suwa. Look for sake lees at your local Asian market, or even better, at a sake-brewery store if there is one near you. The lees give the hot pot a cloudy appearance, similar to miso soup.

Recommended pairing: Masumi Kaya Brown junmai.

Serves 2–4

3½ oz (100 g) sake lees and enough water to cover
Piece daikon radish, about 7 oz (200 g) cut into matchsticks 1–2 in (2.5–5 cm) long
1 Tbsp finely sliced ginger
10–14 oz (300–400 g) thinly sliced pork loin or belly
½ cup (60 g) chopped green onion or scallion, sliced ½ in (1.5 cm) thick on the diagonal

For the soup

½ cup (120 ml) sake (Masumi Kaya Brown sake or other junmai sake)
½–1 cup (120–240 ml) water
1 Tbsp soy sauce
¾ tsp salt, or to taste
¼ tsp sugar

1. Place the sake lees in a bowl with just enough water to cover. Let the lees soften for 1 hour, then using a hand mixer, blend into a smooth paste.
2. Put the sake lees and the soup ingredients in a hot-pot vessel (stoneware or earthenware, if possible).
3. Add the daikon radish to the pot and bring to a simmer. Cook the daikon until tender, about 3 minutes.
4. Add the ginger and the pork. Cover the pot and turn the heat to medium-high until the pot is bubbling, then reduce to a simmer.
6. Add the green onion, and simmer for a further minute.

Sukiyaki

Sakura Masamune Brewery, Hyogo Prefecture

This dish was served to us by chef Toru Takahashi at Sakura-en restaurant at Sakura Masamune Brewery. The rich beef dish, pairs perfectly with Nada-style full-bodied and bold junmai ginjo. You can cook this on the stove top or on a tabletop hot plate if you have one. The quantity in this recipe is for small servings as part of a multicourse meal. You can increase the ingredient amounts to make a filling main dish served with steamed rice.

Recommended pairing: Sakura Masamune Bonds Well With Beef junmai ginjo

Serves 2–3

1 shiitake mushroom per person, fresh or dried
7 oz (200 g) napa cabbage
Bunch of edible chrysanthemum greens, about 1½ oz (40 g), or spinach or mustard greens
Piece of green onion, about 1½ oz (40 g)
Small clump enoki mushrooms, about 1 oz (30 g)
1 small carrot
4 pieces fu (dried, baked wheat gluten), optional
Beef tallow or canola oil for sautéeing
1 raw egg per person
10 oz (300 g) beef tenderloin, thinly sliced
¾ cup (200 ml) Sukiyaki Sauce (see below)

Sake Lees Hot Pot

Sukiyaki

1. If using dried shiitake mushrooms, soak in warm water for 20 minutes to reconstitute.
2. Cut the napa cabbage leaves into bite-sized pieces, and the core into smaller pieces. Cut the chrysanthemum greens into bite-sized pieces.
3. Slice the white part of the green onion diagonally into ¾ in (2 cm) pieces. Discard the bottom part of the enoki and tear the mushrooms into small bunches.
4. Remove and discard the shiitake stems. Quarter the carrot lengthways. Soak the fu (if using) in water to rehydrate, then squeeze the water out.
5. Heat the beef tallow or oil in a large sauté pan over medium-high heat
6. With a fork, beat one egg for each person in individual bowls.
7. Place 1 slice of beef per person in the pan, and enough Sukiyaki Sauce to lightly coat. Brown the beef for a few seconds on each side. Enjoy this beef dipped in egg as your appetizer. Keep the remaining egg to eat with the rest of the hot pot.
8. Put half of the rest of the ingredients in the pan, add the rest of the Sukiyaki Sauce to generously cover the bottom of the pan, and cover with a lid.

9. When steam rises from the pan, check the cabbage is cooked. When all the ingredients are cooked, serve, using the egg as a dipping sauce. Repeat with the second half of ingredients.

Sukiyaki Sauce

This is better made in larger quantities. Save the leftover sauce for use in another recipe.

²/₃ cup (180 ml) mirin
3 cups (720 ml) dashi (see page 203, or powdered dashi using ½ tsp per cup)
⅓ cup (80 g) sugar
½ Tbsp sake
Scant 1 cup (220 ml) dark soy sauce

1. Heat the mirin in a small saucepan over medium-high heat for several minutes. Add the dashi, sugar and sake to the mirin and, mix well.
2. When the pan comes back to a boil, add the soy sauce, and then bring to a boil again. Remove from the heat and allow to cool.

Chapter Twenty-Two

Craft Sake and the World

In 2014, four friends and business partners in Queensland, New Zealand were relaxing and watching replay games of their national rugby team, the All Blacks. David Joll, Craig McLachlan, Richard Ryall and Yoshi Kawamura—all of whom had lived in Japan for extended periods (Kawamura is a Japanese national now based in New Zealand), were connected by their love of Japan, sport and sake. Watching the team that they felt an almost familial love for, they hatched an outlandish plan.

"We realized that we had to be involved in the 2019 Rugby World Cup in some way," Joll later recalled. He had lived in Japan for twenty years, had two advanced degrees from Japanese universities and had also written the Lonely Planet's guide to hiking in Japan. He and McLachlan had been rugby teammates and fellow Japanese language students at the University of Auckland.

The group came up with the scheme of starting their own sake company, aptly naming their brewery and their product Zenkuro, Japanese for "all black." Joll, who had no brewing experience was installed as head brewer. The plan was not as far-fetched as it might seem, given the group's ties to Japan and its members' entrepreneurial backgrounds. Joll, McLachlan and Ryall run an adventure travel company in Queensland that caters to Japanese visitors, and all told, the four partners have headed at least a half a dozen business ventures.

Yet it's still impressive that their five-year plan actually worked out. The umami-filled Zenkuro Rugby World Cup Special Edition tokubetsu junmai sake we drank while sitting on a log in front of Kumorebi in Fukuoka was their dream realized. It not only took the Zenkuro team to Japan to view a number of 2019 championship games, it also had them—along with their special-edition sake collaborators Kumazawa and Kanhokuto breweries—fêted from Tokyo to Fukuoka (Joll's wife Yasuko's

hometown). Japan's team made it to the quarter-finals, and the sake was a sell-out success.

"Initially we thought it was a hobby and a business opportunity," Joll says of Zenkuro. The team figured there were a few hundred Japanese restaurants in New Zealand, and many "forward-

thinking, innovative fusion chefs who know about koji and wanted sake on their drinks lists." If they could just sell a bottle a week to each, they'd be doing all right. There were a lot of questioning glances at first, but Joll says, "Japanese food, pop culture, that wonderful powder snow skiing and then the Rugby World Cup . . . everyone's interested in Japan now, and things have changed much faster than we thought they would." Even the wine industry has taken an interest; demand is growing among wineries for Joll to lead sake talks, tastings and participate in pairing dinners.

Graced with locally sourced soft alpine water, Zenkuro supplements that home ingredient with commercial yeast and Yamada Nishiki and Gohya-kumangoku rice from Japan. Initially the biggest challenge for Joll was gaining sake-brewing

knowledge. There was little available on the Internet when he started, and even with his Japanese-lan-guage abilities, slogging through brewers-associa-tion manuals was nothing like brewing alongside a Japanese master brewer. He spent a month at British Columbia's YK3 sake brewery with brewer Yoshiaki Kasugai and visited small craft brewers in the US. Through an introduction made by Kawa-mura, he also spent time at Yoshikubo Brewery in Ibaraki Prefecture. Joll's efforts have brought Zenku-ro a handful of awards, and the team is spending an increasing amount of time on this side business. His biggest challenge now is how to increase production levels without sacrificing quality.

"I got into sake brewing through my love for Japan rather than the other way around," Joll says, "and I'm aware how sake sales are going down in Japan. We did think that if we can help make sake popular overseas that would help revive interest in Japan. I hope we can contribute to an increased Japanese understanding of and appreciation for their national treasure."

Left At Zenkuro Brewery, David Joll uses lake and river stones in his *fune* press. **Below, left to right** Yuuma Okamoto, Akihito Shimizu, Joll's wife Yasuko Fukuda Joll, and Joll.

Yasutaka Daimon, president of Daimon Brewery in Osaka, played a central role in the early spread of sake education and knowledge.

Craft Sake Leaps Japan's Borders

There are now more than forty sake breweries worldwide, with more in the planning stages. The international landscape is dotted with high-caliber craft breweries: Sequoia and Den in San Francisco; Brooklyn Kura in New York; Nami in Culiacán, Mexico; Ontario Spring Water Sake Company in Toronto; and Les Larmes du Levant in Pélussin, France, to name a few.

You might consider this the second, artisanal wave of sake's worldwide spread, the first dating back to the breweries opened by Japanese immigrants and investors in the late nineteenth century. Our focus is not on mega-breweries like Takara and Ozeki that have been brewing in California since the 1970s, but the recent phenomenon of foreigners (or lone Japanese abroad) making sake, which began in the mid-90s. Its origins can be traced back to a handful of early Western post-ginjo enthusiasts who went on to exert an outsized influence on the spread of international sake culture.

John Gauntner and Philip Harper both arrived in Japan in 1988, as English teachers on the government-sponsored JET (Japan Exchange and Teaching) program. Both stumbled upon the drink that was to change their lives, Gauntner becoming the world's best-known non-Japanese sake educator and an importer, and Harper becoming Japan's first non-Japanese master brewer. Oceans away, future San Francisco sake merchant Beau Timken was undergoing a similar conversion in Cape Town, South Africa, where he was attending business school and drinking sake with some Japanese fishermen during his down time.

All three would come into the orbit of sixth-generation Osaka brewery president Yasutaka Daimon. In 2003, Daimon hosted Gauntner's first sake-professional course at his brewery. Timken, who opened his San Francisco sake specialty store, True Sake, in 2002, was one of three students in that class. In 2003 Harper started working at Daimon brewery as a *kurabito*, becoming *toji* in 2005. In 2009, Daimon and Timken joined forces to offer a sake-brewing-instruction course for people with brewing backgrounds. Kjetil Jikium from Nøgne Ø Brewery in Norway enrolled, and met Canadian brewer Brock Bennett there. The two went on to collaborate at Nøgne Ø, which became the first brewery to make sake in Europe, a brand called Hadak Jima. (Sadly the brewery stopped making sake in 2018 when a downturn in sales forced new owners to shed the sake product line.) Also in that 2009 class was Rick Smith, who, with his wife Hiroko Furukawa, opened the first sake shop in New York City, Sakaya.

It took another early adopter, Blake Richardson, to open the first sake brewery and pub outside of Japan, moto-i, which he did in Minneapolis in 2008. He, too, learned the basics of sake from Gauntner, at a 2006 sake professional course in Kamakura. Among his classmates was the couple Nancy and Tim Cushman, who would go on to open Boston and Mexico City's influential modern sushi spots O Ya, and Johnnie Stroud, who would open the pioneering Seattle sake shop Sake Nomi with his wife Taiko in 2008. These groups would form the nucleus of the Japanese craft-sake diaspora.

Born to Brew: Blake Richardson, moto-i, Minneapolis

As a student at the University of Minnesota, Blake Richardson fell in love with home beer brewing.

Dassai: A Craft-brewing Juggernaut Lands in Suburban New York State

In 2016, the Culinary Institute of America (CIA) in Hyde Park, New York, the country's premier cooking school, approached the makers of the highly successful craft brewery Dassai to gauge its interest in opening a brewing facility near the school. Both the school and the brewery agreed that sake knowledge and expertise in the US and worldwide lagged behind interest in the drink. If Asahi Brewery, Dassai's maker, established a brewery near campus it would give students the opportunity for a hands-on brewing experience, and the two organizations could collaborate on a sake-education program. They imagined a program that would become part of the degree curriculum and cover the areas of tasting, pairing and service.

Asahi president Kazuhiro Sakurai found the artisanal food culture of the Hudson River valley and its proximity to New York City appealing. "We need to change the image of sake from something you only drink with Japanese food, or only in Japan," he says. "It takes adopting a different lifestyle to instill that new mindset. I chose New York because of its strong power to create and disseminate this type of new food culture, and its ability to influence Europe as well."

The Dassai brand is marketed as a super-premium sake, an image burnished by the chic tea salon and restaurant it operates on Paris's rue du Faubourg Saint-Honoré, a partnership with the late French chef Joël Robuchon. Its entire lineup consists of elegant junmai daiginjos, their common denominator being a nearly wine-like, fruity profile. In the US, Sakurai knew that one of the great advantages of brewing locally would be the ability to sell fresh, unpasteurized namazake at an affordable price, without the hefty import markup. Prices abroad can easily reach two to three times the price of the same bottle in Japan. Asahi conceived of a completely new line, Dassai Blue, for the American market, priced in the twenty-dollar range. The brewery will also offer a high-end Dassai bottle in the fifty-dollar range. His goal, says Sakurai, is to "shorten the route to really good sake" for Americans, and to create a delicious and affordable local sake. He also wants to make an American sake that expresses its locality, with local Hudson Valley water, American rice, and eventually, American brewery workers.

The move would also hasten Sakurai's goal of seeing the new mindset he alluded to: Americans ordering sake paired with oysters, pizza, Chinese or French food, just as naturally they would order it at an izakaya or sushi bar. And far from cannibalizing his own brand, he asserts, Dassai Blue and Dassai will be rivals, but rivals who share techniques. By competing against each other, he believes, both will become stronger. Various delays, including the Covid-19 pandemic set the brewery's opening back until spring 2022, when brewing is also expected to begin.

This led to interning at a Colorado brewery after he graduated. On his way back to Minnesota, he got wind of a new beer brewery opening somewhere in St. Paul. "I got in my old, white vinyl-top 1975 Buick Regal and ran it up and down the streets of St. Paul. When I saw a building with tanks in the windows, I went in and said, "Do you guys need a brewer?" He was twenty-three. Three years later he enrolled in the Siebel Institute in Chicago to earn a diploma in brewing technology, and in 1999 opened his Minneapolis beer brewery and bar, Herkimer.

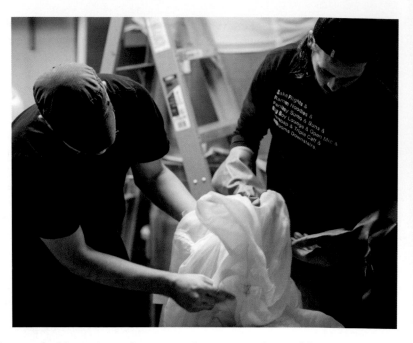

His first sip of sake came at a sushi restaurant in 2003, when he tasted a Masumi junmai ginjo. He fell in love with this strange new drink that paired so well with food. "I knew nothing about it, but was absolutely fascinated with the flavors, the elegance of it, the entire experience," he recalls.

Above At moto-i, owner–master brewer Blake Richardson (left) and lead brewer Nick Lowry (right) pull rice from the steamer. **Right** Sake on offer at moto-i.

Richardson set his mind to brewing sake and opening an izakaya-style pub he named moto-i ("moto" meaning sake starter, and "i" for "izakaya), and looked around for people who could give him help. A sake educator from Vancouver, Elise Gee, who had been one of his first sake education classmates back in 2006, helped him set up the brewery. Later, she called the experience "the hardest, most creative and fulfilling work I have ever done." Richardson sourced a rice washer from Japan, but everything else he used was repurposed or jury-rigged: stainless-steel beer fermenters for starter tanks; wine tanks for the *moromi* mash. They made over a hundred trips to Home Depot, turning plastic chairs into rice-soaking buckets and using pillow cases to hold the soaking rice.

Richardson had a few pieces of equipment custom made: a stainless-steel rice-steaming basket designed to fit into an industrial-sized kettle; a square, stainless-steel box with a spout at the bottom for trying *shizuku* drip pressing; and a rice cooling rack with a fan below it upon which wooden boxes could be stacked. Gee recalls, "there was a lot of stress with many deadlines to meet, launching a large restaurant while also trying to brew several inaugural tanks in time for the grand opening. Throughout it all, we were single-minded in our desire to get it right, to emulate and honor the breweries we had visited in Japan."

For advice, Richardson turned to the only craft-sake brewer operating in the country at the time, SakéOne in Forest Grove, Oregon, which supplied him with milled rice, koji and yeast. Eventually he repurposed a hydroponics tent to grow his own koji, and even found a used rice-milling machine in northern California. Richardson's company, Minnesota Rice and Milling, now mills rice for eight different craft-sake breweries in the US and Mexico.

The biggest hurdle to starting his brewery and pub, he says, was the licensing process and the challenge of "just explaining to people what sake is." The federal government considers his brews "beer until it hits the bottle, and then it's considered wine, but the states are all confused by sake at some level," he says. In Minnesota his sake is taxed at the higher wine rate, but his business is licensed as a brew pub which prohibits him from distributing his product. On top of these bureaucratic and financial hurdles, he learned that compared to beer brewing, "the feedback loop" for sake was much slower. Instead of tasting the outcomes of countless small decisions made in the brewing process in a few weeks as with beer, it takes much longer with sake. "Maturing a sake for six to twelve months gives you a much clearer picture of the final result," he explains. "Then you tweak the recipe and procedures for the next season." In other words, dialing in a really good, precise sake takes at least several years.

SakéOne

In the summer of 1990, Kyota Murai, the son of Aomori Prefecture–based Momokawa Brewery's fifth-generation president Tohru Murai arrived in Oregon to attend Pacific University in Forest Grove. He fell in love with the Pacific Northwest, and so did his family. Being sake makers, they noticed the

similarity between the very soft water from the slopes of Oregon's coastal range with that of their own brewery water, which flows from the Hakkoda Mountains and Lake Towada to their town of Oirase in southeastern Aomori.

In 1992, the company set up a subsidiary in Forest Grove called SakéOne for the purpose of importing sake. By 1997 it had added a brewery. As sake makers, says Steve Vuylsteke, president and CEO of SakéOne since 2009, this corner of Oregon "checked all the boxes—climate, water and good Calrose rice from California." Though Momokawa Brewery sold its shares in the company to Hakut-

suru Brewery, it still serves as import partner to SakéOne. Its export line, Murai sake, is one of seven different sakes the company imports.

Vuylsteke, whose own family was one of the pioneers of the pinot noir revolution in the Willamette Valley in the early 1980s, saw echoes of that time in the Oregon sake scene of the early 2000s: the lack of education among consumers about what sake is, the sense of an emerging region and market and the challenges that come with teaching consumers to understand a new drink. As with pinot noirs in 1980, he believes that what will propel the craft-sake industry in America forward is "a real sense of community, of wanting to promote the region" more than one's own winery or brewery, and "a very quality-oriented mindset."

Looking back at those early days of Oregon wines, he adds, "We had no idea what it would turn into today." From mainly fruit-wine producers and a handful of pinot noir producers, Oregon is now home to nearly eight hundred wineries, with pinot by far its most celebrated grape. He and the Murai family might say the same thing about sake and the advances it has made in Oregon in the last thirty years: Portlanders like to boast that they have the highest per capita consumption of sake in the US.

Exporting Sake-Making Expertise Abroad

Vuylsteke's belief in the power of a collective craft-sake community, that a rising tide lifts all boats, is one that is shared by the sake-brewing community in Japan and around the world. He points to an unusual three-day brewing seminar that unfolded in Sacramento, the heart of California's prime rice-growing region, in late June of 2018. This opportunity for non-Japanese brewers to learn from Japanese masters was sponsored by the Iida Group, an Osaka-based liquor wholesaler with a

On Sado Island in Niigata Prefecture, Gakkogura ("brewery school") offers one-week courses each summer on all aspects of sake making—from rice washing and steaming to koji-making and fermentation.

hand in every different link of the sake supply chain. One of Iida's subsidiary companies, Shinnakano Industry Co., manufactures rice-milling machines and now runs what is known as the largest rice-milling facility in the US. Based in Sacramento, it caters mostly to large Japanese-owned breweries.

From 2015, Shinnakano began fielding more and more inquiries from small North American breweries about buying rice. Iida representative Mitsuhiro Kono went to meet these aspiring brewers, consulting with them on everything from sourcing rice to small-scale equipment to yeast. He saw that the brewers were eager to learn, but had limited opportunity to do so. And even though what they were making was very different from Japanese-made sake, Kono says, "I saw how people who had never had an interest in or tasted sake before were keenly interested in locally made sake. I really felt the potential of the sake that they were brewing." To meet the need for sake-brewing education, the idea for the seminar was born.

The fifteen craft brewers from the US and Canada who attended picked up tips from three well-known master brewers: Kosuke Kuji of Nanbu Bijin, British-born toji Philip Harper of Kinoshita Brewery

and Junpei Komatsu of Komatsu Brewery.

In a blog post he wrote about the seminar, Kuji says, "I've always thought that in order for sake to spread around the world, the level of sake from overseas breweries and brewers must rise." Though many in Japan worry that sharing trade secrets somehow diminishes Japanese sake brewing, Kuji countered by reminding them of the term *sakaya banryu*, meaning "a thousand ways of sake brewing." In other words, even if you tried to make the same sake as another brewery, it would be impossible; the individuality of each brewer is imprinted, like strands of DNA, in his or her brew. Kuji pointed to the wide variety of wines available throughout the world, and how the once upstart Californians eventually produced Opus One, the 1980s Napa Valley Bordeaux blend created by Robert Mondavi in collaboration with Château Mouton Rothschild. He began to wonder which overseas brewer would come up with the sake equivalent of Opus One. With characteristic enthusiasm, he added, "I'm really looking forward to the results in five or ten years! We Japanese brewers will work hard to make even higher quality sake so that we will not lose!"

In Japan, too, sake makers have noted the rising demand for hands-on brewing education, and have responded. In 2017 Daimon Brewery, headed by newly installed CEO and former investment banker

Marcus Consolini, revived its brewer-education course, making it more scientifically rigorous and adding visits to a rice farm, koji maker and sake merchants in the Osaka area. Interest has been strong, says Consolini, with a record number of applicants in 2020. On Sado Island in Niigata Prefecture, Obata Brewery has since 2014 offered a one-week brewing program called Gakkogura ("brewery school") that attracts aspiring brewers from around the world.

Shared Sake Expertise Across Borders

The 2018 Sacramento brewing seminar expressed the Japanese sake industry's desire to grow a global sake-making movement, but it was not a lone statement. Behind every successful international start-up you will find stories of Japan-to-the-world sake knowledge sharing.

At the Ontario Spring Sake Company in Toronto, founder and president Ken Valvur's ties to the Miyasaka family, makers of Masumi sake, gave him a crucial leg up in the industry. He had become close to the family during his years as the founder of Canada's first bento-box company. When Valvur opened his sake brewery in 2011, the Miyasakas came on as consultants, helping him lay out the brewery, connecting him to suppliers and offering training for his first general manager. Valvur's first toji was a woman named Yoshiko Takahashi.

Through an introduction by Gauntner, Blake Richardson at moto-i was able to spend a day with Hiroshi Konno, the Akita mold merchant and Tom Selleck look alike we met in chapter 17. Konno, says Richardson, gave him "the best lesson in koji-kin ever." He adds, "I still practice the things he taught me in the eight hours we spent together."

Brooklyn Kura's Brandon Doughan credits time spent with the brewers at Miyasaka and Nanbu Bijin for the chance to brew alongside their toji, even if for a short while. Although Doughan says his Japanese is almost non-existent, he was still able to glean valuable lessons on how to brew more ergonomically and efficiently, and get close-up looks at top-line equipment that he could then ask his Brooklyn steel fabricator to build. Social media

posts, too, can lead to valuable exchanges. When one Japanese toji posted a series of photos and descriptions of brewing a kimoto sake, Doughan reached out for details. "He helped me understand the aroma changes a kimoto goes through," says Doughan. "It smells bad initially! Without these sorts of interactions, I may have given up on certain things if they didn't go how I expected them to."

Noriko Kamei and Jake Myrick, co-owners and toji at Sequoia Brewery in San Francisco, say the time they spent with toji Shinji Kawabata at Hokkaido's Kamikawa Taisetsu Brewery taught them invaluable lessons about equipment, workflow and where the sake market is headed. "He taught me the importance of developing our own formulas optimized for our local California rice," says Kamei. Kawabata advised Kamei to "try to develop your senses so you know the condition of the fermentation through the look and smell, then turn your experiences into your own formula." Kamei says, "That was eye-opening to me because I had been following written formulas and feeling frustrated at not getting the expected results."

A Brooklyn Sake Inspires Japanese Brewers

Brandon Doughan and Brian Polen, co-founders of US brewery Brooklyn Kura, were dumbfounded when they received the ultimate compliment as foreign sake brewers operating outside of Japan: in the fall of 2019, some of Japan's most promising young brewing talents—Masato Usui of Senkin Brewery in Tochigi and Masayuki Imanishi of Imanishi Brewery in Nara, makers of the Mimurosugi brand of sake—created two versions of a special sake in homage to Brooklyn Kura. They named their special sake From Brooklyn. The Japanese brewers had visited Brooklyn Kura a year before, and, inspired by its owners' passion and quality product (and probably the hipster street cred of its Brooklyn location), had, unbeknownst to Polen and Doughan, concocted their own soft, acid-forward sake tribute to the little American brewery.

That such incredibly talented brewers wanted to represent us was shocking," said Polen. "We felt a really complex set of emotions." The two hope one

The Sake World Cup

Osaka sake aficionado Koji Uenoyama has always been internationalist in outlook. He studied Spanish and discovered the burgeoning international sake movement when he read an article about the sake brewer Seda Líquida in Catalonia, Spain. He also knew that in Japan "sake is not a drink that people think is cool. It's a pretty nerdy world, and unless you have the right friend, it's one that you'll never step into." He decided to use his foreign-language skills to teach foreigners about sake and at the same time show the Japanese how cool sake is becoming internationally.

Uenoyama went from running an international guesthouse where he organized small sake parties to earning an international *kikisake-shi* certification given to sake sommeliers, promoters and educators around the world. Next, he managed a bar, where he held sake classes for foreign tourists. When the coronavirus hit Japan in 2020, he turned his attention full time to an event idea he had hatched back in 2018, which he named The Sake World Cup. Although it sounds like a competition, it is in fact a tasting event for internationally made sake.

In 2018 he had received sake submissions from nine breweries from around the world, and attracted a crowd of seventy people in Kyoto. In 2019, he teamed up with the well-known sake writer and expert Haruo Matsuzaki to much greater success, holding events in both Kyoto and Tokyo. He received submissions from twenty-one international breweries and attracted close to three-hundred guests.

The pandemic put a hold on the 2020 event. Uenoyama is cautiously hopeful. "The bad image that my generation had of sake has been cleaned up a little," he explains. "Young people today now have no image of what sake is." He realizes he has a lot more work to do.

"Tradition is good if you can maintain and respect what it has been, but also take in new ideas and be tolerant of changes," he says, conceding that the last fifteen to twenty years have brought real improvements in sake quality and diversity, and a widening of its fan base to include far more women than in the past. Like Polen, Uenoyama places a high value on the fearlessness of foreign brewers as a way to push the industry forward. "They're mostly very young, and are coming up with creative ways to match their sake with the local food. I like what they're doing."

day to bring both their sake and their brewery's story to Japan.

Head brewer Doughan met Polen, who now serves as brewery president, in Japan in 2013 at a mutual friend's wedding. Traveling together to see the thatched-roof farmhouses of Shirakawa-go in Gifu Prefecture, they ate Hida beef and visited a small traditional sake brewery. "It was the first time we'd seen sake making, and smelled fermented sake," says Doughan. "It made an impression on us."

Polen, who worked in the product and technology side of American Express, had long loved the New York sake bars Decibel and Sakagura, while Doughan, a Portland, Oregon-based biochemist and cancer researcher, had been home brewing beer for the past twenty years. He had dabbled in soy-sauce brewing and wine making, and would ferment any fruit he could get his hands on. The science and practice of brewing sour beers was a special interest of his. Both Doughan and Polen wondered why, in a major metropolitan area like New York City, "where there's a strong consumer base and a real affinity for a thoughtful, well-made craft product," had no one tried making sake? "We wanted to take it one step further and make sake more approachable, affordable and with greater variety—and address a learning gap," says Pollen.

They formed the company in 2016, at first renting a space in Bushwick to start some experimental brews while putting together a business plan. In June 2017, they signed their lease in the retail and business hub Industry City and in early 2018 sold their first sake. It helped that the brewery, with its bright blue door and minimalist tap room, is situated inside a thriving warehouse, restaurant, retail and artist studio complex.

Doughan and Polen's idea was to master quality traditional sakes while slowly adding experimental types. One sign their plan is working are the accolades their flagship Number Fourteen junmai ginjo namazake has received and the increasing popularity of their rosé-colored, dry-hopped junmai ginjo Occidental, aimed at wine and craft-beer lovers. In fall 2020 they sent their first international shipments out to Berlin and Hong Kong.

"France sends nine billion dollars in wine out into the world in a year, Italy six billion and Japan three hundred million in sake," says Polen. "Our ability to bridge that gap is real." He's excited about the arrival of Asahi Brewery in the Hudson Valley because of the "focused investment in sake marketing, education and training" it will bring. Once Americans are comfortable ordering sake as an alternative to beer or wine, that—combined with "production, distribution, boots on the ground servers, retail and hospitality—is when I think we'll to see the growth happen faster," he adds.

Brandon Doughan (left) and Brian Polen (right) founded Brooklyn Kura sake brewery in 2016.

Already, Brooklyn Kura has benefited from being in New York, where large food and beverage producers have invested in agriculture, milling and distribution, "essentially underwriting and in many ways bringing down the barriers to entry," Polen explains, adding, "Without that infrastructure, it would have been much more difficult to achieve the quality we have." Polen tips his hat to established sake brewers in the US, like Gekkeikan, Yaegaki and SakéOne, for similarly bringing down barriers to entry, but also for "giving Americans a taste of how casual and accessible sake can be."

A Sake Research Scientist Begins Brewing in Hawaii

In March 2020, when Chiaki Takahashi launched Islander Sake Brewery in Honolulu's Kaka'ako neighborhood, she had the advantage of a local market that had for years enjoyed locally brewed sake. But the Honolulu Sake Brewery had been shuttered for over thirty years, and Takahashi wanted to carry on its legacy. Her disadvantage though, was that the day after she opened the brewery doors, Honolulu shut down all non-essential business due to the Covid-19 pandemic.

Arkansas rice farmer Chris Isbell has emerged as a go-to source for US craft-sake brewers looking for premium domestic sake rice.

A former research scientist specializing in the effects of stress on brain chemistry at Nippon Medical School, Takahashi had transitioned to investigating the effects of stress on the fermentation process at the National Research Institute of Brewing (NRIB). She dreamed of opening her own brewery in a unique location between Japan and mainland United States that seamlessly blends Japanese and American culture. Takahashi is both president and master brewer at Islander, where one of its most interesting features is the way her scientific research shapes her style of brewing. She carefully calibrates and adjusts temperatures in order to exert maximum beneficial stress on the microorganisms in the fermenting mash. "We increase stress on the microorganisms to make the sake, and we decrease our stress when drinking it," she told *Hana Hou!*, the Hawaiian Airlines inflight magazine.

Sourcing Rice

While Zenkuro's rice is from Japan, American brewers have benefitted from two regions that offer good growing conditions for sake rice: the Sacramento Valley in California and Lonoke County, Arkansas, the latter largely because of one talented, fourth-generation farmer named Chris Isbell, who began growing Koshihikari table rice in the early 1990s and now grows four different sake rices. Sake's growth outside of Japan, Isbell believes, "will be like sushi," meaning exponential, especially, he believes, "as people get educated enough to know there are big differences in quality."

One of the rice varieties that Isbell grows is Wataribune, descended from the first rice seeds Japanese immigrants to California in 1905 brought with them. It grew on the Kanto Plain surrounding Tokyo and did double duty as both a table and a sake rice. The California rice industry rebranded this as Caloro, and by cross-breeding it with another strain known as Caladay, the industry-funded Rice Experiment Station in the town of Biggs developed the powerhouse medium-grain rice Calrose. More tinkering ensued, but it is essentially this descendant of Wataribune/Caloro that most North American sake breweries make sake with. In a tantalizing connection to early sake traditions, Wataribune's own parentage—and thus Calrose's—is thought to connect to our favorite heirloom, the mighty Omachi rice.

Although Isbell can grow Wataribune, he found no takers for this seed that he sourced from the USDA's germplasm bank. Brewers so far prefer Yamada Nishiki, though there is also demand for Gohyakumangoku and even Omachi.

Close to its Rice Source: Sequoia Brewery, San Francisco

In 2010, over a century after the first Wataribune seeds made their way across the Pacific to California, Jake Myrick and his wife Noriko Kamei took their savings from twenty years spent in the IT and non-profit worlds and put it into their San Francisco–based start-up brewery, Sequoia Sake. When they outgrew their garage they moved into a compact space in the Bayview district of the city. They, like most American sake breweries, use Calrose table rice, and they've taken home awards for their Coastal Ginjo label.

The couple have also taken advantage of their proximity to California's rice-growing and wine regions. Their relationship with Sacramento-based Sun Valley Rice led to its increased production of Yamada Nishiki rice. Myrick was also able to source some early Wataribune (now known as Caloro) rice. Partnering with a UC Davis–affiliated research geneticist and the USDA, the team conducted DNA and plant analysis, and in 2019 Sequoia was licensed by the USDA and state regulators to grow it. Sequoia released its first sake made with organic Caloro in 2021, under the name "Sequoia sake rice." Because the rice has little taste of its own, unlike Calrose, Myrick notes, "This allows the koji and yeast to impart their flavors more honestly into the sake, creating more complex flavor with a greater depth."

International Brewing Leads the Way

As these small international sake brewers mature, it is they who may end up showing the way to Japanese sake brewers who are trying to crack the code of internationalization. Both large industrial and craft-sake brewers, from Gekkeikan and Hakutsuru to Hakkaisan and Nanbu Bijin, have beat a trail to Brooklyn Kura and Sequoia Sake because they have a lot to learn from these upstarts. How they are presenting and marketing themselves, how they are expanding the definition of what sake is, which sakes appeal to local audiences: all of this is key information in a craft industry where internationalization is a necessity for survival.

"We're the frontline in the battle to expand the sake market," says Polen. "Most importantly, new makers all seem to share the simple goal of educating consumers. What we're doing gives Japanese producers access to a broad set of regional and local experiments that may offer insights into what we need to grow this market. In a way," he adds, "we are a proof of concept."

International Sake Flight

Sake name: Zenkuro
Sake type: Junmai daiginjo
Brewery: Zenkuro, Queenstown, New Zealand
Brewed with water from New Zealand's Southern Alps, featuring intensity and purity on the palate.

Sake name: Number Fourteen
Sake type: Junmai ginjo nama
Brewery: Brooklyn Kura, Brooklyn, US
Among a raft of cool, well-crafted sakes, this light and crisp brew with understated florals makes a good introductory sip.

Sake name: Izumi
Sake type: Arabashiri junmai muroka genshu
Brewery: Ontario Spring Water Sake Company, Toronto, Canada
The brewery makes super-fresh small-batch sake. Each tank provides a small amount of free-run sake. Fresh green banana and green melon notes with subtle hints of spice.

Chapter Twenty-Three

Where Do We Go From Here?

Sake's future is by no means secure; total domestic sales in Japan have shrunk year after year since peaking in 1973, and the number of breweries has fallen from 1,830 in 2003 to 1,371 in 2018. Japan's population continues to downsize, while worldwide, alcohol consumption is declining, a trend led by marketers' most cherished demographic group, young people. But if you are a sake maker, there's no function to pessimism—imagining a path forward is where sake makers are directing their energies.

Hideharu Ohta, tenth-generation president of Daishichi Brewery in Fukushima Prefecture, predicts that as sake becomes more internationalized over the next ten to twenty years, overseas tastes in sake will shift as new fans of sake get to know it. "When the Japanese started drinking wine for the first time, the most popular variety was fresh and fruity sweet white wine that was easy to drink," he says. Over time "there was a switch to red wine, which continues to the present day." While fruity, aromatic daiginjos might first attract new sake drinkers, he says, "their tastes will shift to more savory styles." That would suit his brewery well; it is known for sticking to the traditional kimoto starter method, which is generally deeper and more full-bodied in style, even as the government advised everyone to switch to the faster *sokujo* method. Ohta adds, "of course, that doesn't mean that the tastes of the world will become the same as those of the Japanese, but each country will reach its own form of maturity."

Ohta also believes that sustainability and ethical practices will become increasingly essential in the future global marketplace. In the world of sake, that means that "wasteful rice polishing just to flaunt

luxury will not be allowed." Instead, he says, "proof will be required that it is indispensable for achieving quality," and brewers will not only have to be able to justify their practices, but also explain how they "can contribute to the world's food culture."

Shinji Kawabata, master brewer at Hokkaido's Kamikawa Taisetsu Brewery, agrees that extravagantly low polishing ratios (meaning shaving off more and more of the outer husk) are no longer the only ways to signify luxury and quality. Ginjo sake, he believes, has run its course—we're now even seeing a bit of a backlash. Instead, brewers are looking for other techniques to make great sake. One of his recently discovered methods is using organic rice, and not because it's on trend, or something the marketplace is demanding. "One way to coax out the innate taste of the rice and its best characteristics is to keep the polishing to a minimum and select organically produced, high quality sake rice," Kawabata explains. "When I first used organically grown Ginpu rice, the off-flavors that I always worried about in conventionally grown Ginpu disappeared. I was surprised to find its taste more full, more expansive. This made me really embrace the idea of organics. Rather than exploring

new varieties of rice, I want to keep improving sake using the varieties I'm already brewing with."

Whether sustainability efforts are driven by reasons of taste, environmental consciousness or consumer demand, no doubt they will continue to expand across Japan as breweries follow the lead of Daishinshu Brewery in Nagano, Obata Brewery in Niigata or Hachinohe Brewery in Aomori, which have taken measures to preserve the natural landscape surrounding their breweries. New lightweight bottle designs and more efficient storage and refrigeration techniques will also continue to evolve.

To hear how the role of sake yeasts might evolve in the coming years, we turned to yeast researcher Takayuki Kazuoka from Tokyo University of Agriculture (Nodai). During our visit with him, he had expressed reservations about brewers' over-reliance on the heightened aromas and punchiness of modern yeasts at the expense of solid craftsmanship. But that caveat aside, he described an appealing future sake world bursting with diversity, filled with niche sake products made possible by high-level craftsmanship and imaginative boundary pushing. "We're already seeing styles ranging from high aroma to gently aged sake with body, or sake brewed with wine or shochu yeasts," he told us. "Brewers are just beginning to explore the yeast affinities of the many new varieties of hybrid rice. And there's still a lot of experimentation to be done on the effect of different brewing-water types on new yeast varieties."

We are already witnessing brewers who feel increasingly free to experiment and question what, in fact, sake is. While much of this license-to-be-crazy attitude toward sake brewing originates in less tradition-bound cultures, its effects do boomerang back to Japan. We recall a delicious sake we had at Gem by Moto in Tokyo—a collaboration called "Afrugem" between Chiba's Kidoizumi Brewery and the bar Gem by Moto—made with *kijoshu* (a rich type of sake in which some of the brewing water has been replaced with finished sake) aged in scotch barrels. There's Masuda Brewery in Toyama, which is aging dessert kijoshu for five years in Henri Giraud oak champagne barrels, or Tomonobu Mitobe's Yamagata Masamune Malola: he figured out how to introduce the malolactic fermentation of wine into sake to create his rich and mellow sake, the perfect match for prosciutto di Parma.

In Fukuoka Prefecture, Yamano Kotobuki Brewery has engineered a sake that for the first time incorporates an aroma compound normally associated with sauvignon blanc, giving it bright citrus and muscat notes. Then there was this one: in a bid to marry two cultures in a can of sake, in late 2021 London Sake introduced its new Session sparkling sake, infused with Japanese wasabi leaf and British apple. All of this experimentation reminded us of a comment that Moriki Brewery's master brewer Rumiko Moriki made to us: "Each maker is thinking about how they will change their product for the foreign market. Changes in flavor, alcohol content, there will be a lot of changes to gain a wider understanding among global audiences. But for us in the domestic market, it's a question of how much do we cater to that?"

On the side of sake service and sake consumption, importer for US boutique import agency Vine Connections and Sake Samurai Monica Samuels is happy to see a new sense of fun and experimentation. "More than ever, people in Japan are just being more playful with sake, in the best possible way," she says. "I've gone to sake bars in Japan where they'll take two sakes and blend them, something that would have been sacrilege a few years ago. In some ways you're seeing things that are more daring and experimental than at wine bars. And when you ask them why they did that, you get a dissertation, it's really thought out, too."

Innovation will also continue on the marketing and financing end. Soccer-star-turned-sake-promoter Hidetoshi Nakata has spearheaded an app, Sakenomy, which supplies consumers with individual label translation, brewery and pairing information. And he's working on bringing more transparency to supply-chain logistics via a digital blockchain ledger system.

Yamagata-based Wakaze Brewery managed to

Above The Yamada Nishiki harvest in Yokawa.
Right Tomonobu Mitobe introduced the malolactic fermentation of wine into sake.

raise $1.4 million in venture-capital money to fund practices like brewing in France using wine yeast, local hard water and locally grown rice; aging its sake in wine barrels; or spiking it with spices or tea.

Satoshi Kodama, whose parents run Kodama Brewery in Akita, returned from a year-long stint working at Azuma-Kirin brewery in São Paulo, Brazil with an affection for the country and how it has adapted sake to the local culture by introducing cocktails that combine sake with mango, passion fruit, or the Brazilian grape jaboticaba. Azuma has also shown Brazilians how to swap sake for the national spirit cachaça in a caipirinha to make the "sakepirinha." Satoshi's father, Shin-ichi Kodama, says where he once balked at the thought of sparkling, or aged sake, his tastes evolved after visiting Brazil and seeing how sparkling or fruit-sake cocktails can express the more free and laid-back culture there. At ki modern japanese + bar where Michael works, he makes a Japanese vermouth using Masumi Okuden junmai and twenty-five different botanicals, fortified with shochu.

Blake Richardson, founder and brewer at moto-i in Minneapolis, foresees American craft sake following the same arc as its craft beer. "At first, microbreweries tried so desperately hard to make beer identical to what they found in stout in England, lager in Munich, or lambic in Bruges, that was the yardstick of quality. But at some point we'll pivot—maybe it will be the discovery of some local yeast, or the development of a new rice, but there will be something that happens," he says, that will allow America to brew a brew a sake as good as the best Japanese sake, but not through simple imitation.

Tetsuo Yamaguchi, eleventh-generation head of Yamaguchi Brewery in Kurume, Fukuoka says, "We will definitely at some point be in direct competition with wine. Already you hear French sommeliers and chefs saying that, hands down, sake pairs better with seafood than wine. If you consider that Japan has only been making seriously good sake for about thirty years, imagine where sake will be in one hundred years. It's going to be way better; it will have advanced that much more."

As overseas sake gets better and better, predicts international sake judge Carlin Kumada, Japanese sake will become what French wine is to the rest of the world's production. "Sure, you can get good Californian or Canadian wine, but for a high-end wine, you go to France," he explains. In the same way, people around the world will consider local sake their everyday go-to, but select a premium Japanese bottle for special occasions.

In the future, a bigger part of that Japanese experience is likely to be sparkling (*awa*) sakes. All agree that Gunma Prefecture's Nagai Brewery makes one of the best sparkling sakes on the market, its Mizubasho Pure. But sparkling varieties—ranging from the earthy, ciderish profiles of

Terada Honke's Musubi and Masumi's Origarami, to Hakkaisan's elegant and clear Awa—will continue to evolve. Sparkling sake may not have yet achieved champagne-level creaminess, but it pairs better with seafood, caviar, egg and meat dishes, points out Kensuke Shichida, president of Tenzan Brewery in Saga Prefecture. "*Awazake* is just more adaptable," he says, adding that as global consumption grows, sake will become widely recognized as more food-friendly than wine.

The Yokawa Yamada Nishiki Harvest

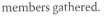

Although we couldn't be in Yokawa for the harvest, we followed it from afar. By October the mature rice stalks that had grown from the seedlings we helped plant had shot up, their heavy golden heads listing toward the ground, their stalks a pale green fading to brown. Kikuhime Brewery's annual hand-harvesting ritual was on 18 October, a gray day when about fifteen supporters and community members gathered.

Each person was given a sickle, and began grabbing rice stalks by the bunch, cutting them at the roots and laying them neatly in the field in rows. The bundles were carefully wrapped in lengths of straw, after which the group constructed the *inaki* bamboo frames upon which the rice would be hung upside down and dried. The inaki, too, were tied together with lengths of straw, a low-tech, centuries-old tradition beautiful in its simplicity. When they were finished, the V-shaped frames were heavy with sheaves of rice and looked like a row of tidy thatched roofs. At day's end, the hard work merited a celebration with draughts of the balanced and umami-filled Kikuhime junmai daiginjo that had begun its life in these fields.

Though this is the traditional harvesting method, almost all sake-rice fields today are harvested using small, farmer-driven combines. Kikuhime's 3,500 bales are harvested in the first three weeks of October, says the brewery's rice expert, Toshiyuki

Ide. The rice is dried and sorted in Yokawa, then transported to the Ishikawa Prefecture brewery to be milled. While planting can be timed for good weather, harvest is another matter. Rice must be harvested at peak ripeness, and the farmer's perennial worry is that rain will force a delay. This year's extreme heat during the first half of the ripening period, from late August to early September has resulted in harder-than-ideal rice, which brewers will have to adjust for during production.

Back Home: A Tasting

Back in Toronto, we decide to hold our own *on-nomi* (a new Japanese term coined during the pandemic to describe drinking digitally with friends) to taste the products of the brewers we visited who source prime Yokawa Yamada Nishiki. Holding up to our noses a glass of Kikuhime's Kinken junmai, we detect notes of caramel, cereal, soy sauce and the nuttiness drawn out during its one-to-two years of aging. Named for the shrine in Tsurugi town where brewers go at the start of every brewing season to pray for a safe brewing year, this is considered one of Kikuhime's softer and gentler sakes compared to its more muscular yamahai junmai. Yet that classic Kikuhime style, a balance of umami, honeyed sweetness and acidity, is there.

This sake is about protecting old brewing traditions and eschewing the modern. Memories of Mt. Haku rising in the distance and the brewery's giant rice-milling facility rush back—a long row of milling machines in front of which prizewinning stalks of dried Yamada Nishiki hung, like championship banners in a sports arena. We picture in our mind's eye president Tatsushi Yanagi, the panache with which he brewed our green tea, the utilitarian, exquisite iron kettle hanging from its heavy chain, and the artifacts of his own making that surrounded him. This junmai sake evokes the craftsman-

Dried rice at Kikuhime Brewery.

ship of the ancient province and the fierce loyalty its maker harbors toward its history and customs.

Next, we turn to the bottle of Sohomare tokubetsu junmai kimoto, only slightly more polished at 60 percent than Kikuhime's 65 percent. Yet it is far lighter, more delicate, more floral on the nose, its unmistakable umami balanced with citrus notes and a pronounced mineral salinity. It is an expression of the waters of Nikko's Mt. Nantai, and the personality of Sohomare president Jun Kono, with his love of wine, champagne and the practice of blending.

In this bottle we find a layered expression of those influences, holding within it perhaps the effects of displacement, of a family that left its ancient seat to move closer to the center of power in Edo. This is the product of a brewery not immune to foreign and modernizing influences, even as it hews to the original kimoto starter method of brewing.

Had we still had a bottle of it we would have next tasted the most traditional of the three Yokawa Yamada Nishiki sakes, Sakura Masamune's Yomigaeri Hyakunen, the one brewed with the rediscovered Yeast No. 1, exactly as it was made a century ago. This is the one Michael nabbed for his sake regionality class, with rice polished to a rough 80 percent, and made with a kimoto starter. To brew the sake, *toji* Norihide Harada used *miyamizu*, the water his brewery's reputation was built upon. Most of its sake is no longer made with miyamizu, so this was a deliberate choice to achieve the utmost level of authenticity. In this sake, prime Yokawa

Yamada Nishiki rice is brewed to maximize body and umami. Michael recalls its taste, the antique yeast yielding little in the way of aroma, yet the brew expressing a beautiful and persistent toasted-cereal quality with just a tiny suggestion of sweet spice, a little citrus and a long, lingering finish.

The Yomigaeri Hyakunen is historic Nada, with its history of technical brewing excellence, captured in a bottle. It is also the only one of the three sakes to fully express the regionality of Hyogo: the ideal Yokawa microclimate generated in the shadow of Mt. Rokko; the ancient clay soil that imbues its Yamada Nishiki with a complex and subtle bouquet of umami, sweetness and rich texture; the frigid winds that rush off the Rokko Mountains to cool the steamed rice; and the sharp, defining, miyamizu water that originates on those slopes before making its way underground. All of that is there in the bottle, orchestrated by skills honed over eleven generations of brewing history.

Three different Toku-A Yokawa Yamada Nishiki sakes, and three very different expressions. The tastes are at once ancient and fresh, the product of centuries old know-how and the latest technical innovations. But what were the through lines? What did they all have in common? In a word, balance. The elements of umami, sweetness, acidity and silky profile were all seamlessly orchestrated—no doubt

in large part by the master brewers—but also by nature. Sakes made from Yamada Nishiki rice might also be defined by what they do not possess, the ornate taste of Omachi, the shorter tail and the drier, leaner style of Gohyakumangoku. Instead, these three Yamada Nishiki sakes shared a spreading fullness, and the opulence and elegance this coveted grain is known for.

We raise our glasses to say *kanpai* to the craft-sake world we have tried to describe. Its diversity has long since burst the confines of cookie-cutter notions of excellence, just as its reach has jumped Japan's borders and circled the world. To continue this story, we can point to any number of countries around the globe, where the next chapter of traditional craft sake's evolution is being written.

Kanpai! to that, we say, and imagine we hear the clinking of glasses.

Toku-A Paddy-to-Glass Flight

Numbers 1–3 are the Toku-A Yamada Nishiki sakes with which we celebrated the end of our journey. Number 4 is one of our favorite sparkling sakes.

1. Sake name: Sohomare **Sake type:** Tokubetsu junmai kimoto **Brewery:** Sohomare, Tochigi Prefecture
2. Sake name: Kikuhime "Kinken" **Sake type:** Junmai **Brewery:** Kikuhime, Ishikawa Prefecture
3. Sake name: Yomigaeri Hyakunen **Sake type:** Junmai genshu **Brewery:** Sakura Masamune, Hyogo Prefecture
4. Sake name: Mizubasho "Pure" **Sake type:** Sparkling junmai daiginjo **Brewery:** Nagai, Gunma Prefecture

Glossary of Sake Terms

amakuchi 甘口 Sweet-tasting sake.

amami 甘味 Sweetness.

amazake 甘酒 Sweet, no- or low-alcohol sake in which rice is broken down into sugars either through the addition of *koji* rice or sake lees.

amino san-do アミノ酸度 The level of amino acids in a sake.

arabashiri あらばしり The first portion of sake out of the press, typically free-run sake. A typical pressing is divided into three parts.

aruten-shu アル添酒 Short for *arukoru-tenka-shu*, or sake made with the addition of high-strength brewer's alcohol before pressing.

Aspergillus oryzae The Latin term for koji mold, or koji-kin.

assakuki 圧搾機 Modern, accordion-style horizontal sake press that separates the main mash (*moromi*) from its lees (*kasu*). Often referred to simply as Yabuta after the most famous and ubiquitous brand of press.

atsukan 熱燗 Hot sake. Typically served at 122°F (50°C) or above.

awazake あわ酒 Sparkling sake made in the traditional bottle-fermented method. Also known as *happo-shu*.

bin-hi-ire 瓶火入れ Sake pasteurized in the bottle. Also known as *binkan*.

binkan 瓶燗 See *bin-hi-ire*

bodaimoto 菩提酛 A ancient fermentation starter that predates *kimoto*, developed by the monks at Shoryaku Temple in Nara Prefecture.

BY Brewing Year. In the brewing world, the brewing year starts in July and ends in June of the following year.

choko or **ochoko** 猪口 or お猪口 A small sake cup.

chozo 貯蔵 Storage and maturation of sake.

daiginjo-shu 大吟醸酒 One of the top classifications in sake making. Often referred to as the pinnacle of sake making (although this viewpoint is changing), made with rice polished to a minimum of 50% of its original size.

daki 暖気 A small bucket- or float-like vessel, often made of wood or metal, that is filled with cold water, ice or hot water, and placed in the starter to control fermentation temperature.

Dewasansan 出羽燦々 An important sake-specific rice variety from Yamagata Prefecture.

doburoku 濁酒 A thick, unfiltered sake that is not legally considered sake due to its lack of filtration.

Echigo Toji 越後杜氏 An important toji guild from Niigata. Echigo is the old provincial name of present-day Niigata.

Edo 江戸 The capital of Japan under the Tokugawa shogunate, present-day Tokyo.

fukuro-shibori 袋搾り Drip-pressing. Cloth bags are filled with the *moromi* (main mash) and hung in a small tank, allowing gravity to press the sake. A traditional method often used for a brewery's top sakes.

fune 槽 A box-like container that holds the bags of *moromi* mash.

fune-shibori 槽搾り Traditional method of pressing sake using a vat or box (*fune*), typically made from wood, which is filled with stacked cloth bags filled with sake mash (*moromi*). Pressure is applied from above to squeeze the sake out.

Fushimi 伏見 The southern ward of Kyoto City, and an historically important sake-making district.

futsu-shu 普通酒 Regular or non-premium sake.

genmai 玄米 Brown, unpolished rice.

genshu 原酒 Undiluted sake.

ginjo-shu 吟醸酒 Premium sake, referring to the top four classifications: *ginjo*, *junmai ginjo*, *daiginjo* and *junmai daiginjo*. Also any sake for which the rice has been polished to a minimum of 60% of its original size.

ginjo-ka 吟醸香 *Ginjo* aromas.

go 合 A traditional unit of measurement, 180 ml (6 fl. oz.) and the basic building-block unit size for measuring sake quantities.

Gohyakumangoku 五百万石 An important sake-specific rice from Niigata Prefecture.

go-mi 五味 The five flavors that formed the traditional way of assessing sake, namely *sanmi* (acidity), *amami* (sweetness), *karami* (dryness), *shibumi* (astringency) and *nigami* (bitterness).

guinomi ぐい呑み A sake drinking vessel that is slightly larger than a *choko*.

hangiri-oke 半切桶 A half-cut barrel traditionally made of wood but more often, in modern times, of stainless steel and aluminum. Often used for the *yama-oroshi* (pounding of the mash) in *kimoto* making.

happo-shu 発泡酒 Sparkling sake. See also *awazake*.

hi-ire 火入れ Pasteurization.

hineka 老香 The aromas associated with faulted, out-of-condition, deteriorating sake.

hinoki 檜 Japanese cypress. A widely used wood in Japan and in sake making, for temples, shrines and the interior of *koji* rooms.

hiochi 火落ち Considered a fault in unpasteurized sake that is caused by the propagation of *hiochi-kin* bacteria.

hi-ochi-kin 火落ち菌 A type of lactic acid bacteria that causes spoilage in unpasteurized sake.

hiragana 平仮名 An indigenous Japanese syllabic writing system, unlike Chinese-derived kanji characters.

hiyaoroshi ひやおろし A sake released in the autumn season that is typically only pasteurized once.

honjozo-shu 本醸造酒 One of the classifications of premium sake, polished to a minimum of 70% of its original size, with a small amount of brewer's alcohol added before completion.

ichi-go 一合 A standard single serving of sake, or 180 ml (6 fl. oz.).

ikkyu 一級 First class. Sake classification from the old Kyubetsu Seido system.

issho 一升 A traditional unit of measurement, 1.8 liters (2 quarts).

isshobin 一升瓶 A large-format sake bottle with a volume of 1.8 liters (2 quarts).

itto 一斗 A traditional measuring unit of 18 liters (19 quarts).

izakaya 居酒屋 A Japanese tavern featuring sake, beer, shochu and casual food.

jizake 地酒 Locally made sake, often craft sake from small boutique producers using local ingredients.

jo-on 常温 Room temperature.

junmai-shu 純米酒 Pure rice sake, made without the addition of high-strength brewer's alcohol, instead only featuring alcohol resulting from the fermentation process.

kakemai 掛米 Steamed rice used in the fermentation starter or *moromi* tank, not for *koji* making.

kanji 漢字 Japan's oldest formal writing system, which originated in China.

kanzake 燗酒 Hot sake.

kanzukuri 寒造り Winter or cold-weather sake brewing. This is a term that originated in the Edo period.

kaori 香り Aromas or fragrances.

karakuchi 辛口 Dry taste.

karami 辛味 Dry flavor.

kasu buai 粕歩合 The percentage, in weight, of the sake lees (*sake kasu*) that remain after pressing. The higher the number, the more delicate the resulting sake.

kijoshu 貴醸酒 Sweet sake, made by substituting a fraction of the water used to make a sake with already-brewed sake.

kikichoko きき猪口 Professional sake tasting cup made of white porcelain, bearing two concentric blue circles on the bottom inside of the cup.

kikizake きき酒 Sake tasting.

kimoto 生酛 An ancient and labor-intensive yeast starter that originated in Hyogo during the early Edo period, involving the use of wooden paddles to pound the rice into a paste in order to extract enzymes.

kire 切れ A very short, "cut" finish.

kobo 酵母 Yeast.

koji 麹 or **kojimai** 麹米 Steamed white inoculated with *koji-kin*.

koji-kin 麹菌 Fungus/mold spores from the *Aspergillus oryzae* family used to convert rice starch into digestible sugars for yeast to feed upon.

koku 石 A traditional unit of measurement equal to 180 liters (47½ gallons).

koshiki 甑 A traditional rice steamer.

koshu 古酒 Aged sake.

kosui 硬水 Hard water.

kura 蔵 Sake brewery.

kurabito 蔵人 Sake brewery worker or workers.

kuramoto 蔵元 Sake brewery owner or owners.

kyokai kobo 協会酵母 Sake yeast distributed by the Brewing Society of Japan.

kyubetsu seido 級別制度 The old classification system for sake, terminated in 1992, which divided sake into *tokkyu* (special class), *ikkyu* (first class), or *nikkyu* (second class) grades.

masu 升 A traditional wooden cedar box used to measure rice and other ingredients. Also used as a drinking vessel.

Miyama Nishiki 美山錦 One of Japan's principal sake rices, from Nagano Prefecture.

miyamizu 宮水 The famous brewing water of the Nada-Gogo area.

moromi 醪 The main fermentation mash.

moto 酛 Sake starter.

moyashi もやし Lit., "sprouts," another name for *koji* spores.

muroka 無濾過 Sake that has not been charcoal filtered.

mushimai 蒸し米 Steamed rice.

Nada-Gogo 灘五郷 Arguably the most important sake-making region in Japan, comprising five villages in present-day Kobe and Nishinomiya cities. Home to *miyamizu* brewing water.

nakadori 中取り The middle and most prized portion of a single sake pressing.

nama chozo 生貯蔵 Sake that is stored as *nama* (unpasteurized) sake and pasteurized only once before bottling.

namazake 生酒 Unpasteurized sake.

namazume 生詰 Sake pasteurized before storage but not given the typical second pasteurization. See *hiyaoroshi*

Nanbu Toji 南部杜氏 One of the most influential *toji* guilds, originating in the former Nanbu province, or present-day Iwate Prefecture.

nansui 軟水 Soft water.

nigami 苦味 Bitterness.

nigori-zake 濁り酒 Roughly filtered, cloudy sake.

nihonshu 日本酒 Since the kanji character 酒 (read as *sake* or *shu*) can refer to any type of alcohol, *nihonshu* specifies "Japanese alcohol," or sake.

nihonshu-do 日本酒度 A measurement system used to determine sweetness and dryness of sake. Also referred to as the Sake Meter Value.

nikkyu 二級 Second class. Unranked sake from the old Kyubetsu Seido classification system.

Nokyo 農協 Japan Agriculture (JA), an association of local farm co-ops throughout Japan.

nomiya 飲み屋 Drinking place.

nuka 糠 Rice bran, a by-product of the rice-polishing process.

nurukan 温燗 Sake-serving temperature of 104°F (40°C).

ochoko お猪口 See *choko*

okan お燗 Warmed sake.

oke-gai 桶買い "Buying tanks." A company's purchase of sake from other breweries.

oke-uri 桶売り "Selling tanks." Sake produced for the purposes of selling to another brewery for sale under that company's brand.

Omachi 雄町 The oldest heirloom sake rice in the sake world, hailing from Okayama Prefecture.

oribiki 澱引き Allowing the particles in sake to settle at the bottom of the tank at the end of fermentation.

orizake 滓酒 Cloudy sake containing fine rice particles.

ote 大手 A term referring to the largest brewers in the sake industry.

roka 濾過 Charcoal filtering the sake to stabilize color and flavor.

Rokko-oroshi 六甲おろし The local winds that flow south down from the Rokko Mountains to the sake breweries in Nada.

sakagura 酒蔵 Sake brewery.

sakamai 酒米 Sake rice.

sakaya 酒屋 Sake shop.

sakazuki 杯 or 盃 A flat, saucer-like sake cup used in ceremonies.

sake kasu 酒粕 Lees, or the rice-based solids that remain after pressing.

sandan shikomi 三段仕込 Three-stage sake-brewing method in which steamed rice, water and *koji* are added in three stages to allow for steady yeast development.

sando 酸度 Level of acidity in a sake.

sanmi 酸味 Acidity.

sanzo-shu 三増酒 Lit., "Tripled sake," a

235

type of sake filled with enough additives to effectively triple it in volume. Sanctioned by the government to cope with wartime shortages, it is no longer legal in sake making.

sasa-nigori ささ濁り Lightly cloudy sake.

seimai buai 精米歩合 Polishing rate of the sake rice.

seishu 清酒 Lit., "Clear sake." An official term for sake along with *nihonshu*.

seme 責め The final, tail-end portion of pressed sake.

senmai 洗米 Rice washing.

shiboritate 搾りたて Just-pressed sake.

shibumi 渋味 A pleasant, mouth-gripping astringency.

shikomi 仕込み Brewing a batch of sake.

shinpaku 心白 The starchy, white heart found in sake-specific rice.

shinshu 新酒 Unpasteurized "new" sake.

shizen-shu 自然酒 Natural, organic sake.

shizuku 雫 Drip-pressing.

shubo 酒母 Yeast starter.

shuzo 酒造 Sake brewery.

shuzo kotekimai 酒造好適米 Sake-specific rice.

sokujo moto 速醸酛 The fast, "modern" yeast starter, developed in the early 1900s.

sugi 杉 Cedar. Its pleasing aroma made it a favored wood for *taru* sake barrels. See *taruzake*.

sugidama 杉玉 A ball made with green cedar branches hung at the entrance to a

sake brewery to indicate brewing is underway.

Tanba Toji 丹波杜氏 An important *toji* guild from the Tanba region of Hyogo Prefecture.

tane koji 種麹 *Koji* spores.

tanrei karakuchi 淡麗辛口 Light, crisp, dry. Often used to describe the sake of Niigata.

taruzake 樽酒 Sake matured briefly in wooden barrels, or *taru*.

taue 田植え Rice planting.

tobin 斗瓶 An 18-liter (19-quart) bottle used to capture drip-pressed sake.

tobin gakoi 斗瓶囲い The sake from the middle of a *shizuku* (drip) pressing into a *tobin*.

Tohoku 東北 The northernmost six prefectures on the main island of Honshu: Aomori, Akita, Iwate, Miyagi, Yamagata and Fukushima.

toji 杜氏 Master brewer or chief brewer at a sake brewery.

toji ryuha 杜氏流派 Guild of sake master brewers.

tokkuri 徳利 Small flask for serving sake.

tokkyu 特級 Special class. The highest classification in the former Kyubetsu Seido classification system.

tokutei meishoshu 特定名称酒 Premium, or special designation sake.

tsuki-haze 突破精 Manner of *koji*-spore propagation featuring light enzymatic

activity and a focus on hyphae reaching the center of steamed rice grains. Most often associated with *ginjo* sake production.

umami 旨味 The sixth taste, often described as "savory deliciousness."

umeshu 梅酒 Plum sake.

usunigori うすにごり Lightly cloudy sake.

Yabuta 薮田 Brand name of *assakuki*-style sake press.

Yamada Nishiki 山田錦 The most widely cultivated and revered sake-specific rice in the Japan.

yamahai 山廃 A type of yeast starter method similar to *kimoto* but without wooden pole mashing.

yama-oroshi 山嵐 The use of wooden poles in the *kimoto* method to pound the rice.

yodan 四段 The fourth addition in sake used to adjust the sweetness of a sake. This addition consists of only *koji* rice.

yongobin 四合瓶 A 720-ml (24 fl. oz.) size bottle, or four *go*.

Zenkoku Shinshu Kanpyokai 全国新酒鑑評会 The National New Sake Appraisal, organized by the National Research Institute of Brewing (NRIB).

Photo Credits

Index

Index

Acknowledgments

This book would not have been possible without the support of the small but rapidly expanding international sake community.

We thank the countless brewers and breweries, researchers, sake sommeliers and agents, sake bars and other sources for opening their arms and brewery doors to us, and for patiently answering endless follow-up and fact-checking questions. Among them, we are especially thankful for the warm hospitality of the Miyasaka family (Masumi Brewery) and their tireless representative Keith Norum, the Maegaki family (Kamoizumi Brewery), the Kodama family (Kodama Brewery), Kosuke Kuji (Nanbu Bijin) and Yoshi Yamamoto (Yucho Brewery). For being such excellent tour guides and sources, we thank Haruhiko Uehigashi and Carlin Kumada.

For enhancing the richness and diversity of this book through tales of their family histories and the history of sake, we thank Miho Imada at Imada Brewery, Jun and Michihiro Kono at Sohomare Brewery, Rumiko Moriki at Moriki Brewery, Masumi Nakano at Dewazakura Brewery, Shigeki Tonoike at Tonoike Brewery, Tazaemon Yamamura at Sakura Masamune Brewery, Mitsuru and Masataka Hanafusa at Muromachi Brewery, Tadayoshi Toshimori at Toshimori Brewery, Goro Yamazaki at Otokoyama Brewery and Tatsushi Yanagi at Kikuhime Brewery.

For deepening our understanding of the role of fungus, mold and yeast in sake making, we are greatly indebted to Hiroshi Konno, Ph.D., Koichi Higuchi and Takayuki Kazuoka. To the many other brewers and sources we do not have space to mention by name, we thank you and hope our book does your stories justice.

We first discussed this book with Hiromi Iuchi of the Japan Sake and Shochu Makers Association and Etsuko Nakamura, Sake Samurai and founder of Sake Brewery Tours. Both were whole-hearted in their encouragement and provided valuable support and information along the way. For their early support of the project and for helping us get this project off the ground, we thank Sake Samurais Richie Hawtin and Kenjiro Monji, and sommelier Pascaline Peltier.

We owe a large debt of gratitude to the team of expert readers who offered valuable comments, corrections and suggestions on the manuscript: John Gauntner, Chris Pearce and Beau Timken. For valuable support in the Snow Country chapter, we thank Hakkaisan Brewery and Timothy Sullivan.

Sake writer and educator Ayuko Yamaguchi was our indispensable fact-checker, whom we thank for her discerning eye, and for being an appreciative and enthusiastic reader. Our thanks go out to Tokyo-based photographer Irwin Wong, who provided many of the beautiful portraits and brewery photographs sprinkled throughout this book, and Eric Medsker for his handsome cover photograph. We are also indebted to the many sake breweries that shared photos with us for this book.

We thank our stellar agent, Max Sinsheimer, for his persistence in finding a publisher for our book and for his excellent editorial guidance.

We thank Nancy's friend, Japanese instructor and translator Mariko Aratani for her cheerful help in translating the poems and literary excerpts we have included in this book.

Michael gives a shout-out to everyone at ki modern japanese + bar, members of the Sake Institute of Ontario and the Independent Wine Education Guild for the opportunities provided that shaped his sake pedagogical skills and made him the sake geek he is today.

For making the recipes chapter accurate, wide-ranging and mouth-watering, we thank the many sake brewing families who donated cherished recipes. We also thank Chef Hing Wong at ki modern Japanese + bar, whose beautiful interpretations of the dishes are pictured in the chapter, and our team of volunteer recipe testers—Kieran Coyne, Tammy Yiu Coyne, Peter Kirby, Hannah Kirshner, Nick Oliveiro, Naomi Mizoguchi, Yasushi Sasaki, Kinuko Peterson, Jennifer Takaki, Junko Tsunashima and Kaoru Tsunashima.

To the team at Tuttle, especially our editor Cathy Layne, we offer our gratitude for so carefully and kindly shepherding our words and pictures into final book form.

Finally, we would like to thank our cherished partners and family members, Grant, Sandy and Kristin, for their support, love and encouragement during this long research and writing project.

Published in 2022 by Tuttle Publishing, an imprint of
Periplus Editions (HK) Ltd.

www.tuttlepublishing.com

Library of Congress Cataloging in Process

ISBN 978-4-8053-1651-1

Distributed by
North America, Latin America & Europe
Tuttle Publishing
364 Innovation Drive, North Clarendon
VT 05759-9436 USA.
Tel: (802) 773-8930 | Fax: (802) 773-6993
info@tuttlepublishing.com
www.tuttlepublishing.com

Japan
Tuttle Publishing
Yaekari Building, 3rd Floor
5-4-12 Osaki, Shinagawa-ku, Tokyo 141 0032
Tel: (81) 3 5437-0171 | Fax: (81) 3 5437-0755
sales@tuttle.co.jp
www.tuttle.co.jp

Asia Pacific
Berkeley Books Pte. Ltd.
3 Kallang Sector, #04-01/02, Singapore 349278
Tel: (65) 6741-2178 | Fax: (65) 6741-2179
inquiries@periplus.com.sg
www.tuttlepublishing.com

Printed in Malaysia   2205VP
25 24 23 22   5 4 3 2

"Books to Span the East and West"

Tuttle Publishing was founded in 1832 in the small
New England town of Rutland, Vermont [USA]. Our core
values remain as strong today as they were then—to
publish best-in-class books which bring people
together one page at a time. In 1948, we established a
publishing office in Japan—and Tuttle is now a leader
in publishing English-language books about the arts,
languages and cultures of Asia. The world has become
a much smaller place today and Asia's economic and
cultural influence has grown. Yet the need for
meaningful dialogue and information about this
diverse region has never been greater. Over the past
seven decades, Tuttle has published thousands of
books on subjects ranging from martial arts and paper
crafts to language learning and literature—and our
talented authors, illustrators, designers and photo-
graphers have won many prestigious awards. We
welcome you to explore the wealth of information
available on Asia at **www.tuttlepublishing.com.**